MAY '68 AND ITS AFTERLIVES

MAY '68
AND ITS AFTERLIVES

KRISTIN ROSS

THE UNIVERSITY OF CHICAGO PRESS • CHICAGO AND LONDON

Kristin Ross is professor of comparative literature at New York University. She is author of *Fast Cars, Clean Bodies: Decolonization and the Reordering of French Culture* (1995) and *The Emergence of Social Space: Rimbaud and the Paris Commune* (1988).

The University of Chicago Press, Chicago 60637
The University of Chicago Press, Ltd., London
© 2002 by Kristin Ross
All rights reserved. Published 2002
Printed in the United States of America
11 10 09 08 07 06 05 04 03 02   1 2 3 4 5

ISBN: 0-226-72797-1 (cloth)

Library of Congress Cataloging-in-Publication Data

Ross, Kristin.
      May '68 and its afterlives / Kristin Ross.
         p.   cm.
      Includes bibliographical references and index.
      ISBN 0-226-72797-1 (cloth : alk. paper)
      1. Riots—France—Paris.   2. France—Politics and government—1958–   I. Title:
May 1968 and its afterlives.   II. Title.

DC412 .R67 2002
944'.36—dc21   2001052762

For my mother and father

CONTENTS

ACKNOWLEDGMENTS

The idea for a book like this came originally from Adrian Rifkin, who urged me to write it, but who shouldn't fear that he will be held responsible for what I have done. I am grateful to him, Donald Reid, Alice Kaplan, Fredric Jameson, and writing group members Molly Nesbit, Anne Higonnet, Margaret Cohen, and Gloria Kury for their support at the early stages of the project. Jean Chesnaux, Jean-Louis Comolli, Paol Keineg, Annette Michelson, Andrew Ross, Michel Trebitsch, Steven Ungar, and Jay Winter each offered helpful research tips at crucial moments. My thanks to Denis Echard, to Adrian again, and to Jonathan Strong for their careful, critical readings of the entire manuscript.

My research for this project received the generous support of the John Simon Guggenheim Foundation, the National Endowment for the Humanities, and New York University. I am also indebted to the Institute for Advanced Study in Princeton for a fellowship year that allowed me to write much of the book in a congenial and stimulating environment, while giving me access to the resources and assistance of a dedicated library staff. In France, I received gracious help from the staff at the BDIC in Nanterre, the Centre de Recherche de l'Histoire des Mouvements Sociaux et du Syndicalisme, ISKRA, and the Institut d'Histoire du Temps Présent. My editor, Susan Bielstein, and her colleagues at the University of Chicago Press responsible for the production of the book have been a pleasure to work with.

For their intellectual energy, generosity, and enthusiastic commitment to the project, my deepest gratitude goes to Harry Harootunian, Alice Kaplan, and Joan Scott, each of whom not only read the entire manuscript, but several drafts along the way. Their conversation and critique— and their example—made me consider things I had been avoiding, and reconsider some of the certainties I had thought self-evident. To Harry, a fellow-traveler, special thanks for his company and for good times while I researched and wrote the book. To B. and W., your absence helped as much as your presence!

Finally, I'd like to dedicate this book to a serious reader, Anita Brown Ross, and to Walter Ross, a serious wit.

INTRODUCTION

I know of no other period in the history of France that has given me the same feeling that something irrational was happening. —*Raymond Aron, 1968*

What is important is that the action took place, at a time when everyone judged it to be unthinkable. If it took place, then it can happen again. . . . —*Jean-Paul Sartre, 1968*

This is a book about May's afterlives: about the way in which May '68 in France, now more than thirty years past, has been overtaken by its subsequent representations. It is also a book about how the event has endured, resisting annihilation, insisting or asserting its eventfulness against the forms of social amnesia and instrumentalization that have sought to undo it, the sociologies that have explained it, and the ex–student leaders who have claimed a monopoly on its memory.

By "afterlife" I do not wish to invoke a catalog of May's errors and accomplishments or to demonstrate the "lessons" that the May movement might hold for us now. I use the term rather to mean simply that what has become known as "the events of May '68" cannot now be considered separately from the social memory and forgetting that surround them. That memory and that forgetting have taken material forms, forms whose history I trace in this book. The management of May's memory—the way in which the political dimensions of the event have been, for the most part, dissolved or dissipated by commentary and interpretations—is now, thirty years later, at the center of the historical problem of 1968 itself.

And yet even to raise the question of the memory of the recent past is to confront the way in which the whole of our contemporary understanding of processes of social memory and forgetting has been derived from analyses related to another mass event—World War II. World War II has, in fact, "produced" the memory industry in contemporary scholarship, in France and elsewhere, and the parameters of devastation—

1

catastrophe, administrative massacre, atrocity, collaboration, genocide—have in turn made it easy for certain pathological psychoanalytic categories—"trauma," for example, or "repression"—to attain legitimacy as ever more generalizable ways of understanding the excesses and deficiencies of collective memory. And these categories have in turn, I think, defamiliarized us from any understanding, or even perception, of a "mass event" that does not appear to us in the register of "catastrophe" or "mass extermination." "Masses," in other words, have come to mean masses of dead bodies, not masses of people working together to take charge of their collective lives.

Whether or not the transposition of pathological categories onto the historical plane is justified in the case of World War II—recent works by Peter Novick and Norman Finkelstein, argue against their use, at least in the American context[1]—it seemed clear to me that categories like "trauma" and "repression," whether collective or individual, would not be relevant to the story of '68. In the affective register, of course, they fell dramatically short of being able to render the range of associations—pleasure, power, excitement, happiness, disappointment—with which many people recalled the 1960s. These categories could tell us little or nothing, I suspected, about how the recent political past, its ambiance and its sociabilities, are remembered or forgotten, how *left* political culture in particular comes to be recast, reconfigured, or obscured.

Within social history, of course, and particularly among historians of workers collectivities, a mode of addressing such questions has evolved. But in that body of work the problem of memory has almost always been formulated as an issue of reinforcing *identity:* reweaving the threads that have unraveled between generations so as to firm up the continuity of this or that subgroup or subculture; strengthening the received dispositions, habits, ways of life, bodily practices that bolster a particular social identity—the identity of militants, for example, or residents of a particular neighborhood, or members of a certain religious group, or the abiding folk in the rural hinterlands. In this view, memory is seen as the property of social bodies, something one can possess, or if it has been taken away, something that can be injected back into the group to enforce its identity. Memory is mobilized in the service of a conquest or a reconquest of identity, and in recent times, increasingly, of an ever more narrowly conceived ethnic or regional identity.

And yet May '68 had very little to do with the social group—students or "youth"—who were its instigators. It had much more to do with the flight from social determinations, with displacements that took people

---

1. See Peter Novick, *The Holocaust in American Life* (Boston: Houghton Mifflin, 1999); and Norman Finkelstein, *The Holocaust Industry* (London: Verso, 2000).

outside of their location in society, with a disjunction, that is, between political subjectivity and the social group. What is forgotten when May '68 is forgotten seemed to have less to do with the lost habits of this or that social group, than it did with a shattering of social identity that allowed politics to take place. The prevailing theories of social memory and forgetting—the catastrophe or "trauma" school and the social identity school—were of little use in coming to terms with the vicissitudes of the memory of a mass political event like May. Even worse, their domination of the intellectual field and the ubiquity of their tropes—the grand figures of the Gulag or the Holocaust on the one hand or the stabilities of the *habitus* on the other—could perhaps themselves be seen as a symptom, a generalized reluctance to consider the very notion of politics or collective political agency in the present.

L ike every cumbersome movement or "obscure event"—the phrase comes from Sylvain Lazarus—May '68 in the last thirty years has been buried, raked through the coals, trivialized, or represented as a monstrosity. But in the case of '68, an enormous amount of narrative labor—and not a shroud of silence—has facilitated the active forgetting of the events in France. Memoirs, self-celebrations, recantations, television commemorations, abstract philosophical treatises, sociological analyses—May has not suffered from too little attention. Only days after the events subsided in June 1968, an astounding proliferation of verbiage began to be published, and this production has continued, with discernible ebbs and flows, to this day. Discourse has been produced, but its primary effect has been to liquidate—to use an old '68 word—erase, or render obscure the history of May.

Now, this isn't uniformly true. If you read Canadian novelist Mavis Gallant's day-by-day account of May and June in Paris, for example, you can derive a vivid sense of the nature of the event from her stray observations, like the fact that the sale of books went up 40 percent in Paris in those months. This may not be so surprising. In a city where there were no schools in session, where no one could mail a letter, find a newspaper, send a telegram, or cash a check, where no one could take a bus, ride the metro, drive a car, find cigarettes, buy sugar, watch TV, hear news on the radio, or get the trash picked up, where no one could take a train out of the city, hear a weather report, or sleep at night in the parts of the city where tear gas filled apartments as high as the fifth floor, in a city like this reading *can* fill the time. In such details lie submerged some sense of what happens to daily life when 9 million people, across all sectors of public and private employment—from department store clerks to shipbuilders—simply stop working. May '68 was the largest mass movement in French history, the biggest strike in the history of the French workers' movement, and the only "general" insurrection the overdeveloped world has known since World War II. It was the first general strike that extended beyond the traditional centers of industrial production to include workers in the service industries, the communication and culture industries—the whole sphere of social reproduction. No professional sector, no category of worker was unaffected by the strike; no region, city, or village in France was untouched.

The suspended moment of the general strike, the vast expanse of possibility that opened up when the strike disrupted and transformed everyday life—only a small number of the texts and documents about May convey, or choose to convey, something about the nature of that experience.

In mid-May 1968, one work stoppage after another across the nation succeeded the violent demonstrations unleashed by students in the early days of the month. France, for some five to six weeks, was brought to a complete paralysis. Among the insurrections that were occurring across the globe in the 1960s—notably in Mexico, the United States, Germany, Japan, and elsewhere—only in France, and to a certain extent in Italy, did a synchronicity or "meeting" between intellectual refusal of the reigning ideology and worker insurrection occur. The rapid extension of the general strike, both geographically and professionally, outstripped all frames of analysis; in a very brief time, three times more workers were on strike in France than during the Popular Front in 1936. The very surplus of an event of this magnitude, the way in which it exceeded—as it was occurring—the expectations and control of even its most alert protagonists, is an important factor, I believe, in two of the subsequent confiscations I trace in this book: the biographical (personalization) version and the sociological. Neither of these defiguring strategies is new. Forgetting, just as much as remembering, is made possible by the work of various narrative configurations—narratives that model the identity of the protagonists of an action at the same time as they shape the contours of events. To reduce a mass movement to the individual itineraries of a few so-called leaders, spokesmen, or representatives (especially if those representatives have all renounced their past errors) is an old, tried and true tactic of confiscation. Circumscribed in this way, all collective revolt is defanged; it doesn't amount to anything more than the existential anguish of individual destiny; revolt is confined to the jurisdiction of a few "personalities" upon whom the media bestows seemingly innumerable occasions for revising or recasting previous motivations.

And sociology has always set itself up as the tribunal to which the real—the event—is brought to trial after the fact, to be measured, categorized, and contained. In the case of May '68, the problem has been compounded.

French academic historians of the present, who inhabit as much as anyone else the landscape of collective memory about '68, have, until quite recently, remained singularly indifferent to addressing the topic as a subject of research—an indifference historians themselves have been the first to point out. "Why," asked Jean-Pierre Rioux in 1989, "have historians of the present—true, not a numerous species—so willingly abandoned the terrain to a grandstanding sociology?" Surveying the field at the same moment, another historian, Antoine Proust, noted the "poverty" of research in France since 1972, condemning an "overly prudent attitude" among historians, who have seriously failed to address or value the already available documentation—a symptom, he suggested, of intellectual slackness. It may be that a society finds it enormously difficult even to formulate a demand for historical knowledge when an event is so ambiguous.[2] Only two volumes by French academic historians, each a collection of conference papers, and a smattering of *mémoires de maîtrise* have appeared to date.[3] Whether preoccupied by Vichy, unwilling or embarrassed to grapple with the peculiar difficulties posed by recent militant culture in today's liberal climate, or reluctant to settle accounts with their own forgotten memories, historians have abdicated their responsibilities and left this event, even more than others, open to a higher degree of instrumentalization. This abdication has helped create an interpretive vacuum that others—namely sociologists and reformed *gauchistes*—have leapt to fill. These two groups of increasingly media-certified "authorities" or custodians of memory have dominated the discourse on May '68 and have worked in tandem, since the mid-1970s, to produce an official history, a discernable doxa. The relatively systematic set of words, expressions, images, and narratives that have set the limits for what is thinkable about May is, to a large extent, their production. And the bulk of that production, in the chronology I chart, was carried out between 1978 and 1988, between the tenth and twentieth anniversaries of May.

The official story that has been encoded, celebrated publicly in any number of mass media spectacles of commemoration, and handed down to us today, is one of a family or generational drama, stripped of any violence,

2. See Jean-Pierre Rioux, "A Propos des célébrations décennales du Mai français," *Vingtième Siècle* 23 (July–Sept. 1989): 49–58; Antoine Prost, "Quoi de neuf sur le Mai français?" *Le Mouvement Social* 143 (April–June 1988): 91–97.

3. One of these books, the result of a four-year seminar at the Institut d'Histoire du Temps Présent, appeared only this year as I was completing this project. During the course of my research, however, I was able to consult many of the workshop papers eventually collected in the volume. See Michelle Zancarini-Fournel et al., eds., *Les années 68. Le temps de la contestation* (Brussels: Editions Complexe, 2000). See also the book that resulted from a 1988 colloquium sponsored by the Centre de Recherches d'Histoire des Mouvements Sociaux: René Mouriaux et al., eds., *1968: Exploration du Mai français*, 2 vols. (Paris: L'Harmattan, 1992).

asperity, or overt political dimensions—a benign transformation of customs and lifestyles that necessarily accompanied France's modernization from an authoritarian bourgeois state to a new, liberal, modern financier bourgeoisie.

The official story does not limit itself to merely claiming that some of May's more radical ideas and practices came to be recuperated or recycled in the service of Capital. Rather, it asserts that today's capitalist society, far from representing the derailment or failure of the May movement's aspirations, instead represents the accomplishment of its deepest desires. By asserting a teleology of the present, the official story erases those memories of past alternatives that sought or envisioned other outcomes than the one that came to pass.

Within that teleology, May was to be understood as an affirmation of the status quo, a disruption in the service of consensus, a transformation of consciousness, a generational revolt of the young against structural rigidities that were blocking the necessary momentum of cultural modernization in France. The official version of May's afterlife served the interests of sociologists in reinserting any rupture into a logic of the same, enforcing the identities of systems and groups that allow the reproduction of social structures, and the interests of repentant militants intent on exorcising their militant past equally well, even though the authority claimed by the two groups differs radically. The ex-leaders claim to speak on the basis of a vast reserve of personal experience and rely on the experiential to deny key aspects of the event or derail them from their significance. By contrast, the sociologists appeal to abstract structures and regularities, averaging and quantification, the elaboration of typologies built around binary oppositions—all of which is grounded in a deep distrust of the experiential. Yet the two groups, despite contradictory claims, have worked together to fix the dehistoricized and depoliticized codes by which May is now understood. In this sense, I am less interested in the revisionist terms of the "official story"—whether it be the great rebellion by angry youth against the restrictions of their fathers or its corollary, the emergence of a new social category called "youth." I am more concerned with how that particular story came to prevail, how the two contradictory methods or tendencies, the experiential and the structural, converged to formulate categories—"generation," for example—whose effects were ultimately depoliticizing. The paradox of May's memory can be simply stated. How did a mass movement that sought above all, in my view, to contest the domain of the expert, to disrupt the system of naturalized spheres of competence (especially the sphere of specialized politics), become translated in the years that followed into little more than a "knowledge" of '68, on the basis of which a whole generation of self-proclaimed experts and authorities could then assert their expertise? This movement swept away categorical territories and social definitions, and achieved unforeseen alliances and synchronicities *between* social sectors and between very diverse people working together to conduct their affairs collectively. How did such a movement get relocated into defined "sociological" residences: the "student milieu" or "the generation"?

M uch of my effort in this book has been taken up in recounting the history of how the official story laid claim to its authority. Indeed, this was the way I first conceptualized the project: how has May '68 been remembered and discussed in France ten, twenty, thirty years after it occurred? But as I worked, a second, no less compelling goal began to take shape: the goal of evoking or retrieving the traces of a political climate and memory—which is to say another, quite distinct "afterlife" to May—that is neither the social of the sociologists nor the testimony of those who have subsequently claimed to incarnate the official truth of the movement. If I wanted to reveal how the official story came to prevail, I also needed to emancipate the history of the May years from the trusteeship held by some of its former actors, those who became the "generation" of stars in the 1980s, no less than from an array of hypostatic sociological categories like "youth rebelling." The event of 1968 was above all else a massive refusal on the part of thousands, even millions, of people to see in the social what we usually see: nothing more than the narrowest of sociological categories. Writing the history of that refusal, and the way it has been remembered and forgotten, seemed to me to involve finding a different form, a writing that would reach, as the movement itself did, both above and below sociology. Above, that is, or toward a level of philosophical critique manifest in those writers and activists whose involvement with the politics of the '68 years has fostered a continuous commitment to interrogating what it is that makes politics possible, to thinking historical action. Thus, my study turns to writers and activists for whom May '68 constituted a pivotal if not a founding moment in their intellectual and political trajectories: philosophers Jean-Paul Sartre, Alain Badiou, Jacques Rancière, Maurice Blanchot, and Daniel Bensaïd, activist and editor François Maspero, or the writers and activists Martine Storti and Guy Hocquenghem. And below, I have looked toward the historically specific language, subjectivity, and practices of the largely anonymous participants in the streets, the people who made up neighborhood and factory committees: workers, students, farmers, and the many others who found themselves assuming the task of posing questions, not at the level of their own social interests, but at the level of society itself, in its entirety.

My own research into the political language of the May movement has extended beyond the initial, invaluable compilation of documents assembled by Alain Schnapp and Pierre Vidal-Naquet in 1969. I have found the filmed documentary footage, small publications, and mimeographed pamphlets from all kinds of groups, the often ephemeral journals, and the interpretations written in the white heat of the moment to be of much more interest and value than any of the interpretive commentaries—by Edgar Morin, Claude Lefort, Michel de Certeau, among others—consecrated in the years afterward. Yet one need only refer to the pamphlets and tracts included in Schnapp and Vidal-Naquet's survey to establish the clear ideological targets of the May movement in France. These were three: capitalism, American imperialism, and Gaullism. How then do we arrive, twenty years later, at a consensus view of '68 as a mellow, sympathetic, poetic "youth revolt" and lifestyle reform? The answer lies in the dominant narrative configurations—mostly reductions or circumscriptions of the event—adopted by the official story. The first of these configurations, a temporal reduction, has produced an abbreviated chronology whereby what we understand by "May" has become, quite literally, what transpired during the month of May 1968. More specifically, "May" begins on May 3, when the forces of order are called into the Sorbonne, initiating student arrests that in turn provoke violent popular demonstrations during the weeks that follow in the streets of the Latin Quarter. "May" ends on May 30, when de Gaulle makes a speech in which he announces he will not step down from the presidency, threatens army intervention, and dissolves the National Assembly. May, then, is May—and not even June, when close to 9 million people, in every region of the country and across all of the different employment sectors were out on strike. The largest general strike in French history recedes into the background, along with the prehistory of the uprising, which goes back at least to the ending of the Algerian War in the early 1960s. The violent state repression that helped bring an end to the May-June events is not invoked, nor is the *gauchiste* violence that continued well into the early 1970s. In fact, a whole fifteen- to twenty-year period of radical political culture is occulted from view, a political culture whose traces were manifest in the growth of a small but significant opposition to the Algerian War and in the embrace by many French of a "third-worldist" north/south analysis of global politics in the wake of the enormous successes of the colonial revolutions. This political culture was also manifest in the recurrent outbreaks of worker unrest in French factories throughout the mid-1960s, in the rise of an anti-Stalinist, critical Marxist perspective available in countless journals that flourished between the mid-1950s and the mid-1970s. The immediate political context in France was in fact one of triumphant Marxism: in large sectors of the workers movement, in the university in the form of Althusserianism, in small groups of Maoist, Trotskyist, and anarchist militants, and in a dominant frame of reference for work conducted in philosophy and the human sciences since World War II. All these developments recede in the service of a narrative in which a "spontaneous" May suddenly "erupted out of nowhere." The exclusion of the Algerian and worker prehistory to May, as well as its *gauchiste* aftermath, is the price that must be paid for "saving" May as a happy month of liberated "free expression."

The limiting of "May" to May has distinct repercussions. The temporal foreshortening reinforces (and is predicated on) a geographic reduction of the sphere of activity to Paris, more specifically to the Latin Quarter. Again, striking workers on the outskirts of Paris and across the nation recede from the picture; successful experiments in worker/student/farmer solidarity in the provinces and elsewhere are erased. By some accounts, provincial France saw more violent and sustained demonstrations than did Paris during May and June, but this is not represented in the official story. What was lived in factories, in Nantes and Caen and far from Paris—a whole constellation of practices and ideas about equality that cannot now be integrated into the contemporary liberal/libertarian paradigm embraced by many of May's former actors—vanishes from view. Thus, to take one vivid example, the birth of a new antiprogressivist agricultural movement in the early 1970s in the Larzac region—a movement that would manifest a distinct "afterlife" in the form of the egalitarian rural radicalism of the Confédération Paysanne, with its attacks on McDonald's and on genetically modified food—plays no role in May's narration.

The political ferment surrounding agriculture today would seem to ratify the suggestion made by Elisabeth Salvaresi and others that a whole terrain of scattered resistances derived from '68 have endured in rural France, far from Paris, far from its new entrepreneurs, philosophers, and journalists and their relentless marketing of the new. Indeed, Salvaresi has suggested that the deepest political resonance of '68 today is found more frequently in the provinces than in Paris. If so—and it has been beyond the scope of this study to conduct the research necessary to do more than speculate—a new optic onto '68 would open up that would make the legendary status of a Serge July or a Daniel Cohn-Bendit recede, allowing other figures to become more visible in the theoretical and political roles they played during May and afterward. Forgotten militants like Bernard Lambert, for example, Maoist and Catholic agricultural activist in '68 and author of a prescient 1970 study of the exploitation of modernized farmers by agro-business—"workers, farmers, *même combat*"—might be looked at anew in light of today's focus on the global politics of food.[4]

4. See Elisabeth Salvaresi, *Mai en héritage* (Paris: Syros, 1988). See also Bernard Lambert, *Les paysans dans la lutte de classe* (Paris: Le Seuil, 1970).

To disguise its narcissistic and truncated reduction of May to the confines of the Latin Quarter, the official story makes expansive gestures toward a version of internationalism. But it does so at the expense of the one international dimension that could be said to have played the most important role in the French uprisings and that united those uprisings to the insurrections occurring in Germany, Japan, the United States, Italy, and elsewhere—namely the critique of American imperialism and that nation's war against Vietnam. Vietnam has distinctly receded from dominant representations of French May (all but disappearing, for example, in the television commemorations of the 1980s in favor of a thematics of sexual revolution), and that erasure has been compensated for by the construction of a new "international" dimension: that of a vast, well-nigh planetary "generation" of ill-defined and inchoate libertarian youth revolt, or quest for personal autonomy—what Serge July once called "the great liberal-libertarian Cultural Revolution." By the time of the twentieth anniversary, when May had been reduced to a quest for individual and spiritual autonomy on the part of its authorized spokesmen, these ex-student leaders then project that quest onto an entire far-flung "generation," a worldwide age cohort for whom the 1980s watchword of "liberty" has definitively (and anachronistically) replaced what I argue in this book to be the properly 1960s aspiration to "equality."

In the official story, the temporal and geographic reductions of what occurred in May now undergird what has become the massive representational privilege accorded to students and the university world in establishing May's cast of characters. We should not, perhaps, be surprised. Barricades, the occupation of the Sorbonne and the Odéon Theater, and, above all, the poetic graffiti—these are the images that recur as ineluctably as the faces of the same three or four aging ex–student leaders on the commemorations of 1968 broadcast every ten years on French television.

And yet the massive politicization of French middle-class youth in the 1960s took place by way of a set of polemical relations and impossible identifications with two figures now conspicuously absent from this picture: the worker and the colonial militant. These two figures, the privileged "others" of political modernity, form the organizational threads of my investigation, both of the May years—which extend, in the periodization I adopt in this book, from the mid-1950s to the mid-1970s—and on up to the present. I use the word "figure" in the sense of historical actors, theorists, and speakers in their own right; as objects of political desire, fictional and theoretical representation, and fantasy; and as participants, interlocutors in a fragile, ephemeral, and historically specific dialogue. French third-worldism was in one sense nothing more than the recognition, beginning in the late 1950s, that the colonized, through their wars of liberation, had emerged as a new figuration of the people in the political sense ("the wretched of the earth"), eclipsing any manifestation of a European working class by universalizing or giving a name to a political wrong that in turn mobilized students and others in the west. The third-worldism of the early 1960s continued after the end of the Algerian War and through the U.S. acceleration of the war in Vietnam in the middle of that decade. For many people on the left in France, it was Maoism that provided the relay, the means to make the transition, to shift the focus from the colonial peasant militant back to the worker at home, and thus to acknowledge, along with striking auto workers in Turin, that "Vietnam is in our factories." In this way, the French worker then becomes the central figure in the social movements of May '68 proper. But Maoism was not the only force at work. Throughout the 1960s in France, themes of anticapitalism and internationalism were spontaneously combined; the discourses of anticapitalism and anti-imperialism were woven together in an intricate mesh. After all, these were times when on a given evening in the middle of the week at a rally at the Mutualité in Paris, three thousand Trotskyists could be brought to their feet by the slogan "Tous debout, camarades, pour la Bolivie socialiste!"

The principal idea of May was the union of intellectual contestation with workers' struggle. Another way of saying this is that the political subjectivity that emerged in May was a *relational* one, built around a polemics of equality: a day-to-day experience of identifications, aspirations, encounters and missed encounters, meetings, deceptions, and disappointments. The experience of equality, as it was lived by many in the course of the movement—neither as a goal nor a future agenda but as something occurring in the present and verified as such—constitutes an enormous challenge for subsequent representation. The invention during the movement of forms of activity that put an end to representation and delegation, that undermined the division between directors and subordinates, practices that expressed a massive investment in politics as the concern of each and every individual and not just the concern of specialists—such an experience threatens everything that is inscribed in our repertories for describing everyday life, all of the various ways we have to represent the social, all of the finite number of representations to which we can appeal. The problem was all the more acute twenty years later amid the ideological climate of the 1980s, when a generalized offensive against equality was launched under the cover of a critique of egalitarianism. This critique made equality a synonym for uniformity, for the constraint or alienation of liberty, or for an assault on the free functioning of the market. When the union of intellectual contestation with workers struggle, when that idea slips away or is forgotten, what remains of '68 cannot be much more than the prefiguration of an "emancipatory" counterculture, a metaphysics of desire and liberation, the rehearsal for a world made up of "desiring machines" and "autonomous individuals" rooted to the irreducible ground of personal experience.

By the mid-1970s, new figures had taken the place of the worker and the colonial militant and now occupied the center of media attention. "The plebe," a spiritualized and silent figure of helplessness, was the immediate precursor to the figure of suffering at the center of today's human rights discourse. And "the dissident" reanchored French attention to a Cold War narrative rather than to the North/South axis that had defined the 1960s. In the new regime of representation of the humanitarian victim then taking shape, the "wretched of the earth" had become, quite simply, the wretched—stripped, that is, of any political subjectivity or universalizing possibility and reduced to a figure of pure alterity: be it victim or barbarian. In France at least, as I argue in chapter 3, the new discourse of ethical morality surrounding human rights—much of it produced by ex-*gauchistes* concerned with distancing themselves from a militant past or with avoiding coming to terms with the disappointments of May— was already a major chapter in the forgetting of '68. Put differently, we could say that beginning around 1976, the need to repudiate May fueled a retreat from politics into ethics, a retreat that distorted not only May's ideology but much of its memory as well. Ex-*gauchistes* who had claimed the role of custodians of May's memory were singularly well placed to recast the meaning of the May events in the light of the "spiritual transformation" they were themselves undergoing. The events and political culture of 1968, which had in fact exhibited a radical, sometimes violent opposition to the kind of moralizing discourse that would prevail after the late 1970s, were reconfigured in the light of personal ethics, not politics. With the advent of what Guy Hocquenghem once called the "warrior moralism" of the New Philosophers, a new phase had been reached. In the second half of the book, I explore the ways in which the need to obliterate the traces of '68 was served by the new discourses about totalitarianism they popularized and by a new regime of representation in which two figures, namely human rights and the Gulag/Holocaust, came to orchestrate good and evil after the late 1970s.

"No one died in '68." This much-repeated phrase is, in fact, false. But its reiteration must be read as a symptom of an attempt to lend a good-natured, *bon enfant*, almost misty quality to the insurrection and its participants—both the militants and the State. Must an event be measured in terms of its body count? No, certainly not, if the event has been classified as a cultural one—and that is what May, in the official story by the late 1980s, had become. During May nothing happened politically; its effects were purely cultural—so went the consensus evaluation, the story learned, authorized, imposed, celebrated publicly, and commemorated, in print and in the television shows I discuss in chapter 3. "Cultural" usually meant any of the many lifestyle changes, transformations in the habits of daily life, and comportments that came about in the 1970s—such things as women wearing pants instead of skirts or the adoption of new forms of familiarity into spoken discourse. Yet how much do the so-called cultural effects of May have anything to do with the specificity of the event? As Jean-Franklin Narot once commented, not everything that appeared during those months was part of the movement, and not everything that came after May can be attributed to May. Most of the lifestyle accommodations and changes in daily life referred to under the rubric of "May's cultural effects" occurred as well in all Western countries that were undergoing accelerated capitalist modernization—whether or not these countries had a " '68."[5]

What if we take a vague term like "cultural effects" to mean something akin to what is called in Anglo-Saxon countries "the counterculture"? Unlike the United States and England, countries that saw flourishing and inventive countercultural developments, particularly in music, during the 1960s and 1970s, French countercultural forms after 1968 were largely imported. In England or the United States, as Peter Dews has suggested, one could conceivably become initiated into a political culture by creeping through the back door of the counterculture; in France or Italy, on the other hand, the "counterculture" of the 1970s mostly represented the waning of what had been a much more vibrant and forceful political militancy than had been generated in the United States.[6] Of course, the '68 events did play a significant role, with philosophy and other modes of intellectual inquiry, in a lively conjuncture, a conjuncture that made the 1970s in France a moment of unprecedented invention and creativity. In the years immediately following '68, seemingly unlimited intellectual projects and original venues for the exchange of ideas came into being—new journals and experimentation in publishing—all in some way concerned with establishing a duration to the events or with displacing political energy onto other, related investigations. In chapter 2 I look at several

---

5. The accommodation by the French and other Europeans to more American-style consumption habits transpires according to a longer postwar temporality, the French version of which I have discussed in *Fast Cars, Clean Bodies: Decolonization and the Reordering of French Culture* (Cambridge: MIT Press, 1995). The event of May '68 constitutes an interruption, not an acceleration, in the narrative of that process.

6. Peter Dews, "The *Nouvelle Philosophie* and Foucault," *Economy and Society* 8, no. 2 (May 1979): 168.

examples of collective experimentation with modes of political representation, journals that sprang up within the field of historiography. But the journals I discuss are representative of a larger phenomenon of which a list, compiled by Françoise Proust, which I cite here only in part, offers some sense of scope. Among the new publishing ventures or series of books within established publishers that sprang up were 10/18 (1968), Lattès (1968), Champ libre (1968), "Points" Seuil (1970), Galilée (1971), Gallimard "Folio" (1972), Editions des Femmes (1974), Actes Sud (1978). Among periodicals and cultural journals were *Change* (1968), *L'Autre Scène* (1969), *Nouvelle Revue de Psychanalyse* (1970), *Actuel* (1970), *Tel Quel* (1972), *Afrique-Asie* (1972), *Actes de la Recherche en Sciences Sociales* (1975), *Révoltes Logiques* (1975), *Hérodote* (1976). Among newspapers were *Hara-Kiri Hebdo* (1969), *L'Idiot International* (1969), *Tout* (1970), *Libération* (1973), *Le Gai Pied* (1979). Risky, affirmative thought like the kind manifested by this list, Proust comments, necessarily generates reaction. In her chronology and that of many others, the beginning of the end of this effervescent flourishing of invention associated with '68 was already palpable in 1976–1978, when a new form of media intellectual, the New Philosophers, arrived on the scene.[7]

In the realm of high-cultural production in France—especially literature—May has made little impact, either thematically or formally. Within the novel form, as Patrick Combes has shown, very few significant attempts have been made to address the figurability of May's politics. The quasi-totality of novelistic representations of '68 after the fact have marched in lockstep with dominant media representations, choosing, for example, to dramatize the events through the perspective of the sometimes caricatured consciousness of an individual living out an anguished existential crisis against a backdrop of barricades—and this despite the fact, as my own research has uncovered again and again, that the content

---

7. See Françoise Proust, "Débattre ou résister?" *Lignes* 35 (Oct. 1998): 106–120. For Proust, a philosopher, the *definitive* end of this period of post-'68 utopian intellectual energy occurs in 1980 with the first issue of Marcel Gauchet and Pierre Nora's journal, *Le Débat*. This journal consecrated several issues to helping Luc Ferry and Alain Renaut's *La pensée 68* (discussed in chapter 4) play the important role it did in the construction of the "official story" of '68. For Proust, *Le Débat* certified the definitive return of a dialogue limited to that between "intellectuals and technicians (in other words, the experts), [through which] the intellectual internalizes democracy: he renounces vain desires to change the world, he understands that representative democracy, its institutions and its rules, is the ultimate horizon of all political groups; from then on his function is to be in constant debate with the decision makers that he advises, rationally thinking through the problems and the political and cultural crises that a modern democracy confronts." *Le Débat*'s editor, Nora, was fond of pointing to the coincidence of the new journal's publication and the death of Sartre, commenting in an interview that he considered *Le Débat* to be "the opposite of *Les Temps Modernes* and its philosophy of engagement."

of an individual's recollections of that time is almost always participation in a social collective. Only within a more popular genre, the detective story, beginning in the 1980s, have I found a tangible effort to narrate the effects on contemporary society of what it means to have forgotten the recent past—the Algerian and '68 ruptures and the politics and distinct political sociability manifest in those moments.

Much of my argument in this book goes against the grain of the efforts made in the 1980s to attribute merely "cultural," if not moral or spiritual effects, to May. In fact, I have tried to show something close to the opposite perspective. In May, everything happened politically—provided, of course, that we understand "politics" as bearing little or no relation to what was called at the time "la politique des politiciens" (specialized, or electoral politics).

For May '68 itself was not an artistic moment. It was an event that transpired amid very few images; French television, after all, was on strike. Drawings, political cartoons—by Siné, Willem, Cabu, and others—proliferated; photographs were taken. Only the most "immediate" of artistic techniques, it seems, could keep up with the speed of events. But to say this is already to point out how much politics was exerting a magnetic pull on culture, yanking it out of its specific and specialized realm. For what does it mean that art should suddenly see its purpose as that of keeping apace with events, with achieving a complete contemporaneity with the present and with what is happening around it?

The incommensurability or asymmetry that seems to govern the relation between culture and politics holds true for the '68 period in France. In fact, that incommensurability *is* what the event is about: the failure of cultural solutions to provide an answer, the invention and deployment of political forms in direct contestation with existing cultural forms, the exigency of political practices over cultural ones. Nowhere is this more apparent than in the experience of the Beaux-Arts students who occupied their school in mid-May 1968, proclaimed it the revolutionary *Atelier populaire des Beaux-Arts*, and began producing, at breakneck speed, the posters supporting the strike that covered the walls of Paris during those months. The "message" of the majority of the posters, stark and direct, was the certification, and at times the imperative, that whatever it was that was happening—the interruption, the strike, the "moving train"—that it simply *continue:* "Continuons le combat." "La grève continue." "Contre offensive: la grève continue." "Chauffeurs de taxi: la lutte continue." "Maine Montparnasse: la lutte continue." Nothing, that is, in the message aspires to a level of "representing" what was occurring; the goal, rather, is to be at one with—at the same time with, contemporary with—whatever *was* occurring. Speed, a speedy technique, was of the essence; students

learned this soon enough when they abandoned lithography early on because, at ten to fifteen printings an hour, it was far too slow to respond
to the needs of a mass movement. Serigraphy, which was light and easy
to use, yielded up to 250 printings an hour. Speed and a flexible medium
facilitated the absolute interpenetration of art and event achieved by the
posters, but speed is not the most important factor in rendering art capable of living the temporality of an event. Writing thirty years later, one
of the militants active in the *Atelier populaire*, Gérard Fromanger, recalls
the genesis of the posters in a brief memoir. His title, "Art Is What Makes
Life More Interesting than Art," goes far in giving a sense of the dizzying
opening created when the social refuses to stay "out there," distinct from
art, or when art achieves presentation, rather than representation:

> May '68 was that. Artists are no longer in their studios, they no longer
> work, they can't work any more because the real is more powerful than
> their inventions. Naturally, they become militants, me among them. We
> create the *Atelier populaire des Beaux-Arts* and we make posters. We're
> there night and day making posters. The whole country is on strike and
> we've never worked harder in our lives. We're finally necessary.[8]

Fromanger describes in greater detail the stages in the dismantling of art
and artists during May: how, as the mass demonstrations got underway in
mid-May, art students first "got down off their horses to gather the flowers," as the Maoists would say, how they left art behind as they ran from
demo to demo. "We artists had been in the movement for ten days, we run
into each other at the demos. We had separated from everything we had
before. We don't sleep in the studios . . . we live in the streets, in the occupied spaces. . . . We no longer paint, we don't think about it anymore."
The next phase describes a retreat to familiar spaces: "We painters say to
ourselves that we have to do something at Beaux-Arts, that we can't let
the buildings be empty, closed up." An old lithograph machine is located;
the first poster, USINE-UNIVERSITE-UNION, is produced immediately. The
thought at that point is for someone to run the thirty copies down to a
gallery on the rue Dragon to sell them to help the movement. But it is at
this point that "the real," in the shape of the movement, literally inter-
venes, short-circuiting the steps that art must take to be art in bourgeois
culture and hijacking it, so to speak, off that path, bringing it into the
now. There is no time, it seems, for the art object to remain a commodity,
even one that had been redirected in the service of the movement. On the

8. See Gérard Fromanger, "L'art c'est ce qui rend la vie plus intéressante que l'art," *Libération*, May 14, 1998, 43. See also Adrian Rifkin, introduction to *Photogenic Painting / La Peinture
photogénique*, ed. Sarah Wilson (London: Black Dog Press, 1999), 21–59.

way to the gallery, the copies are snatched out of the arms of the student carrying them and plastered immediately on the first available wall. The poster becomes a poster.

"Bourgeois culture," reads the statement that accompanied the founding of the *Atelier populaire*, "separates and isolates artists from other workers by according them a privileged status. Privilege encloses the artist in an invisible prison. We have decided to transform what we are in society."[9]

I think it was in the midst of reviewing hours and hours of tapes of television commemorations that I made the perhaps unusual decision, in a book about the social memory and amnesia of May '68 in France, to conduct no interviews during my research. Whom would I have interviewed? To convey something of the nature of a mass event, I was reluctant to turn to the people who have become major figures in the legends of May culture by virtue of the attention that has already been accorded them, many of whom can now be seen occupying those choice positions within the structure of power that are reserved especially for people who once publicly accused it. Nor did I wish to conduct an ethnographic study of some distinct sector—workers, farmers, a particular political tendency—although a few such studies, some very good, now exist, which I refer to in this book. What possible controls could govern my selection of the testimony of participants in a mass movement that extended throughout France, reaching virtually every town, professional sector, region, and age group? Throughout this book, as in any investigation of the recent past, words written by still living witnesses and participants rub up against writing that has already gathered and sifted documentary traces of the event. But published testimonies at least are open to whomever wishes to read them; unlike oral interviews, they are not addressed to a specific interlocutor. Published testimonies, as Paul Ricoeur suggests, are testimonies that have consented to enter the fray, to put themselves out under the gaze of other testimonies. For this reason I have limited myself to the public record, to a no doubt highly unscientific combination of different material traces in all their profusion and diversity (public and private archival documents, tracts, magazine and journal articles, documentary footage, memoirs, the press) to arrive at the tributary stories of various gazes upon and experiences of the events, and the way these events have been recalled and discussed later on. A collage of individual, sometimes ephemeral, subjectivities circulates in what follows, subjectivities that do not add up to any kind of "exemplary itineraries" or biographical life stories. But without these evocations I could not have hoped to render any sense of the specific

9. "Document: L'atelier populaire." *Les Cahiers de Mai* 2 (July 1–15, 1968): 14–16.

forms of political sociability of those times—any sense, that is, of what it is that has been lost. Since I have been concerned with charting both the official story—like all clichés, easily accessible—and its deviations, I have made a special effort to locate memories that do not conform to the predispositions of the present, that do not serve to legitimate contemporary configurations of power.

But the predispositions of the present have been changing recently in France and along with them the available optics onto '68 as well. The mass strikes of the winter of 1995 in France, followed by the events in Seattle a few years later, have surely played a role in figuring a new conjuncture, a new sense of creative political capacity in France and elsewhere. For my own purposes, two other manifestations of a change in the political and intellectual climate in France have been particularly significant. In recent years a number of alternative political narratives of the last thirty years have appeared, written by people active during the '68 years and compelled, now, to recover a past—their own and others'—a past they view to have been distorted, even hijacked, during the Giscard and Mitterrand years. At the same time, younger scholars, mostly historians, have begun for the first time in France to turn to a serious consideration of the Algerian War period and the '68 years. The labor of these two groups of writers constitutes an important new chapter, in and of itself, in the memory of 1968. And it has made my own work less solitary.

THE POLICE CONCEPTION OF HISTORY

SOCIOLOGY AND THE POLICE

"But nothing happened in France in '68. Institutions didn't change, the university didn't change, conditions for workers didn't change—nothing happened." The speaker, a well-known German sociologist, was responding to a talk I had given about the problems presented by the social memory of '68 in France. He continued: "'68 was really Prague, and Prague brought down the Berlin Wall."[1]

Nothing happened in France, and everything happened in Prague—this was an interpretation I had not encountered before in such a succinct form. Certainly, a more international perspective on '68 than the one I offered that day has long been available, one that emphasizes the convergence in the 1960s of the national liberation struggles (Cuba, Indochina), the antibureaucratic struggles (Hungary, Czechoslovakia), and the anti-capitalist and anti-authoritarian struggles that erupted in the imperialist metropoles of Europe and North America. But the direction of this remark was clearly different. Not only had the third world been eliminated from the picture, but now France was disappearing as well. It was not that many different things happened throughout the world in a brief set of time, it was that only one thing happened; it happened in Prague, and what happened in Prague were the seeds that would later fulfill a triumphant Cold War teleology: the end of actually existing socialism.[2] Was this the post-1989 voice of the Cold War victor,

1. Wolf Lepenies, Institute for Advanced Study, Princeton, October 1999.

2. The idea that "Prague '68 brought down the Berlin Wall" in some sort of direct relation of cause and effect in itself raises basic questions of historical causality, particularly since insurgents in Prague in 1968 (unlike those of 1989) did not seem to view their aspirations for more democracy as being at all incompatible with socialism. See Jean-François Vilar, "Paris-Prague: Aller simple et vague retour," *Lignes* 34 (May 1998): 87: "The fact is that no one, in Czechoslovakia [in 1968] envisaged departing from a socialist schema. The fact is also that in 1989–90 almost no

sweeping up everything that occurred in the twentieth century into that one framework, into that one lone narrative? And if something doesn't fit in that narrative, such as May '68 in France, does it then have no significance? Has change become unthinkable outside of that narrative?

The fall of socialism and the seemingly undisputed hegemony achieved by capitalism distances our world from the world of '68 to the point where it becomes quite difficult to imagine a time when people once envisioned a world different in essential ways from the one in which we now live. In this sense, the sociologist's remarks at Princeton are in keeping with much of the post-1989 assessment of May, a recasting or a forgetting that harnesses May's energy directly to the inevitable outcome of the world of the present. Even *French* May, by some accounts now, when it is acknowledged to have happened, had this outcome—the world of today—as its goal.[3] Through a curious ruse of history, the assault from the left on the reformism and bureaucracy of the French Communist Party had the paradoxical effect of sounding the death knells for the hope of any systemic or revolutionary change from that moment on—and this, according to some ex-*gauchistes* claiming an after-the-fact prescience, was precisely what was desired at the time. In this view, the years separating '68 from the virulent anti-Marxism of prominent ex-*gauchistes* in the mid-1970s are erased from memory, so that those counter-movement phenomena can be made to appear as the secret "meaning," the "underlying desire" of the event all along.

Was the succinctness of the sociologist's assessment of French May grounded in the confidence with which the discipline of sociology—the field that has dominated the interpretation of the May events—claims the ability to measure change and even determine the criteria according to which change can be measured? The feeling that "nothing happened" in May is, of course, frequently expressed—with differing political/affective tones—throughout France today. "Nothing happened, except for the women's movement—and look what that has done to the family"—that is, nothing happened, but everything that did happen was regrettable. This is one version. Another version sounds like this: "Nothing happened. The

---

one defended fixing up the social system within the framework of any kind of 'socialism.'" Vilar, a resident of Prague, states that 1968 in the area that was formerly Czechoslovakia today, far from representing the founding liberatory moment in the march to the present, is instead "never thought about, except among friends." At the level of official history, Prague '68 seems best forgotten, its aspirations incompatible with, rather than leading to or causing—as Wolf Lepenies and others like him imagine—the present-day market democracy.

3. See, for example, Gilles Lipovetsky, *L'ère du vide: Essais sur l'individualisme contemporaine* (Paris: Gallimard, 1983).

French State was able to absorb all that political turbulence and now all those guys have fabulous careers and are driving BMWs"—as though those French driving BMWs today were the only participants in the movement then. Or "Nothing happened politically—but culturally the changes were enormous." This is perhaps the most prevalent version heard in France today, an assessment that relies on a view that the two spheres of politics and culture can be definitively isolated the one from the other. And an assessment where the surfeit of culture's visibility—lifestyle, customs, *habitus*—exists in direct proportion to the invisibility of politics, the amnesia that now surrounds the specifically political dimensions of the '68 years.

What, in fact, can be perceived about those years now? It is perhaps when viewing French television commemorations of the '68 events, particularly those that accompanied the twentieth anniversary of May, that the viewer is most clearly left with the suspicion that "nothing happened." Is this their purpose? Frequently, the commemorations create the impression that everything happened (and so nothing happened); a global contestation of just about everything—imperialism, dress codes, reality, dormitory curfews, capitalism, grammar, sexual repression, communism—and therefore nothing (since everything is equally important) occurred; that May consisted of students saying absolutely anything and workers having nothing to say; or, as in this representative conversation between two former *gauchistes* on a 1985 television commemoration:

> R. Castro (a former Maoist leader, since psychoanalyzed by Lacan): May '68 wasn't political, it was a movement purely of words. . . .
>
> R. Kahn (ex-*gauchiste*, converted to liberalism): It's true . . . the terrible evil of replacing reality with words . . . the idea that anything is possible . . . one of the most lamentable periods . . . children who no longer have any culture . . . even the National Front is a result of '68.
>
> R. Castro: May '68 was a crisis of the elites.
>
> R. Kahn: Sure, now we listen better to kids . . . the system of the *petits chefs* was shaken.
>
> Alfonsi (the TV moderator, to Castro): Are you wearing a "Don't touch my buddy" ["Touche pas à mon pote"] button?
>
> R. Castro: Yes, it makes me feel less anxious.[4]

Amid this discursive and syntactic jumble May, once again, comes to incorporate everything and therefore nothing. The mainstream media,

---

4. Maurice Dugowson, "Histoire d'un jour: 30 mai 1968," television documentary, Europe 1, France 3, 1985.

working in conjunction with ex-*gauchistes*, maintain a haziness or blurring of focus on the event, a blurring that succeeds in dissolving the object through chatter. Viewers witnessing the verbal delirium of ex-*gauchistes* on television might well be drawn to form the same conclusion as the sociologist I encountered in Princeton, particularly when the '68 goal of "seizing speech" is represented as having produced nothing much more, in the long run, than the contemporary spectacle of the commemoration as talk show. Still, the starkness of the sociologist's pronouncement bears further commentary. "Nothing happened in France": nothing changed, major institutions remained unaltered. Was this the voice of the professional sociologist, he whose task it is to say why things invariably remain the same, for whom a rupture in the system gets recuperated so as to reinsert it back into a logic of the same, the logic of the continuous, the logic of reproduction? It is for that reason that sociological interpretations of May and other events have always seemed to me to verge on the tautological. And facts seem to be explained according to the terms of their existence. "Youth rebelling" is one such hypostatic sociological category frequently mobilized in relation to May: youth rebel because they are young; they rebel because they are students and the university is overcrowded; they rebel "like rats or other animals, when forced to live at an excessive density in a confined space."[5] This last is the analogy that another sociologist, Raymond Aron, came up with shortly after the events—marshalling an animalizing vocabulary underused since the time of the Paris Commune.

Or was it the voice of the police? "Nothing happened." In a recent text, Jacques Rancière uses that phrase—only in the present tense: "Nothing is happening"—to represent the functioning of what, broadly speaking, he calls "the police."

> Police intervention in public space is less about interpellating demonstrators than it is about dispersing them. The police are not the law that interpellates the individual (the "hey, you there" of Louis Althusser) unless we confuse the law with religious subjection. The police are above all a certitude about what is there, or rather, about what is not there: "Move along, there's nothing to see." The police say there is nothing to see, nothing happening, nothing to be done but to keep moving, circulating; they say that the space of circulation is nothing but the space of circulation. Politics consists in transforming that space of circulation into the space of the manifestation of a subject: be it the people, workers, citizens. It consists in refiguring that space, what there is to do

5. Raymond Aron, *The Elusive Revolution: Anatomy of a Student Revolt* (New York: Praeger, 1969), 41.

there, what there is to see, or to name. It is a dispute about the division of what is perceptible to the senses.[6]

Is the sociologist's relation to the past that of the police to the present? For Rancière, the police and the sociologist speak with the same voice. Even the most discriminating sociology returns us back to a *habitus,* a way of being, a social grounding or set of determinations that confirm, in the final accounting, that things could not have happened in any other way, that things could not have been any different. Thus, any singularity of experience—and any way in which individuals produce meaning that attempts to capture that singularity—is cancelled out in the process. The police make sure that a properly functional social order functions properly—in this sense they put into practice the discourse of normative sociology. The "police," then, for Rancière, are less concerned with repression than with a more basic function: that of constituting what is or is not perceivable, determining what can or cannot be seen, dividing what can be heard from what cannot. For ultimately the police become the name in his view for everything that concerns the distribution of places and functions, as well as the system that legitimates that hierarchical distribution. The police do their counting statistically: they deal in groups defined by differences in birth, functions, places, and interests. They are another name for the symbolic constitution of the social: the social as made up of groups with specific, identifiable ways of operating—"profiles"—and these ways of operating are themselves assigned directly, quasi-naturally, to the places where those occupations are performed. These groups, when counted, make up the social whole— nothing is missing; nothing is in excess; nothing or no one is left uncounted. "Move along, there is nothing to see." The very phrase is a perfect adequation of functions, places, and identities—nothing is missing, nothing is happening.

But if the "police" is the name Rancière gives to the broadest possible agency of sociopolitical classification, that agency includes not only the various sociological, cultural, and medical classifying functions that set up groups and their functions and that "naturalize" the relations between the two, it also includes the police as we customarily understand the police— the cop on the street. Both senses overlap, as in the perhaps apocryphal anecdote recounted by Henri Lefebvre at Nanterre in 1968 who, when asked to provide the deans with a list of the more politically disruptive

---

6. Jacques Rancière, *Aux bords du politique* (Paris: La fabrique, 1998), 177. Here and elsewhere, translations from the French, unless otherwise noted, are mine.

students in his classes, is said to have replied: "Monsieur le doyen, je ne suis pas un flic."[7]

Writing in 1998, Rancière proposes a theorization of politics and the social order substantially informed by the events of '68 in which he participated thirty years earlier. In the immediate aftermath of '68, years that saw a veritable hypertrophy of the French state in response to a palpable panic among the elites, French theory became populated with police figures. The police appear regularly in the 1970s, as characters, as forces, within theoretical speculation: in the status of example (the "hey, you there" of the interpellating cop on the street in Louis Althusser's staging of how ideology functions); in Michel Foucault's vast meditations on state repression (*Surveiller et punir*, 1975); in Jacques Donzelot's Foucauldian analysis of how the family comes to be inserted into an intricate web of bureaucratic institutions and systems of management (*La Police des familles*, 1977). Their presence is a constant in Maurice Blanchot's analyses of the movement written in conjunction with the Comité d'Action Etudiants-Ecrivains, and it can be felt in a 1969 text like "La parole quotidienne."[8] In the wake of '68, a period of massive concern with public order and its breakdown, when the government's tangible fear of the population taking to the streets again had manifested itself in a dramatic increase of police presence everywhere—in cafés, museums, on street corners, wherever more than two or three people gather—philosophy and theory begin to bear the trace of that presence. Thirty years later, the trace of May and its aftermath can still be found in Rancière's theoretical conceptualization of "the police" as the order of distribution of bodies as a community, as the way places, powers, and functions are managed in the state's production of a chosen social order, and in his analysis of politics as the disruption, broadly speaking, of that naturalized distribution.

In what follows I want to keep each of these registers visible. The empirical police, whose activities made up such an essential part of a regime like de Gaulle's, born in 1958 of a military *coup*, will dominate my discussion in this chapter about the proximity of the Algerian War to the May events. In the next chapter, I will turn to the forms and practices developed during May that went about "denaturalizing" past social relations—and, in so doing, disrupting "the police" as a kind of logic of the social: the logic that assigns people to their places and their social identities, that makes them identical to their functions. For May '68 in fact had very little to do with the interests of the social group—students or "youth"—

7. Henri Lefebvre, cited in Kristin Ross, "Lefebvre on the Situationists: An Interview," *October* 79 (winter 1997): 82.

8. See "La parole quotidienne," in *L'Entretien infini* (Paris: Gallimard, 1969), 355–66.

who sparked the action. What has come to be called "the events of May" consisted mainly in students ceasing to function as students, workers as workers, and farmers as farmers: May was a crisis in functionalism. The movement took the form of political experiments in *de*classification, in disrupting the natural "givenness" of places; it consisted of displacements that took students outside of the university, meetings that brought farmers and workers together, or students to the countryside—trajectories outside of the Latin Quarter, to workers' housing and popular neighborhoods, a new kind of mass organizing (against the Algerian War in the early 1960s, and later against the Vietnam War) that involved physical dislocation. And in that physical dislocation lay a dislocation in the very idea of politics— moving it out of its place, its proper place, which was for the left at that time the Communist Party. The logic of the police worked throughout this period to separate students from workers, to prevent contact, to iso- late students in the Latin Quarter, to prevent student-worker interaction during the June battle at the Flins factory and elsewhere. The vehemence with which that work was carried out—whether by CGT functionaries, de Gaulle, the Communist Party, or the police themselves—gives some notion of the threat such a politics posed. May '68 had less to do with the identity or interests of "students" per se, than with a disjuncture or fissure created within that identity. That disjuncture, as Rancière has suggested elsewhere, took the form of a political opening to otherness (represented by the two classical "others" of political modernity, the worker and the colonial subject) that was itself the result of that generation's particular historical and political memory, a memory bound up with and inscribed in decolonization.[9] (And the story of decolonization was a story in which the police, of course, played a starring role). It was that disjuncture that allowed students and intellectuals to break with the identity of a partic- ular social group with particular self-interests and accede to something larger, to politics in the sense that Rancière gives it, or to what Maurice Blanchot has singled out as the specific force of May: "in the so-called 'student' action, students never acted as students but rather as revealers of a general crisis, as bearers of a power of rupture putting into question the regime, the State, society."[10] They acted in such a way as to put into question the conception of the social (the social as functional) on which the state based its authority to govern. The political opening to otherness

9. See Jacques Rancière, interview, "Democracy Means Equality," *Radical Philosophy* 82 (March/April 1997): 33.

10. This text was originally published under the collective authorship of the Comité d'Action Etudiants-Ecrivains. See "Un an après, le Comité d'action écrivains-étudiants," *Les Lettres Nou- velles* (June–July 1969): 143–88; a portion of it, entitled "Sur le mouvement," was later attributed to Maurice Blanchot and reprinted in *Lignes* 33 (March 1998): 177.

allowed activists to create a rupture with that order, to displace, if only briefly, the places assigned by the police, to make seen what was not seen, make heard what could not be heard.

To show this, we must keep up the tension between "May" as at once an event (as a point in time, a moment when, in fact, "something happened"), *and* as a roughly twenty-year period extending from the mid-1950s to the mid-1970s. It was an event, in the sense that Alain Badiou has given the term: something that arrives in excess, beyond all calculation, something that displaces people and places, that proposes an entirely new situation for thought.[11] It was an event in the sense that thousands—even millions—of people were led infinitely farther than their education, their social situation, their initial vocation would have allowed them to foresee; an event in the sense that real participation—much more than a vague, formal solidarity, much more even than shared ideas—altered the course of lives. But it was not, as many have described it since, a kind of meteorological accident arising out of unforeseen planetary conjunctures or, as in the oft-heard cliché, "a thunderclap in the middle of a serene sky." By 1968 the sky was already darkened. It was an event with a long preparation, dating back to the mobilization against the Algerian War and with an immediate afterlife continuing at least up to the mid-1970s.

What the longer periodization allows me to argue is that May '68 was not a great cultural reform, a push toward modernization, or the dawning sun of a new individualism. It was above all *not* a revolt on the part of the sociological category "youth." It was the revolt of an historically situated cross-section of workers and students alike, for some of whom the War in Algeria provided the background noise of their childhood, whose adolescence or adulthood coincided with the massacre of hundreds of Algerian workers at the hands of Papon's police on October 17, 1961, with Charonne and the near-daily attacks of the OAS. These people were not necessarily of the same age, nor were they all embarked on the same political trajectory, but they all saw, in the context of the final years of the Algerian War, to what use the Gaullist regime put their police. The proximity of '68 to the Algerian events a few years earlier would come to be the first and most important of the dimensions of '68 to be forgotten in the official version produced during the 1980s. Even in 1974, however, activist Guy Hocquenghem was alert to the way Algeria and other world regions of intensive French focus during 1968 were fading from collective memory:

---

11. See Alain Badiou, "Penser le surgissement de l'événement," *Cahiers du Cinéma*, special issue "Cinéma 68," May 1998, 10.

Countries, entire continents have dimmed in our memory: the Algeria of the war, Mao's China, Vietnam have sped by on express trains amid the deafening noise of bombs and battles. We had hardly time to even fantasize about them—already these countries have disappeared for us.[12]

MATRAQUAGE

"Any dialogue between *matraqueurs* and *matraqués* is impossible."[13] Sometime around the middle of May 1968, as this slogan suggests, the policeman's club or *matraque* had become for the insurgents in the streets a pure synecdoche for the State. During de Gaulle's long silence and the fumbling government's response to the initial outbreaks of street violence, the police had become the lone, unmediated representatives of the State. On either side of an absolute division lay those two paradigmatic figures, the beaters and the beaten, inhabiting radically separate and unequal "zones" of existence in a state of immediacy, a state in which any possibility of reciprocal recognition or "dialogue" is doomed to futility. The relation between beaters and beaten is an antidialectic of absolute difference and total opposition—a relationship of "pure violence," not unlike the one Frantz Fanon theorized between his paradigmatic figures of "colonizer" and "colonized" in *Les damnés de la terre*. The *matraque*, a short, generally balanced weapon used for bludgeoning, made of a wooden stick, thicker and heavier at one end and covered with hardened rubber, figures prominently in dramatic recountings, documentary film footage, and the political iconography of May-June. Thus, a typical militant tract entitled "How to Avoid the Matraques," distributed on the bloodiest night of the May events, May 24, instructs demonstrators on how best to fold sections of newspapers like *France-Soir* or *"Figaremuche,"* as militants called the right-wing newspaper, *Le Figaro,* to use as protective coating for the shoulders and neck: "The thickness should correspond to that of 'matraquable' skin—about twenty-five pages of bourgeois press."[14] In narratives of *prise de conscience politique* on the part of people who had kept their distance from politics up until that point, the *matraque* frequently serves an almost pedagogical role of "awakening" or revelation. Thus, one activist, writing in 1988, recalls the police violence of twenty years earlier: "It was

12. Guy Hocquenghem, *L'après-Mai des faunes* (Paris: Grasset, 1974), 35.

13. Alain Sauvageot, cited in UNEF et S.N.E. Sup., *Le livre noir des journées de mai (du 3 mai au 13 mai)* (Paris: Seuil, 1968), 40.

14. Alain Schnapp and Pierre Vidal-Naquet, eds., "How to Avoid the Police-Clubs (Matraques)," *Journal de la Commune étudiante. Textes et documents, nov. 1967–juin 1968* (Paris: Seuil, 1988), 433.

an excellent lesson on the nature of a State that maintains itself through the force of a *matraque:* it was direct education."[15] Another witness states, "I saw street battles up close, I saw cops break peoples' heads open. When you see cops charge, it marks you for the rest of your life."[16] A third participant describes his initiation:

> For me, May '68 started when I was hit with a police club [*matraqué*] walking out of an apartment. It was one of the first demos in the Latin Quarter. The cops were charging. I had heard about what was going on out at Nanterre, but that was still very far away for me. I was in high school, in a preparatory class for the *grandes écoles,* I was peacefully pursuing my studies. All of a sudden I started going to meetings, to assemblies. I didn't understand much of it at all.[17]

Police violence in early May brought more and more people onto the streets. But the catalytic role played by the police in creating the mass dimension of the movement began, it seems, even before the *matraques* started to swing. The very presence of large numbers of police, called to Nanterre by a rector, Pierre Grappin, who had himself been active in the Resistance, made the collusion between the university and the police visible to a new degree:

> The reaction of the students, not only to the action of the police, but to their simple presence . . . is a visceral reaction, a reflex allergy. Most of the students were apolitical in the beginning, they disapproved of the incidents at Nanterre. But they were instinctually on the side of the March 22nd group . . . because the police were there and that signified for them an intolerable repression.[18]

Henri Lefebvre recalls the meeting of theory and daily life at Nanterre:

> The essential Marxist works that the students were reading and commenting on were the texts by Marx on the State, on political alienation. I'm convinced that these played a part in the students' slogan: "Down with the police state." This slogan came out of their experience, their experience with the cops, with controlled space, the space of the university, of the suburbs and the shantytowns that then surrounded the campus of Nanterre.[19]

15. Gérald, cited in Nicolas Daum, *Des révolutionnaires dans un village parisien* (Paris: Londreys, 1988), 158.

16. J.-P., cited in Daum, *Des révolutionnaires dans un village parisien,* 251.

17. Yann, cited in Bruno Giorgini, *Que sont mes amis devenus?* (Paris: Savelli, 1978), 119.

18. Epistemon, *Les idées qui ont ébranlé la France. Nanterre: novembre 1967–juin 1968* (Paris: Fayard, 1968), 100. The "March 22nd Movement" (*Mouvement du 22 mars*) was the anarchist-leaning coalition of Nanterre activists that took shape on that day in 1968.

19. Henri Lefebvre, *Le temps des méprises* (Paris: Stock, 1975), 115.

Another activist remembers a physiological response to the sight of the police:

> First of all, the fact of seeing that thick gray and blue wall of police revolted me, that kind of wall advancing toward us . . . and I too wanted to throw something at them.[20]

Alain Krivine and others have emphasized the spark provided by Rector Roche's decision to call the police into the Sorbonne on May 3. Never before had the police entered the Sorbonne—not even the Germans had violated that sanctuary! From that point on, a movement that had very little initial objective begins to converge around slogans like "Liberate the Sorbonne from police occupation" and "Liberate our comrades in prison" (referring to students initially arrested over anti-Vietnam demonstrations). By May 11, the key demand on the part of the students had become the removal of the police from the university. Again and again, the mere presence of the police served to politicize situations. Among lycéens, police presence—on campus or in the vicinity— was of prime concern. An episode of the television show "Les chemins de la vie," entitled "En terminale," screened in mid-May, shows two lycéens arguing the case for "liberty of expression" (by which they mean the right to conduct political action—organizing, distributing tracts, etc.—inside the high school). The dialogue between the two students and what appear to be well-meaning administrators, who assure them that they too believe in "liberty of expression," reaches an impasse. The students cannot accept what is in their view the reiteration of a merely abstract or formal "liberty of expression"; their concerns, they make clear, are immediate and concrete: "Will the police continue to be outside the lycée door waiting to arrest us?"[21] Similarly, the remarks of a worker at the Sochaux Peugeot factory, commenting on the violence that erupted on June 11, when the government sent in troops of CRS (paramilitary riot police) to take over the striking factory, make clear the politicizing effect that police presence has on a situation not previously viewed as such: "We were against the boss, the factory management, not the CRS—now it's a political fight, we had to defend ourselves. I didn't go there initially to fight, it was a trap. They leapt on top of everyone who fell and kept hitting them after they were on the ground."[22] The worker speaking lost a foot in the battle on June 11; two others, Henri

---

20. Anonymous activist, cited in Jacques Durandeaux, *Les journées de mai 68* (Paris: Desclée de Brouwer, 1968), 13.

21. "En terminale," episode of television series, "Les chemins de la vie," producer Pierre Cardinale, 1968.

22. Worker, speaking at the funeral of slain worker Pierre Beylot, cited in Collectif de Cinéastes et travailleurs de Sochaux, *Sochaux 11 juin 68*, film documentary, 1970.

Blanchet and Pierre Beylot, were killed by the CRS, and 150 other workers were seriously wounded. The instrumental role of the police in securing not only order, but a specifically capitalist order in which workers must fulfill the social function allotted them, could not be more obvious. As the slogan says, there is no possible dialogue between *matraqueurs* and *matraqués*.

As police violence accelerated throughout the first half of May, the tendency, particularly on the part of the CRS, to conduct "blind attacks," which encompassed activists and passersby indiscriminately in a whirlwind of blows, had the effect of producing sympathy in middle-class observers and bystanders not initially well-disposed toward the demonstrators. "The cops were hitting absolutely everyone in their vicinity: I remember seeing a woman passing by with a baby in her arms being beaten [*matraqué*] to the ground."[23]

> One day a professor was walking out of a book store where he had bought some books, and he passed by a group of CRS who immediately began to beat [*matraquer*] him. Their chief must have noticed that the man wasn't a student but rather someone more respectable, and he ordered his men to stop. One of them yelled out, "But chief, he was carrying books!"[24]

The vast sympathy extended to the insurrection on the part of the general population in the first half of May is most often attributed to the effect produced by what the onlookers saw, or thought they were seeing, happening on the streets: a conflict between students and the police. In that drama, one could only be on the side of the students, even if some of them were clearly, in the view of some observers, "troublemakers," and even if some of the students were not really "students." But that sympathy receded markedly when the general strike began after May 13, and a different dynamic—one more clearly resonant of "class warfare"—replaced the violent, athletic skirmishes of early May.

But those skirmishes were certainly instrumental, if we turn to the very few accounts by young workers to be found, in producing an almost instant familiarity on their part with students through the basis of shared experience ("*Matraques, we know them well!*").[25] Workers initially expressed a merely sentimental or abstract solidarity with student demonstrators against police repression. "We were all anti-cops," says one automobile worker. "Among young workers there has always been hatred of

23. René, cited in Daum, *Des révolutionnaires dans un village parisien,* 211.
24. Nicolas, cited in Daum, *Des révolutionnaires dans un village parisien,* 211.
25. Sochaux worker, cited in Collectif de Cinéastes et travailleurs de Sochaux, *Sochaux 11 juin 1968.*

the cops."[26] Another militant worker points out that "It's the same cops, the CRS, who shuttle back and forth between the factory gates and the university gates."[27] But violence very quickly provided a way of progressing from such abstract identification to the more intense and immediate solidarity of combat, as these remarks suggest: "We should be with them [the students] in their combat, participate in their demonstrations at their sides.".[28] Unlike parents and middle-class onlookers, in other words, workers were not moved by pity toward the gassed and the beaten, but rather by a sentiment of admiring respect for the direct action taken by the students—a solidarity that was not charity.

The verb *"matraquer"* that appears so frequently in the literature of May-June takes on a figurative meaning for the first time only after '68. It is only then that the French begin to speak, for example, of the *matraquage* of televisual images, or of other sensory experiences of incessant repetition: no longer literal blows raining down, but the droning staccato of repeated advertising jingles, the refrains of popular music. After '68, the word is most often used in the context of certain kinds of media or advertising "saturation" campaigns, when advertisement slogans descend like cluster bombing, creating the bland monotony of received ideas or doxa, the whole reiterative logic of "the society of consumption." Emmanuel Terray, to take just one example, speaks of the *matraquage* "dear to our advertising executives," conducted by French media in the 1980s around the idea of the "end of history."[29] But during the year 1968 the word *matraquage* was suspended between its future connotations and its colonial past: the word derives originally from the Algerian Arabic, *matraq,* or "club." In 1968, the same word contained both the future announced by its figurative sense, which was just appearing, and the materiality of past colonial violence. In the future lay the way in which the values of the dominant ideology (the market, profits, the firm) find their praises sung—or hammered out (*matraqué*) by the dominant media. But the colonial origins

26. Citroën worker, cited in Michèle Manceaux, *Les Maos en France* (Paris: Gallimard, 1972), 74.

27. CFDT tract, "Zoom sur les jeunes," May 8, 1968, cited in Jacques Baynac, *Mai retrouvé* (Paris: Robert Laffont, 1978), 3.

28. CFDT tract, May 9, 1968, cited in Baynac, *Mai retrouvé,* 74.

29. Emmanuel Terray, *Le troisième jour du communisme* (Paris: Actes Sud, 1992), 9. The *Dictionnaire Grand Robert* gives the original derivation of the word, dating from 1863, from the Algerian Arabic *matraq,* meaning "club" or "big stick." For the post-'68 connotations, it cites this 1970 example taken from Gilbert's *Dictionnaire des mots nouveaux:* "In the language of radio professionals there exists a term, as vulgar as it is significant: *matraquage.* It is a process that consists of filling the listeners' ears with a new slogan or tune that they want to have a commercial success. Specialists say that it's virtually infallible as a technique."

of the word remind us of that long national history and of other bloody confrontations in the not so distant past—confrontations in the colonies and in France that preceded and set the stage for the altercations of May.

By 1968, the idea of direct, physical confrontation with the police as the representative of state power had, for many militants, already acquired substantial validity. Much of that validity had been established by a series of factory strikes that erupted throughout France in the mid-1960s, "savage" or wildcat strikes that began more or less spontaneously in one workshop of one factory, and then spread to the whole enterprise, city, or industrial sector. These strikes were directed against the union leadership as much as against the factory management. Earlier, in 1963, miners had conducted a violent strike and resisted the return to work that the unions had decided; in 1964, Renault workers at Flins, chanting "We want time in order *to live*," demanded a reduced work week. Spontaneous strikes that were longer and more violent than those conducted by the unions occurred in Nantes in 1964, in the naval shipyards of the Midi in February 1966, at Redon, at Le Mans, where workers erected barricades, and at Rhodiaceta in Lyons and Besançon, where the strike lasted the whole month of December 1967 and spread to all the factories of the group in the Lyons region. At Caen, in January 1968 rioting occurred after a strike was savagely repressed; students, farmers, and workers filled the streets together; and over two hundred people were wounded in street fighting with the police. All regions of France, in other words, were touched by labor unrest in the years immediately preceding May '68, unrest that took the form of strikes initiated by workers who resisted any attempts by the labor management to render their strikes symbolic. These strikes were the first since 1936 to involve occupation of the factories by workers. Workers' demands were not always limited to merely economic gains, but began to veer toward a questioning of the model of production, the power structure of the unions, and beyond that, the model of Gaullist society itself. For some student activists, then, these experiments in direct action provided a model or, as Sartre put it more accurately in another context, they "expanded the field of the possible."[30] It was these strikes, during which, as one worker commented, "More was gained in ten hours of street fighting than in ten months of committee meetings,"[31] that offered one scenario of direct action or confrontation. "It was clear before *22 mars* [the March 22 movement] that effective direct action that doesn't temporize on its objectives once those objectives have been set, as in Caen, Redon, etc.—

30. Jean-Paul Sartre, "Sartre par Sartre," in *Situations IX* (Paris: Gallimard, 1972), 127.

31. CFDT delegate at Caens, cited in "The Story of a March 22nd Movement Militant," in *"This Is Only a Beginning,"* ed. Philippe Labro (New York: Funk and Wagnalls, 1969), 82.

well, it works."[32] One of the earliest '68 tracts, distributed by Maoists in the workers' suburbs surrounding Paris, attempted to create a direct link between students' insurgency and the workers' strikes of '67: "Students are not afraid of the cops. When the bourgeoisie's cops repress progressive movements, they don't make the law. Workers at Caen and Redon inflicted a severe lesson on them. Students who support peoples' struggle will go to the school of workers and peasants."[33]

Indeed, it was the documentary film on the Rhodiaceta strike made by Chris Marker and the SLON workers' film collective, broadcast on Antenne 2 in February of 1968 and shown again at a number of film clubs and to students at Nanterre, that provided many militants with some knowledge they may not have otherwise had of the politically turbulent atmosphere within French factories.

> The first important thing that happened to me, a little before May '68, was the discovery of workers' exploitation. Through school I happened to do some training for three months working in a coal mine. I lived with miners. I discovered their habits, even how they ate—something I knew nothing about. It really had an effect on me.
>
> Around the same time I saw a Chris Marker film on TV about the Rhodiaceta strike. It was very important to see that film at the same time, because I could have said to myself, well, miners, that's something special, an older working class. But Rhodia was one of the foremost branches of capitalist accumulation, and that strike brought with it demands and forms of struggle that prefigured May and post-May especially.[34]

The film, entitled *A bientôt, j'espère,* concludes with these words from a worker: "The bosses must not think that we have lost. We will meet again and we will win. A bientôt, j'espère."[35]

But for most of the participants and observers of the May events in Paris it was another set of associations, those evoked by the colonial origins of the *matraque,* that resurfaced during the street fighting. The shock provided by the sheer physical density of the police presence in the streets, a show of state force unseen in Paris since the early 1960s, provoked an immediate association back to the violent ambiance that accompanied the final months of that war. "Streets thick with police cars—reminds

32. Labro, *"This Is Only a Beginning,"* 82.

33. Maoist tract, signed "Comité de défense contre la répression," cited in Baynac, *Mai retrouvé,* 46.

34. Alain, an engineer, cited in Giorgini, *Que sont mes amis devenus?* 85–86.

35. Chris Marker and Mario Marret, *A bientôt, j'espère,* film documentary, 1967.

me of Algerian War,"[36] noted Mavis Gallant. Another witness set the scene in more detail. "Saint-Germain-des-près. There, the first ambulance medics, some with their shirts stained with blood. A hundred *gardes mobiles*. For the first time since Algeria, I am face to face with the enemy."[37] The shock seems to have dislodged a kind of bodily memory in some participants and observers, a sense of *déjà vu*. One participant describes the sensation of being involuntarily transported back in time:

> When we got to the Saint-Michel station, once the doors of the cars were opened, an unbearable odor of chlorine gas emerged, and it became even worse since several people, their heads cracked open and bleeding, had crowded into the station, taking refuge in what was still free space. Suddenly, my throat tightening and my eyes burning, I rediscovered the horrible sensation of tear gas inhaled during the demonstrations against the war in Algeria.[38]

What one observer sees on the street below him immediately recalls the violence of the Algerian period: "At the building windows, the curtains rustle imperceptibly. We watch, shocked and afraid, the cops beat the students the way they had "ratonné" (rat-trapped) the Arabs a few years earlier."[39] For Mavis Gallant, not only the sights, but the sounds produce the association just as strongly: "In the night, that familiar wave of sound, as during the crisis of 1958."[40] Gallant evokes a set of bodily postures, positions adopted instinctively in the choreography of street violence, that recur, creating a kind of palimpsest or layering of the two moments:

> the head bashed in by the *matraques;* fractures of the wrist and forearm, the arm having been raised to protect the head; fractures of the ankle after a fall (running), the pursuer having smashed down on whatever he could reach. (This last thing I saw here in Paris ten years ago this month during the Algerian crisis . . . I see it—the kid tripped, down, the grown man . . .)[41]

Even the vocabulary at hand to describe the way militant students are systematically hunted, chased, cornered in their altercations with the police must be borrowed from the colonial arsenal. *Ratonnade*, a word used only

36. Mavis Gallant, "The Events in May: A Paris Notebook—I," *New Yorker*, Sept 14, 1968, 106.

37. Pierre Peuchmaurd, *Plus vivants que jamais* (Paris: Laffont, 1968), 24.

38. Maurice Rajsfus, *Le travail à perpétuité* (Paris: Manya, 1993), 157.

39. Jacques Baynac, *Mai retrouvé*, 93.

40. Mavis Gallant, "Paris Notebook—I," 58.

41. Mavis Gallant, "The Events in May: A Paris Notebook—II," *New Yorker*, Sept 21, 1968, 55.

up until that moment in reference to the hunting of Algerians (*"ratons"* or "little rats" according to the racial slur) by the police or army, is taken up to refer to similar police operations against students. "In order to avoid *ratonnades*, systematic beatings (*matraquages*), and the snatching of isolated individuals, always disperse in groups of fifty to a hundred . . ."— such is the advice offered by one tract.[42] Later in June, at Flins, "chasing down students, the *ratonnades* are permanent;" "the CRS riot police, their arms slung across their backs, hunt down, flush out (*"ratonnent"*) the students."[43]

The proximity of the Algerian War to the '68 events is explicitly evoked by those activists whose political formation took shape in Paris during the militant antifascism of the early 1960s—an antifascism associated with that war which reawakened, on French soil, a sense of direct confrontation between extremes. "In '68, Algeria was still very close: the left was the left, and the right was the right."[44] In the Latin Quarter in 1961 and 1962, amid a constant police presence, ultraright groups attacked leftist students in the vicinity of the Sorbonne and at the lycées Louis-le-grand and Henri IV. Distributors of journals advocating Algerian independence were attacked on the streets, while the apartments of intellectuals holding similar views were regularly bombed by the OAS. Leftist newspapers and journals were frequently targeted: in February and March 1962 alone, a bomb exploded across from the building housing *Le Monde;* another was discovered in *l'Humanité*'s offices; and an attack destroyed the offices of *France Observateur.*

Militant Pierre Goldman recalls his adolescence in the late 1950s:

> I discovered fascism. Or rather, that there were fascists, that the species didn't die off with the defeat of the Axis and the liberation of France . . . I believed that fascists, absolute evil, had disappeared from reality. That their existence was as incongruous as that of distant ghosts. [In high-school in 1959,] I met young people who defended the Vichy regime, professors too, as well as active fascists, members of the Young Nation [Jeune Nation]. This was the time of the return of de Gaulle, the beginnings of the far-right machinations in Algeria.[45]

A teacher, active in '68, describes the political polarization of the final years of the war:

---

42. Schnapp and Vidal-Naquet, "Comment éviter les matraques," 434.

43. Ibid., 520, 524.

44. Student at the Ecole Nationale d'Administration, cited in Jean-Pierre Beaurenant's 1990 film documentary, *L'examen ou la porte!*

45. Pierre Goldman, *Souvenirs obscures d'un juif polonais né en France* (Paris: Seuil, 1975), 33.

When I first arrived in France, meeting partisans of French Algeria had the effect of instantly propelling me into the other camp.[46]

Dominique Lecourt evokes the immediacy of the war and its politicizing effects:

Long after the fracas of 1958 and the sound of boots that had accompanied the return to power of General de Gaulle, the imminence of a fascist "coup" kept us on alert. And the OAS bombs, in those blue nights, like the almost daily combats on the rue Saint-Jacques, mobilized the most pacifist among us.[47]

A direct, violent response to the threat of fascism was, for another militant later active in '68, the only solution:

But I was antifascist. That was how I was socialized. Others wielded the dialectic—I wielded the *matraque*.[48]

On one side of the two extremes was a composite masculine "type" made up of the merging of an array of paramilitary figures: the CRS, the *gendarmes*, the *légionnaires* and other elite forces within the career military, and, above all, the *parachutistes*. Where other elite regiments were dispersed within the army, the *parachutistes* constituted an internal block or specialized sect, complete with their own uniforms, rituals, passwords, hermetic language, songs (frequently adopted from German S.S. songs)[49] and *esprit de corps:* an army within the army. Incarnated by colonels like Bigeaud and Massu, the somber and romantic aura of the *parachutiste* was imposed on a mass French readership during the Algerian War by photo spreads in *Paris-Match* and *France-Soir*. The mythical figure of the warrior, possessed of a cold, steely, faraway gaze, a distinctively rugged camouflage uniform, sunglasses, sunburn, and a special manner of walking, was best represented, perhaps, in the scene in Pontecorvo's *The Battle of Algiers,* when the newly arrived Colonel Matthieu—Massu, in reality—strides down the main street of Algiers. "[The *para*] does not like speeches, discussions, assemblies. His vocation is to put all that in order. Against speeches, discussions, assemblies he opposes his body and his weapon. . . ."[50]

46. Denis, a teacher, cited in *Libération,* May 13, 1978.
47. Dominique Lecourt, *Les piètres penseurs* (Paris: Flammarion, 1998), 26.
48. Jacques, a member of Pierre Goldman's *service d'ordre* (militants trained in direct, physical street confrontation), cited in Isabelle Sommier, *La violence politique et son deuil. L'Après 68 en France et en Italie* (Rennes: Presses universitaires de Rennes, 1998), 81.
49. Gilles Perrault, *Les parachutistes* (Paris, Seuil, 1961), 56.
50. Ibid., 154.

The distinctive visuals provided by the *parachutiste* were to lend themselves to an array of stereotypes and caricatures that proliferated during the Algerian war and on into the early 1970s. The figure of the *parachutiste*, no less than that of de Gaulle, was a staple of *gauchiste* political cartoons of the period. Siné, for example, who along with 120 other French public figures, signed the Manifesto of the 121 in September 1960, the statement "respecting and judging justified the refusal to take up arms against the Algerian people,"[51] went on to play a vigorous role in illustrating ephemeral newspapers like *Action* and *L'Enragé* that sprang up during May '68. His first political drawings, produced for *l'Express* in 1958, were a series on the *parachutistes*.

But in the early 1960s, what the left was already calling a fascist praetorian guard produced in some of its adversaries a distinctly military response like the one expressed by Pierre Goldman:

> I am shocked by the passivity of the organized left toward the OAS and that the efficacious fighting is mostly being conducted by specialized government units. For the pogromist police of the *ratonnades* of October '61 I have a fierce and Jewish hatred. I cannot understand why the victims assassinated during Charonne have not been avenged.[52]

Goldman's political trajectory was, of course, not unique; another militant describes the stages of a shared itinerary:

> Before May, my activities were mostly of the anti-fascist type . . . I knew nothing about the composition of classes in France. I had no idea about the exploitation workers underwent. . . . It was fairly common at that time to become engaged first of all on the anticolonialist and then the anti-imperialist front. . . . [53]

Goldman and lycéen Michel Recanati were among the militants responsible for organizing and coordinating the "services d'ordre": small groups specialized in physical street combat with the police, or with far-right groups like Occident, Ordre Nouveau, or Jeune Nation, whose leaders, by the mid-1960s, were often former *légionnaires* or *parachutistes*. Using

51. The Manifesto of the 121, formally called the "Déclaration sur le droit à l'insoumission dans la guerre d'Algérie," was written by Maurice Blanchot, Dionys Mascolo, and Maurice Nadeau, and signed by a number of people who later were active in May '68, including Siné, Sartre, Henri Lefebvre, Marguerite Duras, Daniel Guérin, Maurice Blanchot, Dionys Mascolo, François Maspero, Madeleine Rébérioux, Hélène Parmelin, Christiane Rochefort, Pierre Vidal-Nacquet, and others. The text of the document and its signatories is frequently reprinted; see, for example, Hervé Hamon and Patrick Rotman, *Les porteurs de valises: La Résistance française à la guerre d'Algérie* (Paris: Albin Michel, 1979), 393–96.

52. Pierre Goldman, *Souvenirs obscure d'un juif polonais né en France* (Paris: Seuil, 1975), 40.

53. Alain, quoted in Giorgini, *Que sont mes amis devenus?* 85.

antifascism as an elementary instrument of mobilization, the "services d'ordre" provided an offensive capacity on the streets and regular direct, collective action. The activities of the "services d'ordre" and their sometimes spectacular techniques of urban guerilla warfare began before May-June '68 and came to a definitive end only in the Parisian street battles of June 21, 1973. This mobilization against the far-right group Occident, who had been allowed by the police to stage a rally at the Mutualité, left eighty members of the "services d'ordre" seriously wounded and prompted the government the next day to outlaw the militant group who organized the demonstration, the Ligue Communiste. Formed from the shards of the Jeunesse Communiste Révolutionnaire, which had been outlawed by the government in June 1968, the Ligue had at the time as its slogan: "Arm the masses with the desire to arm themselves."

The lifespan of the "services d'ordre," as well as the uncompromisingly antiparliamentary nature of their activities and self-definition, provides one means of periodizing what I am calling '68 culture. Their existence was coterminous with an entirely new form of political struggle, one in which, as the Japanese students, the Zengakuren, had discovered before the French, "the police are not necessarily the stronger": the uniform, is no longer magic, the cop no longer invulnerable. The spectacular military actions of what were called the *noyau dur* (hard core) did not fall into the category of spontaneous or uncontrolled violence. Rather, they formed half of a specific tactic known as "escalation-provocation." Escalation-provocation called for a sequencing of actions whereby a violent interaction with the cops or fascist groups by the "noyau dur" would be followed immediately by a large and legal demonstration. The first action provoked the authorities and drew attention, while the second politicized larger circles of people by drawing them in and associating them with the action.

Goldman's quasi-military response is an extreme version of a widespread political awakening occasioned by the Algerian war and its repercussions in France. At the most general level, the end of the war saw the birth of a new form of political thought and subjectivity in France, whose accomplishment was the great political, philosophical, and intellectual ruptures of the end of the 1960s.[54] Algeria defined a fracture in French society, in its identity, by creating a break between the official "humanist" discourse of that society and French practices occurring in Algeria and occasionally within France as well. "Through the struggle against the

<hr />

54. Marc Kravetz, among others, makes this argument in the context of analyzing the ideological role played by Sartre's journal, *Les Temps Modernes*, in those years. See Herta Alvarez-Escudero's 1997 episode of the television series *Qu'est-ce qu'elle dit, Zazie?* entitled *Les Temps Modernes*.

war, in demonstrations, draft resistance, secret organizing, aiding the Algerians, discussions about their revolution, a minority of students became
conscious of what they opposed in *their own* society. . . . Algeria was the
occasion," wrote Cornelius Castoriadis in 1963, "the catalyst for an opposition in search of itself, becoming more and more conscious of itself."[55]
It is around Algeria that the official left—the Communist Party—first becomes "*la gauche respectueuse*," what Sartre defined as "a left that respects
the values of the right even if it is conscious of not sharing them,"[56] and
thus a political form to be denounced. Typical of the French Communist
Party's attitude to the Algerian liberation struggle is the statement made
by Waldeck Rochet, secretary-general of the Party during 1968, to the National Assembly on June 5, 1956, openly taking a position that advocated
a continuing French presence in Algeria and North Africa:

> As communists we are convinced partisans of negociation, because we
> don't want our youth dying in North Africa for the interests of a mi-
> nority of exploiters and, in addition, because we are certain that the
> only path allowing us to save the French presence in Algeria and North
> Africa is to attempt negociation with qualified representatives of the
> Algerian people in view of establishing links that are freely consented
> to and conforming to the interests of the French people and the Alge-
> rian people—including, of course, the immense majority of Algerians
> of French origin.[57]

In the perspective that arose in opposition to the "wait and see" attitude
adopted by the PCF, a view that saw the PCF advocating assimilation and
becoming the guardian of the interests of the French nation as an entity
existing over and above classes, the radical left is born, along with a new
attitude toward official communism. "The Algerian War," writes Marie-
Noelle Thibault, "opened the eyes of a whole generation and was largely
responsible for molding it. The deep horror felt at the atrocities of the
colonial war led us to a simple fact: democracies are imperialist countries
too. The most important feature . . . [was that] political action, including support for national liberation struggles, was conceived of as a mass
movement."[58] For another intellectual, the war produced a widespread

55. Cornelius Castoriadis (with Claude Chabrol), "La jeunesse étudiante," *Socialisme ou Barbarie*, no. 34 (March 1963): 56.
56. Jean-Paul Sartre, "Plaidoyer pour les intellectuels," *Situations VIII* (Paris: Gallimard, 1972), 421.
57. Waldeck Rochet, cited in "Le PCF et la question coloniale," *Révolution* 7 (March 1964): 98.
58. Marie-Noelle Thibault, "Souvenirs, souvenirs," in *May '68: Coming of Age*, ed. D. L. Hanley and A. P. Kerr (London: Macmillan, 1989), 192.

disidentification with the State. "The unglorious way in which the Algerian War ended, the blast of hate that was the OAS and what it revealed about our society, all that was not in the nature of reconciling us with our country."[59] When we turn to personal narratives of this *prise de conscience politique*, many individuals highlight the role played by the police:

> Several of us as high school students went to our first meetings against the "dirty war" in Algeria. Our first demonstrations were those in which Papon's police bloodied the streets of Paris. In other words, we knew that politics could touch and shake up someone's daily life.[60]

> In 1968, I had already been political—since the war in Algeria. In 1962, at the end of the war I was twelve. I barely noticed the war taking place, I was too young. But in '61 there were many demonstrations in my neighborhood against the OAS, and bomb scares in school. It's what led me to become aware of political problems. From that moment on I made a kind of choice—it was relatively clear that I wasn't going to be on the side of the right, the police, and the OAS.[61]

ALGERIAN FRANCE

Perhaps the best evocation of the remembered incidents that make up a political trajectory in the early 1960s, a trajectory that bears some claim to being both individual and collective, occurs in a 1986 detective novel, *Bastille Tango*, by Jean-François Vilar. Vilar was a Trotskyist militant during '68 and journalist for *Rouge*, the daily newspaper published by the Ligue Communiste Révolutionnaire (LCR). In *Bastille Tango* the "clues" all bear some relationship to the way traces of political violence are both inscribed on the physical city and forgotten: the corrosion of forgetting facilitated by the violence of mindless urban renovation. A question asked by a friend of Vilar's narrator, an *ancien soixante-huitard* turned photographer, jars loose a past made up of moments of political crime that have left their traces on the city's physiognomy, a whole poetics of political memory:

> —At what moment did you first (he was looking for the right words) become politically aware?
> It was unexpected but it was a real question. When? The end of the war in Algeria? Charonne? Yes, Charonne was an important date. My first demo. The meeting place was in front of the Lux cinema. My

59. Emmanuel Terray, *Le troisième jour du communsime*, 16.
60. Lecourt, *Les piètres penseurs*, 25–26.
61. René, cited in Daum, *Des révolutionnaires dans un village parisien*, 213.

father held my hand. He never went to demos. But that one, he said
he had to go to. I said take me along and he said OK—in a tone that
was a little bit serious. We were far from the metro station when the
charge began. Very far. But we still had to take shelter under a garage
door on the rue de Montreuil to protect ourselves when the cops were
unleashed . . . When did I first become involved in politics? Around
the same time there were the riots on the boulevards. A school friend
who lived near there had also told me about the drowned bodies, the
Algerians found floating in the canal Saint-Martin . . . The dead that
the newspapers didn't talk about, that we weren't supposed to know
about.[62]

Vilar's account has the merit of not only highlighting the two most disas-
trous of the police altercations presided over by Prefect of Police Maurice
Papon in the early 1960s, but of organizing their representation into a
now familiar palimpsest. His character's musings dramatize a common
historical layering, a sequencing that the events follow as they resurface in
the character's memory. The first event has a name, Charonne, the name
of a metro station; it is the French child's first political demonstration,
and the occasion, in real life, of the death of nine people crushed by a
police rampage on February 8, 1962. Charonne was a "French" event, a
mass demonstration of Parisians organized by left parties and trade unions
against a particularly gruesome OAS attack, one in which a bombing attempt on André Malraux's apartment went awry and ended up blinding
the little daughter of Malraux's concierge. As the demonstrators who had
gathered to protest the OAS were dispersing, the police charged, and people pinned and cornered against the closed entrance to the metro station
were trampled and beaten to death by the police—police who made use, as
'68 demonstrators would use against them seven years later, of the metal
grills that surround Parisian trees. In Vilar's narrative, "Charonne," almost a screen memory, lies close to the surface, to his character's conscious memory—it is his first response to the question of when he first
became politically aware. Charonne's horrors were unseen by the child
in the novel, he was too small or too far away. But their circumstances
have been registered on his body—the crush of the crowd, the sight of the
police, the worry in his father's voice, the feel of his father's hand, as they
crouched for cover from the police. These horrors were unseen by the
narrator, but are representable historically: the dead, in February 1962,
including a boy of sixteen, were counted and acknowledged; their bodies
were found and identified. Charonne, the metro station, gives its name

62. Jean-François Vilar, *Bastille Tango* (Paris: Presses de la Renaissance, 1998), 112–13.

to the event, a place and an event that "took place," whose horrors were public. Something happened. A crowd of over 500,000 people turned out to mourn the dead of Charonne five days later. It was the first of what was to become a series of exemplary *gauchiste* funeral rituals in the streets of Paris—a series that would draw to a close only with the funeral of Jean-Paul Sartre in 1980 and that would include along the way those of militant *lycéen* Gilles Tautin in 1968, Pierre Overney in 1972, and Pierre Goldman in 1976.[63]

But behind Charonne lies a second event, one that for Vilar's character has no name and can only be evoked by means of a haunting image: drowned Algerian bodies floating in the Seine. In most nonfictional accounts, this event has come to be designated by a date, "October 17, 1961." Unlike Charonne, whose name denotes a circumscribed place—the metro station where the bodies were found, crushed and piled on one another—what occurred on October 17, 1961, was perhaps too large to designate with a place name, for its site was Paris in its entirety. And the entire police force of the city was mobilized. Vilar's character does not personally experience the second event as he did Charonne, he is told about it by a friend (but told what? what happened? why were there bodies in the Seine?). The contours of the event remain shadowy for the schoolboys, the stuff of stories: just the floating, unnamed corpses of drowned Algerians as traces—corpses whose existence is no sooner evoked than it is immediately censored, removed from perception: "dead bodies that the newspapers didn't mention, that we weren't supposed to know about": dead bodies that to this day remain uncounted.

On October 17, 1961, the first mass demonstration of the 1960s occurred, organized by the FLN to protest a recent curfew set by the prefect of police that prohibited Algerians in the Paris region from being on the street after 8:30 P.M. Informed in advance of the demonstration, the police, along with the CRS and the mobile *gendarmerie*, are armed with *bidules*, a longer version of the *matraque* with greater leverage and range, capable of breaking a skull open in a single swing when adroitly applied.

63. The June 15, 1968, funeral of Gilles Tautin, a Maoist high school student drowned while fleeing from the police during the Flins demonstrations, drew a crowd of 5,000 mourners; an enormous portrait of Tautin, produced by Beaux-Arts students, was carried by two Flins workers. That of Maoist Renault worker Pierre Overney, shot by a security guard in front of the factory, drew some 200,000 people on March 5, 1972. Although the funeral procession/demonstration was permitted by the government, an astonishing number of CRS and other police were brought to Paris from the provinces for the event. The September 20, 1979, funeral of Pierre Goldman, shot by unknown assailants, brought 15,000 people into the streets, while 25,000 people joined the funeral procession for Sartre on April 15, 1980. See Isabelle Goulinet's 1993 work, "Le gauchisme enterre ses morts" (Mémoire de maîtrise, Université Paris I, Panthéon-Sorbonne 1993).

The police have also been virtually exonerated in advance of any "police excesses" that might occur; in the preceding weeks Papon has visited the various commissariats, imparting these messages: "Settle your affairs with the Algerians yourselves. Whatever happens, you're covered,"[64] and "For one blow, give them back ten."[65] And, to overcome the scruples of certain more hesitant members of his forces, he adds: "You don't need to complicate things. Even if the Algerians are not armed, you should think of them always as armed."[66]

The Algerians—between thirty and forty-thousand men, women and children—are, in fact, unarmed, and the demonstration is peaceful. Many of the Algerians are wearing their best "Sunday" clothes, in the interest of impressing the French and the international communities with their peaceful motives. Nevertheless, police open fire almost immediately. Confrontations occur simultaneously throughout the city wherever the Algerians are concentrated. Police "combat groups" charge the crowd in the main thoroughfares and boulevards, while other police ranks stand behind in the side streets, blocking escape routes and splitting the crowd into small pockets of two or three individuals, each of whom is then surrounded by police, and men and women are methodically clubbed. Along the Seine, police lift unconscious and already dead or dying Algerians and toss them into the river. A document published soon after the massacre by a group of progressive police describes what went on in one part of the city:

> At one end of the Neuilly Bridge, police troops, and on the other, CRS riot police, slowly moved toward one another. All the Algerians caught in this immense trap were struck down and systematically thrown into the Seine. At least a hundred of them underwent this treatment. The bodies of the victims floated to the surface daily and bore traces of blows and strangulation.[67]

64. Maurice Papon, cited in *Ratonnades à Paris* [unauthored, but compiled under the name of Paulette Péju] (Paris: Maspero, 1961), 54.

65. Maurice Papon, cited in Union régionnale parisienne, CFTC, "Face à la repression" [mimeographed pamphlet], Paris, October 30, 1961.

66. Maurice Papon, cited in *Ratonnades à Paris*, 54. I should note that a literature exists holding the FLN accountable as well for the deaths of October 17, 1961, whether on the grounds that the leadership foresaw the massacre and didn't care or that they should have foreseen the massacre is not clear. Pierre Hempel, for example, writes that "Algerian nationalist leaders, helped by gauchiste "porteurs de valise," pushed hundreds of Maghrebin workers to throw themselves into the jaws of death, the massacre in the middle of Paris by armed official gangs of the Prefect Papon. . . ." See his *Mai 68 et la question de la révolution* (Paris: Librairie "La Boulangerie," 1988), 135–36.

67. Cited in *Ratonnades à Paris*, 52.

Some of the arrested men and women are taken to the courtyard of the prefecture of the police where, as Pierre Vidal-Naquet reports, "If I believe the testimony of one policeman, gathered immediately after the event by Paul Thibaud and that I've often had occasion to evoke since then, Papon had several dozen Algerians beaten [*matraqué*] to death in front of his eyes in the courtyard of the police prefecture."[68] Some six thousand others are taken to several sports stadiums reserved by the police for that purpose. In all these places, people die while in custody—of wounds they had already received or of new blows administered by police "welcoming committees" arranged in a kind of gauntlet outside the entrance to the sports arenas.

On the night of October 17, the police publish a communiqué stating that the Algerians had fired on police, who were then forced to return fire. The official death count, originally two, was revised the next morning by Papon's office to three. The almost total news blackout that surrounded the event makes it very hard to determine the exact number of Algerians—for no police were injured—who actually died. Most knowledgeable estimates put the number at around two hundred.[69]

African-American novelist William Gardner Smith put the figure at "over two hundred" in his 1963 novel, *The Stone Face.* It is a mark of the success surrounding the official blackout of information about October 17 that Smith's novel, written by a foreigner in France and published in the United States (it could not be published in France), would stand as one of the few representations of the event available all the way up until the early 1990s—until the moment, that is, when a generation of young *Beurs*, as the children of North African immigrants call themselves, had reached an age at which they could begin to demand information about their parents' fate. Professional or academic historians have lagged well behind amateurs in the attempt to discover what occurred on October 17; investigative journalists, militants, and fiction writers like Smith, or the much more widely read detective novelist, Didier Daeninckx, kept a trace of the event alive during the thirty years when it had entered a "black hole" of memory.[70] While investigating a completely different crime, the detective in Daeninckx's novel, *Meurtres pour mémoire*, pieces together, through classified and declassified archival documents, film footage, and interviews, a version of what occurred that night. What he learns about

68. Pierre Vidal-Naquet, *Mémoire, tome II. La Trouble et la lumière, 1955–1998* (Paris: Seuil, 1998), 150.

69. See Jean-Luc Einaudie, *La bataille de Paris: 17 octobre 1961* (Paris: Seuil, 1991), for the most thorough study of the massacre; for his estimations of the deaths, see especially pp. 266–68.

70. Thus even progressive historians of the period fail to register the magnitude of the event. Bernard Droz and Evelyne Lever, in their *Histoire de la guerre d'Algérie, 1954–1962* (Paris: Seuil, 1984), devote one paragraph to the massacre.

October 17 sheds light on still earlier government crimes. The detective, a cop, picks his way through layers of bureaucratic cover-ups, making astute use of a policeman's understanding of police systems of surveillance and management of information, for the prefectural archives where the state controls and disseminates information are so comprehensive in their logic that records are kept of documents requested and of the citizens who request to see them. By following the traces left behind at that level of surveillance, the detective both exposes the way the state and police archives limit what is perceivable or knowable by the public, and names that limitation as the crime itself, the crime whose solution he sought.

Daeninckx's novel mirrors the efforts that have recently accelerated in France to undo the cover-up surrounding October 17, efforts that are far from over today. Despite the airing and official recognition of the massacre that took place, in the context of Papon's 1998 trial for the crimes he committed under Vichy, and despite heroic recent efforts on the part of individual archivists to disseminate information, the facts of the event remain obscure. Continuing bureaucratic obstinacy limits access to the documents that still exist—except to a few state-approved historians—a problem compounded by unexplained "losses" of crucial documents in the archives at the prefecture de police.[71]

If Daeninckx's novel works to expose the repressive logic of the state and its police, Smith's *The Stone Face* comes at the same problem from a different angle and perspective: that of a young African-American painter in the Paris of the early 1960s who leaves his own world behind and is drawn instead toward an impossible identification with Algerians in struggle. Smith's story is one of a political awakening, a new political subjectivity taking shape through cultural contamination. Initially swept up in the joyful escape from American antiblack prejudice ("out from under that *pressure*"), the protagonist, Simeon, frequents a world of high-living black American literati expatriates in Paris who have been welcomed warmly by the French. He is only dimly aware of the Arab-French hostilities that surround him: "He passed a black woman who walked with an easy gait holding hands with a Frenchman. Newspaper headlines shouted: MOSLEMS RIOT IN ALGIERS. FIFTY DEAD."[72] The protagonist's *prise de con-*

71. For an account of the most recent state of archival access to police documents on October 17, 1961, see Claude Liauzu, "Mémoire, histoire et politique: À propos du 17 octobre 1961," *Tumultes*, no. 14 (April 2000): 63–75. At present, a growing number of political figures, artists, and intellectuals have formed the "Association 17 octobre 1961: contre l'oubli," and have signed a document demanding state recognition and acknowledgement of the crime. The text had nearly 3,000 signatures on December 1, 2000.

72. William Gardner Smith, *The Stone Face* (New York: Farrar, Straus, 1963), 7. Tyler Stovall's work alerted me to the existence of this novel. See his "The Fire Next Time: African-

science is triggered by the paradigmatic scene he observes of the police beating an Arab:

> At the corner, they saw a policeman clubbing a man. Although he had fallen to the pavement, the policeman kept on swinging his long white nightstick down on the man, who was trying to protect his head from the blows with his arms. The man was screaming in a language Simeon could not understand.[73]

The violent scene of *matraquage* jars loose a flashback in Simeon who relives his own beating at the hands of police in Philadelphia, now so distant in time and space from a France where he is respectfully called "vous" by the police, welcomed into elite clubs and restaurants, and treated, from the perspective of the Algerians he now begins to befriend, as white. But his progressive identification with the Algerians is not merely predicated on a shared existential experience of racism and violence, or on the way the blows he watches fall on the body of the Algerian come to be felt anew on his own body through the memory of his treatment by American police. Nor can this identification be attributed to a kind of easy pan-Africanism. Identifying with the Algerians means for Simeon first breaking with his own milieu and its values. It means first *dis*identifying with his own social group, the black Americans in France. Simeon begins to perceive that group as merely floating atop the frothy waves of expatriate society, as oblivious to a form of French racism not directed at themselves as they are horrified and unwilling to participate in the early moments of the civil rights movement back in the States. Increasingly, Simeon turns his steps away from the café on the rue de Tournon where the black writers generally meet and toward the Arab district, the *Goutte d'or*, entering as much as possible into that mode of life and into a wholly different Paris. Swept up as a concerned bystander in the police arrests on October 17 when he assaults a policeman, Simeon, the only American arrested and taken with the rest of the police prisoners to the sports stadium, is greeted by some, but not all, Arabs as "brother," and is quickly freed by a police logic that views the presence of a black American in the company of Algerians to be matter out of place, a category mistake. In the weeks that follow the insurrection, he is unable to locate his Arab friends. The novel makes it clear that it is Simeon's disidentification with his own black compatriots, the physical movements he makes venturing outside of his proper social place to frequent the Algerian insurgents, that accounts for his new

---

American Expatriates and the Algerian War," *Yale French Studies* 98 (2000), 182–200, for a detailed account of Smith's context in the Paris of the early 1960s.

73. Smith, *The Stone Face*, 38.

political subjectivity. He is motivated less by any sense of duty toward the oppressed than by the desire for the other world represented by the Algerians in their struggle with the French. It is that displacement which allows him to see what the other black expatriates, in their clannishness, do not—that something is happening. Even Simeon's decision at the end of the novel to return home, to take up a stand in civil rights struggles in the States, should be read in the light of the fissure opened up in his social identity that occurs when he initially disidentifies with his own group. Political subjectivity, the novel suggests, is formed by way of the Other. In this sense, *The Stone Face* is very much a part of the prehistory of May, for Smith recounts the construction and experience of a specific political subjectivity, formed in part by the shattering of the social determinations held in place by the increasingly naked logic of the police—an experience, a formation, a subjectivity, that would be shared by many of May '68's participants as well.

The police stampede that left nine people crushed to death at the metro station of Charonne registered in French public memory, and the police massacre of October 17, 1961, did not. During May '68, Charonne returned as a frequent reference point or refrain, appearing in slogans, graffiti, and posters: "Nouveau Charonne à Paris" or "CRS: Assassin de Charonne." An article in *Combat* on May 7, 1968, warns of "the foul shadow of the police. . . . Soon you will see, they will perform another Charonne." An anonymous tract distributed on the Boulevard Saint Michel on May 21st read: "The atrocities of the night of May 10th–11th are not only the acts of a Fouchet, a Grimaud or a Peyrefitte, but are the result of a totalitarian and repressive regime—illustrated by Charonne."[74] Observing the street warfare during May, François Truffaut registers an acceleration in the level of violence in his account by introducing the word "Charonne": "The ordinary police had been replaced by the CRS. And the long riot truncheons appeared, the Charonne truncheons."[75]

Today, "Charonne" serves as a metonymy for the Algeria-related violence of the early 1960s, that which comes most immediately to mind when that time is evoked: "The violence? Oh yes, Charonne." One example of such a metonymy occurred during a recent representation of the period on the evening network news on French television. In October 1999, Maurice Papon made a short-lived escape to Switzerland to avoid serving the prison term for his conviction of crimes against humanity

74. Anonymous tract, "Vive la grève illimitée avec occupation des usines," distributed in the vicinity of Boulevard Saint Michel, May 21, 1968.

75. François Truffaut, cited in John Gretton, *Students and Workers: An Analytical Account of Dissent in France, May–June 1968* (London: MacDonald, 1969), 101.

during the Vichy period. Reporting on his flight from the country, the evening television news broadcaster on Antenne 2 made a passing reference to Papon's responsibility, as prefect of police in Paris, for police violence related to the Algerian War in the early 1960s. (Indeed, it was only Papon's trial in the winter of 1998 that reawakened attention to the Algeria period, leading to a call for the opening of the police files from October 17). But the collusions and collisions of memory caused the newscaster to make a curious error: in a kind of shorthand, he gave the name of "Charonne" to "October 17, 1961," essentially conflating the two events into a single instance of police violence, and by so doing, giving precedence once again to the nine French dead over the uncounted Algerians. Since many French people today have a sense of what occurred at Charonne, without necessarily knowing the date, the conflation brought the facts of Charonne back to mind, while the Algerian dead recede once again, "disappeared."

M aurice Papon was not prefect of police during May 1968—he missed the occasion by a little over a year. In January of 1967, Papon left his post and would not reappear in the national limelight again until the mid-1970s, when he was appointed minister of the budget under Giscard d'Estaing. Even though he had left the prefecture in 1967, Papon did not become a mere spectator when the insurrection erupted the following year. When he left the police, the ambassadorship that de Gaulle had wanted to give him apparently wasn't immediately available, so Papon's long peripatetic career in the French bureaucracy took him to western France, where he became president of the large Sud Aviation Factory. Four months later, on May 14, 1968, it was that same factory, Sud Aviation—in part, perhaps, responding to Papon's managerial style—that became the very first of the French factories to go out on strike (they sequestered their *patron*!), setting an example that quickly spread to Renault, across the entire manufacturing sector of western France and to the nation as a whole. The general strike of mid-May erupted ten years to the day after the *coup d'état* that returned de Gaulle to power on May 13, 1958.

In Paris, Papon's successor as prefect of police, Maurice Grimaud, benefited from the image of his predecessor. By contrast, Grimaud himself appears—increasingly, over the years—"liberal" and antiracist. He is now widely credited, even mythologized, for minimizing the number of deaths in '68, for not allowing his men, for example, to shoot into the crowd. But the forces under his command, unleashed against students and workers in '68, were the forces created by Papon and formed during the Algerian crisis. Police powers put in place by de Gaulle and Papon during the Algerian years were ready for use in '68.

Who were the police at the end of the Algerian War? The question, as phrased, cannot really be answered, for it presupposes a division of labor, a job definition, that had largely broken down as a result of the contradictions and obfuscations that war had engendered. For the "war" then was not a war being conducted in a distant land, but rather a "police operation," as it was then called. And the Parisian police under Papon had increasingly come to be made up of soldiers and to function as soldiers. "At the heart of that army of civil functionaries that terrorized Paris from the first days of May '68, there were many who had not finished settling their accounts with the *fellagha*."[76] The police, as Balzac once remarked, like the Jesuits, have a long memory.

It was not until September 1999 that the French Assembly voted for the first time that the Algerian War, which had ended thirty-seven years previously, be officially called by that name—a war, that is, and not by any of the various euphemisms in wide usage—"la guerre sans nom," "the crisis," "the pacification effort," "the events," "operations for the maintenance of order," or most pertinently, "a police operation."[77] The latter term underlines the way in which Algeria, for the French, represented much more than a distant colony. Algeria was, after all, very close by, it was a place where a significant number of French had lived for a long time, and it had been fully integrated, "departmentalized," and put under the charge of the Minister of the Interior as long ago as 1848. Algeria constituted three full departments in France. As such, France could not—so the logic went—be at war with itself, and what was occurring in Algeria could not be a civil war nor even, exactly, a war. It was rather best understood as a domestic, interior affair, a prolonged but local skirmish to be settled by "the police."

A 1987 detective novel, *Mon Colonel* by Francis Zamponi, depicts the dilemma of the French career military man faced with this new confusion in the definition of his *métier*. (Zamponi himself was a member of the March 22 group at Nanterre during '68; afterward he became a journalist for Lyon-*Libé*.) The novel creates the portrait of a French colonel in Constantine, the poorest and largest region in eastern Alge-

76. Maurice Rajsfus, *Mai 68. Sous les pavés, la répression* (Paris: le cherche midi, 1998), 13.

77. "I forbid you to pronounce the words 'Algerian War,'" the President of the Tribunal said to Francis Jeanson during the latter's trial on September 19, 1960. As recently as 1996, Jacques Chirac, dedicating a monument to the "victims and soldiers dead in North Africa, 1952–1962" continued to respect the terminology dating from the time of the conflict. He never once used the word "war" in the course of the ceremony.

ria, and his growing distress over having his job transformed from one of soldiering (fighting and combat) to one of "policing" (gathering information, establishing files). The fact that his police work is invariably conducted by means of torture does not, in and of itself, bother this colonel greatly; he is neither squeamish nor morally opposed to such procedures, and he insists on presenting full documentation of grisly interrogation practices to the various state and army functionaries who show up from France to inspect the operations—functionaries who, intent on putting a clean face on the war back home in France, quickly bury the reports and attempt to silence the colonel. The colonel's crisis evolves rather within what is for him a strict, hierarchical yet rugged, definition of the *métier*. He is not depicted as a racist—the Algerian is simply another soldier, the enemy. The colonel suffers from claustrophobia brought on by having his combat exploits reduced to a series of grim yet quasi-secretarial operations: the forceable extraction of information (demanded, yet officially "denied" by his commanders in France) from "suspects" (not necessarily soldiers), the maintenance of a bureaucracy involved in establishing identification files on the personal lives of the Algerians in the village. Zamponi's novel displaces the moral question of torture onto another register. The question, for the colonel, is not whether he is a fighter or a torturer, but rather, whether he is a fighter or a file clerk.

The colonel's situation in Zamponi's novel is one fictional response to effects created by actual French government directives. The "Instruction 11" of 1955, for example, shifted the orientation the army should follow in its fight against Algerian rebels away from military action and toward *"renseignement"*: "the search for information must be the constant concern . . . as little adapted as it might be to a struggle that is more police-like than military in nature, the Army's mission is to perform these tasks."[78] The "Special Powers" Act of 1956, voted by the socialist government with the full support of the Communist Party, suspended most of the guarantees of individual liberty in Algeria, allowing "exceptional measures" to be taken to establish order, protect people and property, and safeguard the territory. It allowed the powers of the police to pass into the hands of the army—in effect, creating a normalization of torture, since a prolonged detainment of "suspects" in what had become houses of torture was now effectively legalized. In Zamponi's novel, the French officials who arrive to inspect operations in Algeria have their counterpart in real life in the "Commission de sauvegarde des droits et libertés individuelles

78. Cited in Claire Mauss-Copeaux, *Appelés en Algérie. La parole confisquée* (Paris: Hachette, 1998), 170–71.

en Algérie" established by de Gaulle, a powerless commission that in the end served to mask the violence of an army that had received from its leaders the order to win the battle, as General Massu once succinctly put it, "by any means."[79]

Just as the domestic, "internal" functions of the police seep into army operations in Algeria, so army activities come to form part of the job description of the policeman in the large cities of metropolitan France. During the course of the war, the Parisian police are regularly called upon to perform operations that have their counterpart in the "police operations" being conducted by the army across the sea. Consider, for example, the implications for French wartime strategy and operations, of the fact that the four hundred thousand Algerian immigrants living and working in France during that period, earning salaries considerably higher than those of their peers in Algeria, were in effect financing the greatest part of the war at home in Algeria.[80] The war, for the Algerians, in other words, was financed largely from France, from the earnings of Algerian *travailleurs immigrés* living on the outskirts of Paris. For the FLN, the difficulty lay not in collecting the money from Algerian inhabitants of the makeshift *bidonvilles* (slums) surrounding large French cities like Paris, but rather in transporting the cash through the city (where any person appearing to be an Arab driving a car was immediately suspect and searched) and ultimately out of the country. Thus, the services rendered the FLN by Henri Curiel, Francis Jeanson, Félix Guattari, cartoonist Siné, and the network of other French supporters of the Algerian cause, the "porteurs de valise," consisted mostly in moving cash, not arms, across the city, and over national borders. But their activities created a new set of tasks and responsibilities for the metropolitan police, since it was they who were assigned the task of blocking the physical movement of FLN cash within the city and out of the country.

It is perhaps at the level of the literal transfer of personnel from one place to another that the infiltration of the French Army into the police can be seen most distinctly. Papon's own career, which seamlessly merged the two functions of the police and the military and which spanned the entire postwar period, provides the best example. A bit of police history is in order. In 1945, immediately after the Liberation, at a moment when Papon was deputy director of Algeria in the ministry of the interior, the institution of the police passed through a brief, but significant,

79. General Massu, cited in Pierre Viansson-Ponté, *Histoire de la république gaulliènne, Mai 1958–Avril 1969* (Paris: Robert Laffont), 15.

80. Abdel Krin Cherqui, former treasurer of the FLN, makes this point in Gilles Perrault, *Un homme à part* (Paris: Barrault, 1984), 289.

"progressive" period in France. Former members of the resistance joined the force, as well as the newly founded national police, the CRS (Compagnie Républicaine de Securité) established that year, taking the places left vacant by the seven thousand officers who were let go or "purged" for having been too compromised under Vichy. Two years later, when the Socialist minister of the interior, Jules Moch, sent the CRS to repress a workers revolt in the autumn, several CRS companies, notably those in Bordeaux and Marseille, disobeyed orders and refused to go. These companies were then dissolved, and a kind of "counter-purge" of all branches of the police force began, to eliminate "communist sympathizers," a purge conducted after 1951 by Parisian Prefect Jean Baylot, assisted by the man he then chose to be his secretary general—Maurice Papon. Baylot took charge of reintegrating those police officers who had been purged immediately after the war and who had been surviving up until that point as a kind of shadow or "parallel" service to the official police, conducting surveillance of trade unions and the Communist Party—specialists, as such, in anticommunism. Under Baylot, these troops specialized in the violent repression of demonstrations. Serving throughout the years of the French War in Indochina, Baylot created an atmosphere that nourished an indiscriminate police hatred for those who were "selling out" the Empire—intellectuals, progressives, Communists, trade-union militants—all viewed as "enemies of the nation" manipulated by Moscow.

When Baylot, Papon's mentor in police matters, was fired by Mendès-France in 1954, Papon quit as well, resurfacing across the ocean in the role of secretary general of the protectorate of Morocco, where he was put in charge of police operations involved with rounding up and detaining Moroccan nationalists. In June 1956, Papon was back in Algeria, which was now at war, and he was once again placed in charge of the police. This was his third administrative stint in North Africa between the Liberation and when he took up his duties as prefect of police of Paris in 1958.

Once in Paris, Papon found the classical structures of the police inefficient for conducting subversive war; he quickly decided to bring back, under a new form, some of the structures ("Sections Administratives Spécialisées"), personnel, and techniques ("psychological action") he had helped develop in rural areas of Algeria. Under Papon, the ranks of the Parisian police swelled with more and more *anciens combattants* from Indochina and ex-army officials and *parachutistes* from Algeria. The end of the series of colonial wars (Indo-China and Algeria) and the reduction of the conventional army because of the creation of the *force de frappe* [de Gaulle's consolidation of French military autonomy and rapid strike po-

tential, including nuclear weapons] caused a certain number of career non-commissioned officers to transfer to analogous positions in the police."[81]
For aggressive interrogations of Algerians in Paris, Papon even created a police force made up entirely of *"harkis"* (Algerians who fought on the side of the French during the war): a kind of "parallel" force, working in conjunction with and in liaison with the police to conduct indiscriminate sweeps of Arab neighborhoods and extract information. Supplementary forces made up entirely of "indigenous" troops had long been a tradition in Algeria and other colonies—now they appeared for the first time in the metropole. Under Papon, torture was installed in Paris.

This confusion or merging of the domestic and the international, the police and the army, has its origin, of course, in the thought disorder that is colonialism and in the particular intensity that disorder acquired in France's relations with Algeria during the late 1950s and early 1960s. Is this a war or is it a police action? If this is not a war then is it a civil war? Is the Algerian a foreign (external) enemy, or is he a citizen? Is he a *Viet*, or is he a brother? Is the Algerian French? The answer to the literal question of citizenship was of course, yes; Algerians, as the March 7, 1944, ordonnance established, were French citizens, "enjoying all of the rights and bearing all of the responsibilities of non-Muslim French." But nowhere is the confusion that nevertheless reigned over all of these questions more apparent than in the tensely worded document that issued from Papon's prefecture on October 5, 1961, the document whose instigation of a curfew affecting Algerians in the Paris area prompted the Algerian demonstration of October 17, 1961. The communication begins in this way:

> In view of bringing an immediate end to the criminal activities of Algerian terrorists, new measures have just been taken by the Prefecture

---

81. Labro, *"This Is Only a Beginning,"* 171–72. Similarly, a document written by the CFTC after the October 17, 1961 massacre describes police personnel "recruited for some years on the principle criteria of anti-communism, counting in its ranks 'veterans from Indochina and Algeria,' of a racist and fascistic mentality, trained to employ methods valued during the colonial wars." Cited in *Ratonnades à Paris*, p. 47. In *The Stone Face*, William Gardner Smith provides an oblique gaze onto changes in the make-up of the Parisian police force in the early 1960s. His protagonist Simeon begins to notice:

> a metamorphosis in the police—or so it seemed to Simeon—during the year since his arrival in Paris. Simeon had never liked police, but the French police had impressed him more favorably than most. Once polite and attentive, now they slouched on street corners with the insolence of power, cigarettes hanging from their lips, occasionally signaling with obscene gestures to young girls who passed by. Simeon learned that this change in the police was not accidental. The police department had been purged of officers who had shown softness with Algerians in France. (174)

of the Police. In view of facilitating their execution, Muslim Algerian workers [*travailleurs musulmans algériens*] are advised most urgently to abstain from walking about during the night in the streets of Paris and the Parisian suburbs, and most particularly during the hours of 8:30 P.M. to 5:30 A.M.[82]

The wording has been carefully chosen: Algerians are "advised," and not ordered, to stay off the streets—but advised "most urgently" [*conseillé de la façon la plus pressante*]. What is the status of this advice? Certainly, the police will interpret and act upon the communication as establishing a set of orders, and the existence of the curfew will have the side effect of making employers all the more reluctant to hire or continue to employ Algerians. But nothing, in theory, forces Algerians to pay attention to police "advice"; later in the document, a similar wording is used: "it is very strongly recommended" [*il est très vivement recommandé*]. The time period specified, 8:30 P.M. to 5:30 A.M., has been obviously determined by the desire to give workers who live on the periphery of the city just exactly enough time to transport themselves to and from work; they are then off the streets, in the sense of in their place and locatable at all times: either at work or asleep at home. The document continues:

> Those who, because of work, are obliged to be on the streets during these hours can apply to the sector of technical assistance [*secteur d'assistance technique*] in their neighborhood or their district for a temporary permit, which will be granted them after verification of their request. Furthermore, it has been determined that the terrorist incidents are, for the most part, the result of groups of three or four men. Consequently, Muslim French [*français musulmans*] are strongly advised to move about on their own, since small groups run the risk of appearing suspicious to the police on their rounds. Finally, the prefecture of police has decided that cafés [*débits de boisson*] operated and frequented by Muslim French from Algeria [*français musulmans d'Algérie*] must close each day at 7:00 P.M.

The "secteurs d'assistance techniques" or "SATs" were an invention of Papon: centers where an Algerian immigrant has to present himself to obtain any of the various official papers—passports, visas to return to Algeria, work certificates—he might need. Any visit to an SAT meant an extensive police interrogation and the establishment of a *fiche* (file) on that individual. The curfew thus created the secondary gain for the

---

82. Communication by Maurice Papon, October 5, 1961, cited in Einaudie, *La bataille de Paris*, 85. See also Michel Levine, *Les ratonnades d'octobre* (Paris: Ramsay, 1985).

police of potentially funneling more Algerians into the SATs, Algerians who may have slipped through the net up until that point. But if Algerians are only being advised to stay off the streets, why must they get a special document to walk about during the proscribed hours? But no, once again, they "can apply," not "must apply"—is the curfew obligatory or not? In fact, the only place where the verbs pass unequivocally from advice to command is in the final sentence that obliges certain bars and cafés to close at 7 P.M.—the opening and closing of bars and cafés falls squarely within the regulative domain of the police prefecture. The hour, 7 P.M., once again makes certain that no Algerian can stop off for a drink after work and that restaurants be closed for the unique meal of the day; no leisure or conversation, no activity remains except that of working or sleeping—if, that is, sleeping is indeed possible in the overcrowded rooms where many immigrant workers lived and where access to beds was frequently staggered, with those who were not sleeping usually making room for the others by going out. But which bars and cafés have to close? Do twelve Algerian drinkers make a café "frequented by" Algerians? Do three? And this, of course, raises the more fundamental problem posed by the document. Do three drinkers who *appear* North African or Arab make it a bar or café "frequented by Algerians"? More importantly, who, exactly, is being forbidden to be on the streets? Who is being designated? Algerians? Presumably not, for "pieds-noirs" or "French Algerians" are also, at this time, Algerians. But even if we ignore that problem, a more fundamental one remains. Can one category of French be forbidden to move about? Algerians, supposedly, are French—"with the full honors and duties of French citizenship"—as French as Corsicans or Bretons. And yet Corsicans and Bretons are never singled out specifically by an official document: they are simply French. This is why the administration had to come up with designations like "Muslim French from Algeria." But here a new problem arises in the introduction of a religious category to differentiate one group of French from other "French." The army, at this point in time, had developed a related circumlocution: FSNA, *français de souche nord-africaine* (French of North African extraction"). What in any case cannot be avoided by any of the circumlocutions is that racial characteristics are the only criteria proffered by the text of Papon's order: people who might appear to be Algerians must stay off the streets at night and avoid walking around in groups of three or four. But this, of course, created other confusions since people who appear to be Algerians might include *harkis* working on the side of the French police, not to mention Moroccans, Tunisians, and other Arabs—even Jews. Anyone, in other words, who resembled an Arab was de facto targeted.

In the days immediately following the savage repression of the October 17, 1961, demonstration, the Communist Party newspaper, *l'Humanité*, wrote several long articles about the violence, attempting to report on an event that other newspapers—*Le Monde, La Croix, France-Soir*—were not talking about. But *l'Humanité* stopped short of calling for a demonstration to protest the massacre. Only two very small groups, the Comité Anticolonialiste and the Comité du Front Universitaire Antifasciste (FUA) took to the streets to protest the police action. Both were student groups, and both groups had only come into existence that fall, in a largely successful attempt to rid the Latin Quarter of OAS commandos and far-right groups like Jeune Nation and Occident. The significance of their protest, however, far outweighs their actual membership numbers, for in their activities we can detect the first appearance of a durable radical current within the student milieu. By this I mean the first instance of an intervention at the national level in a new mode, of students as a political force, for a cause that was not a defense of student interests. Although the large student union, the UNEF, had organized a mass demonstration against the war in March 1960, their protest had concerned the limitation placed upon draft deferrals, and although this clearly showed the perceived necessity of conjugating student union struggles with the struggle against the Algerian War, the defense of student interests was still the mobilizing factor for the demonstration; UNEF, in that sense, remained "corporatist." The FUA, on the other hand, took the initiative in the student struggle against the war in interventions and "direct actions" that gave its members a direct hold on general problems of French society—and not the problems of students per se—and thus the beginning of a critique of the bases of the Gaullist regime. True political force, it would seem, lay outside the official student union apparatus. Through their struggles against the Algerian War, the experience of the FUA, and their support for the FLN (on the day of the proclamation of Algerian independence, FUA members hung an FLN flag from the Sorbonne), students acquired their own traditions of struggle, forged independently of the existing apparatuses and parties. They formed their own organizations, and in so doing, a whole new conception of mass movement began to emerge: political action organized around a clear objective—in this case Algerian independence—and utilizing "hard" or direct physical combat, as against the fascist groups. The struggle against the war could and should, in their view, be the departure point for the reestablishment of a whole new revolutionary combat or, at the very least, for the return of a workers movement that would be aggressive and no longer on the defensive.

Writing about the police massacre of Algerians on October 17, 1961, Jacques Rancière makes a similar point. For him, the police operation was a double one: to sweep up or cleanse the city space of the demon-strators' manifestation of a wrong, along with an attempt to sweep up or cleanse the record of that act. For the French, Rancière points out, the second of these "cleansings" was perhaps more significant than the first. For not only was October 17, then, the first mass demonstration of the 1960s in France, but it was the inaugural experience, for many French, of "the cover-up": the news blackout that sought to keep the event from view, that tried to prescribe what could be seen and what could not, what could be said and what could not. The attempted news blackout, perhaps even more than the murders themselves, became the occasion for the first experience of a dislocation or a chasm opening up in many peoples' iden-tity as French, in what it meant to be French—a severing of identification with a state that had done this in the name of the French and then tried to remove it from their view. This is what Rancière has in mind when he locates political "subjectivation," as he calls it—the manifestation of political subjectivity—first and foremost in an experience of disidentifi-cation or declassification, and not in an experience of shared community. For the crisis provoked in many young French by the police and military actions might have given rise only to a purely moral or ethical identifi-cation with the drowned victims in the Seine, a sentiment of pity, were it not for the rupture that occurred in their allegiance to the established political system, be it parties or the State. The student movement from that point on had less to do with the university than with fleeing it; the movement was not about being a student and embracing the interests or aspirations specific to students but with introducing a disparity into the student identity and the identity of what it meant to be French—a dis-parity that allowed for a political way to espouse the cause of the Other. A slogan like "We are all German Jews," as Rancière points out, which would be chanted by tens of thousands of French people on the streets of Paris in mid-May '68, is in some ways a deferred explosion, unthinkable without those earlier exercises in establishing ways of including or allying with the Other premised on the refusal to identify with a certain self.[83] In that peculiar construction of an impossible "we," a subjectivation that passes by way of the Other, lies an essential dislocation or fracturing of social identity that would define much of the political experimentation of May '68. "We are all German Jews": the "we" of the slogan assem-bles a collective subject through the identification with a group—German Jews—that, through its proclamation as a shared name, becomes no longer sociologically classifiable.

83. See Jacques Rancière, "La cause de l'autre," in *Aux bords du politique*, 148–64; trans. David Macey as "The Cause of the Other," *Parallax* 7 (April–June 1998): 25–34.

Consider that "we," the "we" of the slogan "We are all German Jews" in relation to the rival "we" of the May–June 1968 events, the one that materialized on May 29, 1968, during a displacement or a dislocation of a very different kind. On that day, President de Gaulle, by most accounts weakened, confused, and dispirited by the general strike that had gripped the country and by the unabated violence in the streets, flew to Baden-Baden to meet with the former leader of the *parachutistes* and symbol of "Algérie française," General Jacques Massu. De Gaulle, presumably, was anxious to see whether Massu, as well as the 70,000 French troops under his command in Germany, had remained uncontaminated by the winds of madness. Would the army be well disposed to doing its duty to prevent exterior and interior subversion, and, if necessary, to "bring order back to France?" Much has been made of the unpredictability of de Gaulle's behavior and intentions regarding this new flight to Varennes, and of the secrecy surrounding his absence from Paris, a secrecy that seemed to show the typically military contempt in which he held his subordinates (Pompidou, de Gaulle's prime minister, upset about being kept out of the loop, announces in frustration that he will resign—he didn't).[84] But consider the union, the "we" that was unveiled when de Gaulle, the former hero of the resistance and leader of Free France, embraced General Massu, the intimate associate of the fascist generals who had mounted the putsch against de Gaulle in 1962. In the image of that simple conversation shrouded in mystery between the former resistance hero and his former enemy Massu, a perfect crystallization of the see-saw in the idea of antifascism, which pervades the French 1960s, begins to take shape. The underbelly of Gaullism is laid bare, its fierce confiscation of democracy during Algeria and beyond: the Gaullist state's reliance on Papon and Massu, the police chief and the army general, an alliance whose members were called upon throughout the long 1960s to unite their efforts against the common enemy. In de Gaulle's flight to Baden-Baden, what looked to be a defection, a vacillation or abandonment of power, was in fact its consolidation, for de Gaulle, who had made use of the military the first time in 1958 to take power, returned to the military a second time in 1968 in order not to lose it. Brought to power in 1958 by a military coup supported by the prosperous classes, de Gaulle, the man on horseback and unifier of the nation, had pretended to represent the superior interest of the country as a whole. And for ten years he had allowed the bourgeoisie to reinforce its economic power by forg-

84. "I think I am going to quit. I can no longer continue to work in these conditions. . . . Understand, it's not possible that we be confronted like this with a *fait accompli*. Things are being hidden from us that are being told to others. On the strength of that, my decision is made, I'm going to quit." Pompidou, cited in Jacques Foccart, *Le général en Mai. Journal de l'Elysée*, vol. 2, 1968–69 (Paris: Fayard, 1998), 49–50.

ing the myth of a great, strong independent State, "above class division." In 1968, the national political crisis becomes in the hands of Gaullism one more occasion to realize a Bonapartist ideal: the State as lone political force. But the price paid for such a consolidation of state power is a shift in its image or rather an unveiling of its true face. "Nor is Gaullism a regime like the others," commented Jean-Pierre Vernant at the time. "Born of a riot, it has suppressed or weakened all the representative institutions of parliamentary democracy that can, during periods of grave crisis, play a role of intermediary or buffer between power and the people."[85] To fight off the menace caused by a strike that now millions of workers had joined, the Gaullist State can no longer in May of 1968 promote the myth of itself as "unifier of the nation" as it had done successfully in the past; rather it has to call forth a unification of the bourgeoisie; the bourgeoisie has to declare its class character; politics has to be supplanted by the direct domination of the bourgeoisie. If de Gaulle can no longer unite the nation, he can at least unite the various fractions of the bourgeoisie. And to that end those fractions have to descend into the streets of Paris and show themselves. Vernant notes, "De Gaulle, who is not a general for nothing, did not let the occasion pass. When the day came he imposed his own strategy, contesting the mass movement on the very terrain where it had developed against him, that of the street."[86] On May 30 1968, the day after his return from meeting with General Massu in Baden-Baden (and, appropriately, the feast day of Joan of Arc), a powerful summons was issued to all the different fractions of the middle class to unite against the common enemy. The Pétainists and the *anciens resistants*, "the whole criminal fringe of Gaullism, its administrators and its cops, the parasitic body of the regime that represents its surest social base,"[87] were called out by Gaullist organizations to form civic action groups called CDRs, or *Comités pour la défense de la république,* and to demonstrate in favor of the regime. Over 300,000 pro-"order" supporters filled the Champs-Elysées on May 30 to rally behind de Gaulle. In that parade Gaullists like Chaban-Delmas and Malraux joined hands with detachments from "Occident"; intellectuals like Raymond Aron marched beside the lumpen dregs created by the colonial wars—the secret societies, parallel police, hit men, strike breakers, *anciens combattants,* and hired thugs that had rallied to de Gaulle's summons. The slogans that resounded on May 30, "La France aux français," "les ouvriers au boulot," or "Cohn-Bendit à Dachau," were in themselves a profound

85. Jean-Pierre Vernant, cited in Schnapp and Vidal-Naquet, *Journal de la commune étudiant,* 788.

86. Ibid., 790.

87. Daniel Bensaïd and Henri Weber, *Mai 1968: une répétition générale* (Paris: Maspero, 1968), 208.

indication of the disruption May '68 had caused in the logic of assigned roles and stations, the logic of "the police." Let students study, workers work, teachers teach, and France be French—these were the terms of the call to order. As these slogans were chanted on the street that afternoon, they were punctuated by the familiar klaxon signal—three short, then two long horn blasts. This brief but powerful mnemonic device, a kind of soundtrack to the whole of the Gaullist regime, was sounded out loud one more time; the rhythmic honking signal that had once meant "De-Gaulle-au-pouvoir" in 1958, and then "Al-gé-rie fran-çaise" during the following years, and "O-A-S vaincra" most recently, was now sounded to signify "de-Gaulle-n'est-pas-seul."[88]

The rhythmic honkings of the old nationalist horn were designed to drown out what was for the forces of order the most terrifying sound of May '68: the catcalls and hisses from Billancourt workers that greeted Georges Seguy, head of the CGT, when he announced to them on May 27 the terms of the Grenelle agreement hastily negotiated to try to bring an end to the strike. Would the strike continue indefinitely? It was those whistles, that continued refusal on the part of workers, that propelled de Gaulle to Baden-Baden into the arms of his old adversary. In the face of the greater enemy, as in a mirror, the two generals embraced. The final days of May '68 move very quickly. The day after the immense pro–de Gaulle rally parades down the Champs Elysée from the Concorde to l'Etoile, a new picturesque character makes his appearance: Raymond Marcellin, appointed minister of the interior on May 31, 1968. A new character and yet somehow familiar—in Marcellin, the man called upon to bring a definitive halt to 1960s insurgency and liquidate any sequels to May, Maurice Papon would find an appropriate double, a perfect book-end to the chapter Papon had helped open ten years earlier. Like Papon, Marcellin had distinguished himself early in his career by proving effective at breaking up the workers' strikes of 1947–1948 when he served as undersecretary of state. An accomplished clean-up man ("The will of the country is order"),[89] it would fall to Marcellin to enact de Gaulle's dictum that "Nothing more must happen, neither in the streets, nor in public buildings."[90]

If nothing more must happen, then something *was* happening. The hypertrophy of the State in the years immediately after May—years of

---

88. Viansson-Ponté, *Histoire de la république gaulienne*, 648.

89. Raymond Marcellin, *L'importune vérité* (Paris: Plon, 1978), 297.

90. Charles de Gaulle, cited in Comité d'Action Étudiants-Écrivains au Service du Mouvement, *Comité* 1 (October 1968): 1.

crackdown and repression that are eliminated from the now dominant representation of a good-natured, "counter-cultural" May—provides at least one recognition of the magnitude of the event.

Raymond Marcellin was the first of the sociologists of May '68, and perhaps the most thorough. His task, as he described it, was to enforce a "French political will" that grounds its force in "social cohesion and not in the struggle between classes or categories." Thus, he writes, "the following principle of social justice must be applied with energy and perseverance: 'To each his place, his share, his dignity.' "[91] To each his place: the distribution of groups and functions, disrupted during May, must now be reconstituted, and it is the job of the police to ensure the fabrication of the social order. To this end, Marcellin's first act, after being appointed, was to assemble the most complete collection possible of the some 20,000 tracts, documents, journals, and texts of the '68 movement and personally read them. His study, of course, had in view the massive police identification, classification, and roundup of all known *gauchistes* and other militants—workers, students, and others—that then rapidly ensued. By June 6, he had already established a list of militants, classified according to the far-left organizations to which each adhered; he had also streamlined operations in his own camp by recreating the Bureau de Liaison, a kind of centralized clearinghouse for all the different branches of the police. In August, he published a pamphlet on "revolutionary groups organized in view of the violent seizure of power," evoking the significant presence during May of "foreign influences," accomplices in a vast, international conspiracy.[92] The jails soon filled with the first political prisoners since the Algerian War. But the jails had first to be emptied of some significant occupants, the former leaders of the OAS. The *gauchiste* peril put an end to the vestiges of divisions over Algeria, and the government, in the face of that greater peril, reached out its hand to the old rightwing generals. On June 15, 1968, only days after all *gauchiste* organizations had been outlawed, some fifty convicted OAS assassins, among them the far-right generals including Raoul Salan who had attempted the putsch against de Gaulle, were amnestied, allowed back into France, or released

---

91. Marcellin, *L'importune vérité*, 297.

92. See Ministère de l'intérieur, "Les Objectifs et les méthodes des mouvements révolutionnaires," August 1968. Marcellin found a wholehearted supporter for these views in self-described fascist Maurice Bardeche: "Certainly nothing was less improvised than the riots in the Latin Quarter. The groupuscules . . . were financed, informed, and managed by specialists that were furnished to them from abroad. . . . Who furnished the money and the arms? The elements of a conspiracy exist, and the Minister of the Interior has them at his disposition. . . ." See his "Comédie de la révolution," in *Défense de l'Occident* (Paris: Edition Nouvelles Editions Latines, 1968), 4–6.

from prison—which did not go unnoticed by militants at the time. "Just when he [de Gaulle] launches a witch-hunt against the students and workers that he calls "uncontrollable elements," he frees the fascists Bidault, Salan, Lacheroy. He calls for the formation of civic action groups led by the thugs (*barbouzes*) and former OAS guys."[93] Demonstrations on public streets were forbidden for eighteen months, all politically "nonneutral" foreigners were immediately deported, and any showing of film footage of the '68 insurrection was repressed. Having attached great importance to the revolutionary tracts of May, Marcellin was assiduous in controlling what could be seen and what could be said about May from that point on, both on the streets and in print. These were the years of a pitiless pursuit of newspaper vendors, poster hangers, and cartoonists associated with the radical May press, years when publications hostile to the United States like the journal *Tricontinental* were seized, years when the least political slogan hostile to the government (or deemed as such) led to prison, when "insulting the police" becomes a charge for which people are regularly brought to trial.[94]

For many of those active in the uprising, after-May was a sinister time, inhabited by ghostly images of combat and a sense of continuous surveillance. Even the boredom and melancholy of work taken up again reluctantly carried the indistinct but indelible traces of the previous violence, as workers taken by management to have been political leaders (*meneurs*) during the strike were moved to more onerous work-stations in the factory or simply let go, and as many young militants sought to avoid arrest by going underground.

During a press conference held in November 1971, Marcellin summed up his philosophy as follows:

> For too long it was thought that resolving social and economic problems would fix everything. This is not the case. In periods of trouble and insurrection when even the most ancient institutions hesitate and no

93. Comité d'Action Travailleurs-Étudiants, "Les Elections: Que Faire?" tract dated June 15, 1968. The eleven leftist groups dissolved by the government, their publications forbidden were the JCR, the Voix Ouvrière, 'Révoltes,' the Comité de liaison des étudiants révolutionnaires, the UJC (m-l), the PCMLF, the Parti communiste internationale, the Fédération de la jeunesse révolutionnaire, the Organisation communiste internationale, and the Mouvement du 22 mars. Marcellin, it seems, was particularly proud of the decision to release the OAS military prisoners, commenting that "the liberation of the former OAS has produced an excellent effect." Foccart, *Le générale en Mai*, 202.

94. See Maurice Rasjus, *Sous les pavés, la répression* for the most thorough account of the repression of the early 1970s. Rasjus gives particular attention to the censorship and seizures directed at the radical press, including journalism, books, theatrical plays and films, in those years, as well as to forms of repression enacted in the high schools.

longer play their role, the State alone serves as a fortification or buttress for the population against the consequence of mental disorders.[95]

The more quantifiable aspects of Marcellin's philosophy of the fortified state could be gauged at the end of his regime in 1974: a full 42,000 cops had been added to the force for the reconquest of Paris, its factories and its campuses—an increase of 50 percent over six years. The government exhibited a manifest terror of any further taking to the streets on the part of its citizens. When, for example, a demonstration against the Vietnam War was called for November 15, 1969, the government forbade the demonstration; 11,000 demonstrators showed up nevertheless, and they were greeted by 12,000 police. But the newly fortified state of post-May was all the more insidious in that it was less attached to the old paramilitary visuals, the colorful iconography of *parachutistes* and CRS, the visors and the *matraques*. The police were more numerous; anyone who visited Paris in the early 1970s will recall the concentration in the metros and on the sidewalks of armed police, the CRS vans stationed at regular, close intervals throughout the central city. But there was also a less visible, less easily identifiable police presence in the streets. One of Marcellin's innovations was the "policemen-students": cops chosen among the new young recruits to pursue a university education in exchange for informing on what was going on on the campuses. Surveillance and censorship took precedence over *matraquages*. Activist groups like the "Secours rouge" were founded to try to combat police terror or what one of their slogans called "the all-powerfulness of the cops (in their multiple uniforms)." Under the Pompidou/Marcellin regime, a high school teacher could be fired or suspended for a whole array of crimes: distributing a tract to students, being pregnant and unmarried, studying texts about homosexuality in class, hanging an anti-imperialist poster in a high school corridor.[96] For Maurice Blanchot, writing in July 1968, the whole atmosphere of post-May, the palpable everyday ambiance of the State's fortification and its paranoia, its extension into all domains of social life, was condensed in the newly ubiquitous figure circulating on the streets of Paris, the plainclothes policeman:

> An unmistakeable sign: the invasion of the street by plainclothes police. . . . They are everywhere, in any place they deem suspicious, near movie houses, in cafés, even in museums, approaching whenever three or four people are together talking innocently: invisible, but all the same

95. Raymond Marcellin, cited in Comité de vigilance sur les pratiques policières, *POLICE: Receuil de coupures de presse* (Paris, Charles Corlet, 1972), 64.

96. See Martine Storti, *Un chagrin politique: De mai 68 aux années 80* (Paris: L'Harmattan, 1996), 117.

very visible. Each citizen must learn that the street no longer belongs to him, but to power alone, which wishes to impose muteness, produce asphyxia.[97]

97. Comité d'Action Etudiants-Ecrivains, "La rue," tract dated July 17, 1968. Rpt. with attribution to Maurice Blanchot, *Lignes* 33 (March 1998): 144.

2. FORMS AND PRACTICES

More than anything else, May '68 was in my view a vast aspiration toward equality.
—*Daniel Lindenberg*

THE CRITIQUE OF SPECIALIZATION

How much was the "seizure of power" by militants in 1968—the failure of which has constituted in retrospect what many still mean when they speak of the failure of May—a narrative or an agenda itself imposed primarily by the state? How much was the "taking of state power" and the set of problems related to such a goal the state's own centralizing fantasy, created mostly in the final week of May 1968 when de Gaulle, in his speech of May 30, evokes the threat of massive state violence and the intervention of the army to forestall what he calls an impending "communist dictatorship" in France? In the last few days of May, time accelerates markedly; the state decides to put an end to the *chienlit* (disorder)[1] and impose its own temporality. Do you want power? If thousands of you are in the streets then this must be the case. Fine, try to seize it from the army and its tanks. Given the extreme military proportions of de Gaulle's reaction, it bears recalling that the demonstrators in the streets were unarmed and that, as Sartre commented later, "A regime is not brought down by 100,000 unarmed students, no matter how courageous."[2]

1. "La réforme oui; la chienlit, non": one of the lone comments made by de Gaulle during May about the events transpiring in France. In the sixteenth century, the word *chienlit* referred to a carnival mask; literally, of course, "chier-en-lit" evokes the idea of fouling one's own nest. The *Larousse* dictionary lists the year 1968 as the first time the term was used to refer to a "disordered or chaotic situation." De Gaulle, however, was not the first to use the term in the context of '68; that honor, according to Keith Reader and Khursheed Wadja, goes to the neo-fascist weekly newspaper *Minute*, on May 2: "We will not abandon the street to the disorder [chienlit] of insurgents [enragés]." See their *The May 1968 Events in France: Reproductions and Interpretations* (London: St Martin's, 1993), 3.

2. Sartre, *Situations VIII*, 194.

Militant Pierre Goldman was among those who lamented the fact that
the demonstrators in the streets were unarmed:

> The student revolt began to grow. The movement that had erupted
> on the campuses was now joined by the determining presence of the
> workers. They began a general strike. I was excited but I cannot hide
> the fact that I sensed in that revolt obscene emanations. It seemed to
> me that the students spreading out onto the streets, in the Sorbonne,
> represented the unhealthy tide of an hysterical symptom. They were
> satisfying their desire for history using ludic and masturbatory forms.
> I was shocked that they were seizing speech and that they were happy
> with that. They were substituting speech for action. This seizure of
> power was an imaginary power. My opinion was that they gravely mis-
> understood the government's tactic and that that tactic was subtle and
> effective. They thought they were in insurrection, in violence, but it
> was paving stones they were throwing, not grenades.
>   . . . Nonetheless, I hoped that this collective, delirious onanism
> would lead to a revolutionary situation. The presence of the workers—
> their strike—was in effect of a different order. I knew some militants
> who were very involved in the conduct of the student combats. I went
> to see one of them, he belonged to the March 22 Movement, and I pro-
> posed an armed action to him. I told him that despite everything the
> situation remained peaceful and that it had to explode. . . . He looked
> at me like I was a madman, a mythomaniac. . . .
>   . . . De Gaulle left for Germany and came back. He spoke. What he
> said was simple. In his pitiless discourse he recalled that the forces he
> represented, force itself, was capable of wars and history. He sentenced
> his adversaries to impotence and dream. To castration. It was a chal-
> lenge and no one took him up on it. Power chased away imagination.
> The festival was over.[3]

Despite his recognition of the "determining presence of the workers" and
the fact that their strike was of a "different order" than the frenetic and, to
his mind, delirious, activities of the students in the streets, Goldman nar-
rows his perspective to focus on a confrontation between an all-powerful
military state and powerless, masturbatory students adrift in a purely
symbolic realm. His scenario is not so very different from that of someone at the very opposite end, from Goldman, of the political spectrum:
Raymond Aron. (Whereas Goldman sought to provoke the movement to
armed insurrection, Aron, a professed anti-Gaullist, marched nevertheless arm in arm with the Gaullist forces of order down the Champs Elysée

3. Goldman, *Souvenirs obscurs d'un juif polonais né en France*, 70–71.

on May 30).[4] Like Goldman, Aron—famously—viewed '68 to be "the event that turned out to have been a non-event."[5] Nothing happened, in other words. In fact, Aron was the very first of May's commentators to pronounce May a non-event. Aron and Goldman offer renditions of the conclusion to the non-event that are strikingly similar. Goldman: "De Gaulle left for Germany. He spoke. . . . The festival was over." Aron: "General de Gaulle spoke for three minutes. The whole affair was over and the atmosphere transformed."[6] In each of the accounts, de Gaulle returns to the source of his strength, the army, the threat of a military situation is evoked, and the students evaporate into the thin air of the imaginary.

It seems accurate to say now that the government's military threat was directed less at the students in the streets than it was at providing a context of crisis in which the various labor union organizations, primarily the CGT, could regain the power they needed to effectively corral or strong-arm workers into a swift acceptance of the rapidly negotiated settlement called the Grenelle Accords, after these had been refused by workers not only at Billancourt, but at Citroën, Sud-Aviation, Rhodiaceta, and elsewhere. This was the perspective adopted at the time by a group of writers and workers active in the movement: "De Gaulle is inciting violence . . . we will not enter into the process . . . the strike must continue."[7] A Renault worker concurs: "Chaos and revolution, he [de Gaulle] is the only one talking that way; we don't use those words."[8] And it was a perspective reiterated firmly by a worker, Anne-Marie Schwartch, when she insisted years later during a panel discussion in one of the early television commemorations of May that:

> the problem at that moment was not one of making revolution, but rather that the CGT not sell out the strike. [Turning to Guy Hermier, a PCF deputy on the panel with her:] *You* went around from shop to shop in the factories, from factory to factory, telling us that the others had gone back to work, saying that it was all over. . . .[9]

4. Raymond Aron, *Mémoires: 50 ans de réflexion politique* (Paris: Julliard, 1983), 473.

5. Aron, *Elusive Revolution*, ix. Historian Pierre Nora is perhaps the most recent commentator to reiterate Aron's assessment that "nothing happened in '68" in the conclusion to his *Lieux de mémoire:* "[N]othing tangible or palpable occurred at all." "The Era of Commemoration," in *Realms of Memory*, vol. 3 (New York: Columbia, 1998), 611.

6. Aron, *Elusive Revolution*, 25.

7. Tract, Comité d'Action Ecrivains/Etudiants/Travailleurs, undated but after May 30.

8. Renault worker, cited in Gudie Lawaetz, *Mai 68,* film documentary, 1974.

9. "Mai: Connais Pas," episode of TV show "Vendredi," May 13, 1983, prod. André Campana, FR3.

Indeed, what is most striking about the terms negotiated between management and union leaders is the relative poverty of the gains for workers in relation to the amplitude of the movement. A higher percentage of French workers than ever before, across every sector and in every region of the country, had been on strike for the longest time in French history. And yet the immediate principal results of the Grenelle Accords, negotiated between May 25 and 27, were a small augmentation in the minimum salary and the extension of union rights in the factories.[10]

The threat to which the government was responding in May–June '68 was less the violent contestation of students aiming to "seize power" than the fact that a quite inconsistent student maelstrom had succeeded, thanks to the violent repression it had encountered at the hands of the police, in attaching its wagon of insurgency to a mass strike. What was at stake was not, immediately, the question of state power. The workers' strike, by erupting outside of the confines of the big French labor confederations and outside the desiderata of any of the various left parties, particularly the Communist Party, had come to threaten the very existence of those institutions and organizations. As one worker said, "It's we who went on strike, it's not up to anyone else to decide for us."[11] When de Gaulle took his helicopter trip to the Black Forest to negotiate a new alliance against the communist menace with Massu and the army, that menace already no longer existed. A new, more corrosive communism had formed outside the structure of the party. The other—official communism—had already known for a long time the moment when to end a strike: the day before its victory. Focusing attention on the Latin Quarter, even after the mass strikes began on May 14, was the main element in the government's strategy to isolate the street violence and quarantine it away from the workers—enclosed, for the most part, in the occupied factories. The May 11 decision taken by Georges Pompidou, de Gaulle's prime minister, to reopen the Sorbonne to the students two days later, a decision widely criticized by his advisors at the time, by Aron soon afterward, and castigated by de Gaulle as collaborationist ("C'est du Pétain," he told his

---

10. Daniel Cohn-Bendit was correct in assessing "the grand maneuvers of Grenelle" to be "the biggest theft [escroquerie] of the century. All the powers come together to save their own power. . . . Pompidou saving the P.C. and the C.G.T., Seguy upholding the powers that be before he drowns." Daniel and Gabriel Cohn Bendit, *Le gauchisme—remède à la maladie sénile du communisme* (Hamburg: Rowohlt Taschenbuch Verlag, 1968), 142. Workers gained far less from Grenelle than they had in 1936 when the Matignon Accords brought an end to the unprecedented strikes that followed the victory of the Popular Front. For a detailed analysis of the terms of the Grenelle Accords, see Cornelius Castoriadis, aka Jean-Marc Coudray, *Mai 1968: La brèche: Premières réflexions sur les événements* (Paris: Fayard, 1968), 122.

11. Citroën worker, cited in *CA 13: Comité d'action du 13ème*, film documentary, Collectif Arc, June 1968.

closest advisors),[12] was in this light perfectly consistent with the overall aim Pompidou would sum up in a single sentence: "I wanted to treat the problem of the youth separately."[13] After students had been dissociated from strikers each group would settle back into the confines of their "sociological" identity, and both would lose: the strike would be contained as a purely salary—bread and butter—issue; the student demands would be rechanneled and redefined as "education" issues. And "violence" as a quality would come to pertain only to students and not to the peaceful, law-abiding workers. "Before May 13, it was above all about making sure, by circumscribing their struggle, that the students not enter the Latin Quarter. After that date it was above all about doing everything possible to prevent them from leaving."[14]

Given the government's strategy of separation and containment, the most effective political forms and actions the movement could develop were those that attempted what has variously been called the "dialogue," "meeting," "relay," "alliance," "solidarity," or even "alloy" (*alliage*)—the term is Jacques Baynac's—between workers and students. Consider two examples of the *prevention* of such a "meeting," one that transpired on the streets, the other in the factories.

On May 24, a crowd of some 100,000 demonstrators attempted to march from the Gare de Lyon to the Bastille; one participant, Pierre Peuchmaurd, writes: "Everyone is there. All of us. The CGT too, but without banners, directors or delegates. The *true* CGT, and several federations of the CFDT and the FO. Fifty percent workers at least. . . . We were circulating and exchanging tracts. A very beautiful tract from the March 22 movement, addressed to the workers who were everywhere that day, 'Your struggle is ours,'—undoubtedly one of the best attempts to define why we were all there."[15] Peuchmaurd mentions another slogan of the day: "No success is definitive in a capitalist regime." But one tract, signed jointly by all of the various Comités d'Action, best captures the tone of that day's demonstration:

> No to parliamentary solutions where de Gaulle leaves and management stays.

12. See Aron, *Mémoires*, 475–78; de Gaulle, cited in the television documentary, "La dernière année du Général," an episode of the series "Les brulures de l'histoire" (prod. Patrick Barberis, 1995) that discusses at some length Pompidou's strategy of dissociating the demands of striking workers from those of the students.

13. Georges Pompidou, *Pour rétablir une vérité* (Paris: Flammarion, 1982), 185.

14. "Le mouvement de Mai: De l'étranglement à la répression," *Analyses et documents*, no. 156 (June 27, 1968): 5.

15. Pierre Peuchmaurd, *Plus vivants que jamais* (Paris: Robert Laffont, 1968), 115–16.

No to negotiations at the top that only prolong a moribund capitalism.

No more referendums. Enough of the circus.

Don't let anyone speak in our place.

But as the demonstrators neared their goal, they were met with a wall of CRS riot police who blocked them from the Bastille and steered them back to their own barricades in the Latin Quarter, barricades that from that point on could now clearly be seen to have been tolerated, tacitly, by the forces of order as the only viable or apt "expression" of the students' movement. "At the Bastille, it's over. A deployment of police to make you dizzy. . . . A victory on the terrain until the retreat (*repli*) back to the Latin Quarter." Later, Peuchmaurd criticizes the students' willful self-enclosure within the imagery of the Latin ghetto, speaking of the demonstrators' "political errors: especially that of returning to the Latin Quarter, all of us regrouping there like assholes, like moths. We should have split up into small groups, saturated the city. . . . The other error was not to free ourselves in time from the myth of the barricade."[16] Sequestration of the demonstrators within the Latin Quarter ghetto as a deliberately chosen tactic by the government is clearly visible from this point on through the last large demonstrations of June 10 and 11.[17]

The second example concerns the practice of "factory occupation" by striking workers, a practice that had been invented in 1936 and not used again by workers movements until just before 1968. Occupation was generally viewed as a mark of the strength and the seriousness of the strike, since it meant a clear departure from tired, artificial forms like meetings and petitions, or the partial "symbolic" strikes that bore the trappings of the trade-union movement and no longer mobilized workers. "Occupying the factories means something other than parading in the streets in order to obtain—or often not to obtain—professional or salary demands: it means the will to be master of one's own workplace."[18] Was the model of occupation adopted by the two factories that unleashed the strike, Sud-Aviation and Renault-Cléon, patterned on the students' occupation of the Sorbonne, as many *gauchistes* have since maintained? Or did it derive from the workers' own tradition, going back to the historical model of the 1930s or to the more recent 1966 and 1967 strikes at Rhodiaceta, Caen, and elsewhere? Most likely, the decision to occupy was taken less as an imitation

16. Ibid., 120–21.

17. See "Le mouvement de Mai: De l'étranglement à la répression," *Analyses et documents* 156 (June 27, 1968).

18. Anonymous pamphlet, dated April 25, 1968.

of students' tactics than in response to the perceived vacillation, the weakness, even defection, of the government. But in either case, occupation—in which the director is either sequestered or expelled or at times allowed to stay within the occupied factory—involves the assumption of services like security, food, and the organization of leisure by workers, and thus a clear reversal of the director's authority. "Occupation is a consolidation of the strike such that the factory doesn't function. It's a way of protecting the strike."[19] Advocates of occupation see it less about taking charge of the factory as a center of production, than about taking charge of a non-neutral space in which the opposing class is constituted as an adversary: taking possession of the logical categories that govern institutions and not the institutions themselves. Occupation is in this sense akin to the student barricade: the dominant class is never as present as it is at the moment of occupation; the enemy is never clearer than when seen across a barricade. Occupation, like the barricade, *reveals* class conflict, the relation to the adversary. According to the case made for occupation, the appropriation of the space of the dominant power would ideally be accompanied by an expansion of the workers' movement outside of the limits of that space.

But was it? Perhaps the streets were a better mixing place, a more conducive place for the expansion of the workers' movement than were the occupied factories. Because of the way that May '68 has been consistently represented, it is easy to forget the extent to which the streets, from early May on, were *already* mixed. As the street battles progressed, students were joined by more and more young workers, stifled by the protocol of the unions, and by unemployed workers—a group whose role and sheer number has been consistently downplayed, both at the time of the insurrection and even more in subsequent representations. Evelyne Sullerot points out the way in which workers' presence on the streets was erased by the vocabulary used by the mainstream media during May as they reported the events:

> One cannot leave unmentioned the crystallization of a vocabulary that was to play a part in the orchestration of an overwhelming fear and in the isolation of the students. The word "barricade," for example, was employed to designate a little heap of a few packing cases and various other refuse. "Students" was a convenient term, which was justified during the first days of May. Later, there was cautious use of "non-students," a discreet way of avoiding the use of "workers." The "non-students" were always left in some mysterious shadow land, where they

19. Worker cited in Daniel Vidal, "Les conditions du politique dans le mouvement ouvrier en mai-juin 1968," in *Grèves revendicatrices ou grèves politiques?* ed. Pierre duBois (Paris: Anthropos, 1971), 514.

were joined by the underworld (*pègres*) and the thugs (*katangais*) as the occasion arose. Even on those occasions in which authentic students were an active but not the majority element in the mass of demonstrators, the radio continued to say, "The students have taken refuge here," "The students retaliated. . . ." etc.[20]

What was true on the streets of Paris was true elsewhere—in fact more so. In Nantes, Rennes, and throughout the provinces, crowds of students, workers, and frequently farmers occupied the streets for a longer period than in Paris.[21] From May 6 on, young workers and unemployed joined students in Clermont-Ferrand and in Grenoble; in the May 7 demonstration in Toulouse it was impossible to distinguish student from "nonstudent" or worker on the streets.[22] Once the mass strikes began, however, how much did "factory occupation," a practice that effectively enclosed many workers in the factories and kept them off the streets, serve the interests of union leaders in controlling and limiting a strike that had already "generalized" without CGT sanction? Not only did occupation anchor workers back in their proper, habitual place, preventing contacts with students, more importantly it broke interfactory communication and much of the informal kinds of information transmission that had ensued during the large street demonstrations between workers of different sectors, and even different regions.[23] With workers still safely in the workplace—even if nonfunctioning—occupation may have lessened any extension via coordination between different factories; it may have blocked communication at variance with the union leadership's representation of the strike. "For the government, as to a certain extent for the workers' unions, it's better that the strikers be in the factories than in the streets."[24] And it's better that the students were in the Latin Quarter—even if the universi-

20. Evelyne Sullerot, "Transistors and Barricades," in Labro, *"This Is Only a Beginning,"* 196–97. "Katangais" referred to a particularly tough group of street-fighters, rebels to any discipline or organization, some of whom claimed to have fought as mercenaries in Katanga.

21. Thus this assessment from the prefect of the Loire-Atlantique region: "The Parisian situation was less serious and less significant than that of the Loire-Atlantique." Cited in *1968: Exploration du Mai français*, vol. 1, *Terrains*, ed. René Mouriaux et al. (Paris: L'Harmattan, 1992), 255. See also Danielle Tartowsky, "Les manifestations de mai-juin 68 en province," in the same volume, 143–62.

22. Hempel, *Mai 68 et la question de la révolution*, 51.

23. "The occupied factories must be opened to all worker and student comrades to establish contact so that we can decide together what we want." Tract, Comité d'Action Travailleurs-Étudiants, undated but after May 15, 1968.

24. Pamphlet, "Le syndicalisme à l'épreuve," cited in Hempel, *Mai 68*, 62. The principal reason for the isolation of workers in the factories, was "a deliberate will, on the part of union leadership, to break off liaisons." "Contribuer à la liaison travailleurs-étudiants," *Cahiers de Mai*, no. 3 (Sept. 1, 1968): 3.

ties and lycées weren't operating—than on the Right Bank. When workers remained cloistered in their factories, union bosses could more easily decide in the workers' place, "sector by sector," through controlling the monopoly of information. Something like this interpretation can be gleaned from the remarks of worker Anne-Marie Schwartch cited earlier; it is also dramatically validated by one of the rare documents of "worker May" that we have: the short documentary film *La reprise du travail aux usines Wonder*. In that brief footage, a woman worker cries out against the decision to return to work, shouting that the vote to end the strike and resume work has been tampered with. Around her, three labor management representatives—*gros bras*—try to "handle" her: "But no." "We'll negotiate all that later on." As she continues to refuse their version of "the end of the strike," the three men grow increasingly impatient, and increasingly physical in their attempts to pressure the woman back into the factory: "It's a *victory*, don't you understand!"[25]

Pierre Goldman's and Raymond Aron's narrative of May as a failed seizure of power revolves around two diametrically opposed choices. These poles—de Gaulle or the students? revolution or psychodrama? revolution or hysteria? event or non-event? revolution or festival? ludic or serious? words or actions? seizing speech or seizing power? imaginary or real?—have largely set the terms of much of the discussion about '68, in the form of analyses or "judgments" of the event itself as well as in the turns taken by theoretical discourse in the 1970s. The thematics of "power," both in its centralized form and in its more microlevel locations and vicissitudes, would dominate a certain Foucauldianism, for example, and would receive full media-sponsored diffusion during the mid-1970s in the diatribes of the New Philosophers. And a media fascination with the question of "armed violence" would dominate the European 1970s in the focus on spectacular actions by Italian and German groups, the Red Brigade and the Baader-Meinhof faction, both of which derived from '68 movements.

But the real question, I believe, lies elsewhere, outside the parameters of revolution, failed or not. Why did something happen rather than nothing? And what was the nature of the event that occurred? The attention given to the problematics of power has effaced another set of problems at issue in May, and 1960s culture more generally, which we might begin to group under the heading of a no less political question—the question of equality. I mean equality not in any objective sense of status, income, function, or the supposedly "equal" dynamics of contracts or reforms, nor as

25. Jacques Willemont and Pierre Bonneau, *La reprise du travail aux usines Wonder*, June 1968.

an explicit demand or a program, but rather as something that emerges in the course of the struggle and is verified subjectively, declared and experienced in the here and now as what is, and not what should be. Such an experience lies to the side of "seizing state power;" outside of that story. The narrative of a desired or failed seizure of power, in other words, is a narrative determined by the logic of the state, the story the state tells to itself. For the state, people in the streets are people always already failing to seize state power. In 1968, "seizing state power" was not only part of the state's narrative, it expressed the state's informing desire to complete itself—that is, to totally assimilate the everyday to its own necessities. Limiting May '68 to that story, to the desire or the failure to seize centralized power, has circumscribed the very definition of "the political," crushing or effacing in the process a political dimension to the events that may in fact have constituted the true threat to the forces of order, the reason for their panic. That dimension lay in a subjectivation enabled by the synchronizing of two very different temporalities: the world of the worker and the world of the student. It lay in the central idea of May '68: the union of intellectual contestation with workers' struggle. It lay in the verification of equality not as any objective of action, but as something that is part and parcel of action, something that emerges in the struggle and is lived and declared as such. In the course of the struggle, practices were developed that demonstrated such a synchronization, that acted to constitute a common—though far from consensual—space and time. And those practices verified the immediate irrelevance of the division of labor—what for Durkheim was nothing more and nothing less than that which holds a society together and guarantees the continuity of its reproduction. As such, these practices form as direct an intervention into the logic and workings of capital as any seizure of the state—perhaps more so.

The opposition (revolution or festival, seizing power or seizing speech) that has dominated discussions of May is a false one. As Bernard Lacroix has commented, just because it took many people a certain amount of time to understand that May did not announce a coming "revolution," this does not then lead to the conclusion that it inaugurated its opposite, a "return to individualism."[26] It is wrong to conclude, in other words, that because the movement failed to seize state power it was either radically indifferent to the question of power or the prototype of a 1980s form of consumer consciousness. A focus on centralized state power was not absent from May; in her discussion of May '68 in Italy, Luisa Passerini describes revolutionary aspirations close to those of the French:

26. See Bernard Lacroix, "A contre-courant: Le parti pris du réalisme," *Pouvoirs* 39 (1986): 117–27.

We realized that, notwithstanding its fascination, the idea of a seizure of power like the assault on the Winter Palace was archaic, and we couldn't say what form the transfer of power to the oppressed classes would take. But certainly a hard shove would be required, it couldn't be a painless transition.[27]

But more central to the movement's aspirations than any such "hard shove" was its realization of forms of direct democracy and collective self-organization. In these forms and practices lie the beginning, in and of itself, of a different social organization, of a universalizable objective of the kind usually ascribed to revolutionary undertakings or at least to their beginnings.

The distinction I am making can perhaps be illustrated by comparing a Leninist tendency to one deriving from the theories of Rosa Luxemburg. Both tendencies share, as did all the radical groups in '68, an anticapitalist goal. But a Leninist party is in essence a radical intelligentsia that says we have the right to rule. Their goal of "seizing power" is as much determined by that objective as it is by the adversary it confronts: the bourgeois state. In the hope of conquering that adversary, the party borrows the adversary's own arms and methods; in a kind of underanalyzed fascination, it imitates the enemy's organization down to the last detail. And it becomes its faithful replica, particularly in the hierarchical relation between militants and the working masses, reproducing the social division that is the very foundation of the existence of the state. But a dominant aspect of May—closer to Luxemburg than to Lenin—focused instead on that social division, on avoiding the hierarchy inherent in Leninism, and as such produced organizations that were an effect of the struggle:

> The rigid mechanical-bureaucratic conception cannot conceive of the struggle save as the product of organization at a certain stage of its strength. On the contrary, the living, dialectical explanation makes the organization emerge as a product of the struggle.[28]

From Luxemburg's perspective, the destruction of the capitalist regime and its replacement with socialism must be conducted from below, *à la base*, beginning with the situation at hand. The movement must continually adapt itself to the political exigencies of the situation, developing practices in contradiction to the bourgeois state and, by so doing, creating

27. Luisa Passerini, *Autobiography of a Generation: Italy, 1968* (Middletown, Conn.: Wesleyan University Press, 1996), 111.

28. Rosa Luxemburg, *The Mass Strike, The Political Party and the Trade Unions*, trans. Patrick Lavin (New York: Harper Torchbook, 1971), 64.

the embryo of the new society to which it aspires as it goes. An anonymous tract dated June 1, entitled "We continue the combat," expresses this clearly:

> The absence today of a leader at the head of our movement corresponds to its very nature. It is not a question of knowing who will be at the head of everyone, but rather how everyone will form one head. More precisely, it is not a question of some political or trade-union organization pre-existing the formation of the movement appropriating the movement.
>
> The unity of the movement should not and cannot derive from the premature presence of a celebrity at its head but from the unity of the aspirations of workers, farmers and students.[29]

Nowhere was what I am calling this "Luxemburgian" or situational tendency more apparent than in the workings of the most significant form invented in May, the *comités d'action*. Small groups of perhaps ten or fifteen people, most of whom had belonged to no pre-formed political group, began to organize—by profession in some cases, by neighborhood or factory in others—after the general strike began in mid-May, largely with the goal of providing material aid to the strikers and producing agitprop to extend the strike. By May 31, over 460 such committees existed in the Paris region alone; "action committees" had appeared in the high schools (CALs) as early as February. In addition to their commitment to power to the workers, these groups shared a hostility to recognizing Pompidou as a viable political interlocutor, a reluctance to being themselves "recuperated" into traditional, mainstream political organizations, and, above all, a definition of their struggle as one of anticapitalism: "Coordination in *comités d'action* implanted in the factories, the neighborhoods, in high schools and university campuses, of union and non-union militants engaged in the same combat: an anticapitalist combat."[30] Some of the neighborhood committees, like that of the Marais, continued to exist for years following May.

> When you think that we kept an "Action Committee" alive for four years, with at least thirty people present at the weekly meeting, without a secretary, without an office, without regular obligatory dues, without a reliable meeting place—only the meeting day was set! In that we had a prodigious libertarian experience.[31]

29. Anonymous tract, "Nous continuons le combat," dated June 1, 1968.
30. Undated tract, "Projet de plate-forme politique des comités d'action."
31. Denise, cited in Daum, *Des révolutionnaires dans un village parisien*, 149.

In part, the "action committees" had emerged as an answer to the question of how best to retain the unorganized, the "mass" unaffiliated who had come out onto the streets for the fighting and the demonstrations. How could these people be catalyzed, organized? The answer, obviously, could not resemble the heavy bureaucratic apparatus of the modern state or party; rather, it must take the form of a supple kind of organization, with no defined a priori platform, and its workings have to transcend the distinction between leadership and mass activity. The *comités d'action* tried and succeeded in bringing into being in factories and neighborhoods other forms of organizations than those that functioned by adherence and election:

> Our functioning was very different from that of the traditional parties or the "groupuscules" that some of us had known. We had no imposed ideology, something that permitted people, whoever they were, to participate in its elaboration—people who weren't used to speaking up, people who had no former political experience, no political culture. Those who were more politicized had the opportunity of confronting their analyses with the point of view of others . . . the C.A. brought together people of different ages and different social milieux.[32]

In the words of the Students-Writers Action Committee:

> We push our refusal to the point of refusing to be assimilated into the political groups that claim to refuse what we refuse. We refuse the refusal programmed by institutions of the opposition. We refuse that our refusal, tied up and packaged, bear a trademark.[33]

Or, in the succinct words of one tract, "The fundamental goal of the *comités d'action* is to define a common political line from the bottom up (*à partir de la base*)."[34]

The history of the "action committees" and the way in which their workings seemed to respond to what one tract called "the fundamental democratic need of the masses"[35] don't correspond to official political history or to the narrative of state power, whether seized or not. Nor do the

32. Ibid., 145.

33. Comité d'Action Etudiants-Ecrivains, later attributed to Marguerite Duras, "20 May 1968: Description of the Birth of Students-Writers Action Committee," in *Green Eyes*, trans. Carol Barko (New York: Columbia University Press, 1990), 55.

34. Bulletin de Liaison Inter-Comités d'Action (B.L.I.C.A.), July 22, 1968.

35. Tract dated May 15, signed "La coordination de la région parisienne," cited in Schnapp and Vidal-Naquet, *Journal de la commune étudiant*, 475.

official commemorations of May have much to say about their history, about the dominant role played by women, for example, in their day-to-day workings.[36] But their existence is the best illustration of what Luxemburg called a "living dialectical evolution." By evoking Luxemburg, I do not want to suggest an explicit or conscious influence of her ideas, or anyone else's for that matter, on the behavior of May militants. I find it impossible to evaluate the role played by radical ideas or revolutionary theories transmitted from the exterior on the eruption and evolution of the insurrection. To do so, I would have to believe that consciousness precedes action or that a movement is born from a model, a blueprint, an idea, or a set of ideas, and not from a struggle—which I don't. The relation between ideas and modes of political action is always a conjunctural or situational one. Nevertheless, for the tendency I am describing, "Luxemburgian" seems to me more accurate than a range of shorthand terms—"anti-authoritarian" or "anarchist," for example—frequently used in writings about May, whose connotations veer toward a kind of chaotic individualism. In a mass movement, what matters is the concrete form that the real movement takes and the meaning individuals attribute to their actions. And what is most striking about revisiting, particularly from the vantage point of today, the actual documents of May—the films and documents that show the activities of the action committees in the high schools, to take one example—is the high degree of organization and coordination that prevailed. Within a mass movement new practices and new horizons cannot be separated. New practices like the "action committees" invented after May 13 and lived at the level of new social relations could only develop because the direction of the movement had become enlarged and modified. And the figuration of new horizons could only be accomplished because new political practices were being invented.

Thus came the return throughout the culture of May to what we could call a thematics of equality: overcoming the separation between manual and intellectual work, refusing professional or cultural qualification as a justification for social hierarchies and systems of political representation, refusing all delegation, undermining specialization—in short, the violent

---

36. The two best sources for the neighborhood *comités d'action* both show the equal role played by women. The documentary by the Collectif Arc, *CA 13: Comité d'Action du 13ème* (June 1968), focuses on one of the most successful of the committees, and its involvement supporting the strikers at the Citroën factory in the 13th *arrondissement*. Nicolas Daum's *Révolutionnaires dans un village parisien* contains interviews conducted twenty years later with members of the CA of the 3rd and 4th *arrondissements*, one of the most long-lasting of the committees. See also "Journal d'un comité d'action de quartier," in *Cahiers de Mai*, no. 3 (Aug.–Sept. 1968): 13–16.

disruption of assigned roles, places, or functions. By starting with a refusal of the roles or places predetermined by the social system, the May
movement veered throughout its existence toward a critique of the social division of labor. Aron, to his credit, recognized the political violence
contained in such contestation when he wrote: "Social organization will
decompose on the day when individuals refuse to accept the solidity and
division of labor, and refuse to submit to the order imposed by all on all."[37]

There is evidence that a kind of "after-the-fact" Leninism emerged in
some militants as part of the disappointments and bitterness associated
with the end of May. To look back at a moment after it has passed—
a moment when ministers, the prime minister, and the president of the
republic had all vacillated and lost consistency, when the government had
become a shadow and had all but evaporated into smoke or dust like the
witch in the *Wizard of Oz*—is to raise the question in all its poignancy
of a missed opportunity, despite the fact that the notion of "seizing state
power" was for the most part not central to the workings of May. Writing
ten years later, a Maoist militant offers the best description of the complex
set of ambivalent emotions associated with the end of May and the defeat
of the left in the June elections called by de Gaulle, an electoral defeat that
mattered less at the time than the fact that the elections had taken place
at all:

> Then there was June. The right pulled itself together, the left had
> nothing to propose in the way of an ideology—even a reformist one. . . .
> I came out of it all with one idea: never do that again, never take power
> from the ground up [*à la base*], never seize speech without seizing
> power. I was overcome with a certain bitterness and resentment against
> the fragility of everything we had done. The question of seizing Power
> (with a capital "P"), political power—I felt it all the more strongly in
> that we had the impression of already having it in the streets, of doing
> what we liked.
>
> The end of that experience was very painful. It's for that reason
> that all those discourses that tend toward taking partial powers, that
> propose ideas of molecular revolutions, leave me extremely skeptical.
> I profoundly loved May '68 for its antiauthoritarian aspect, but I had
> the profound feeling in June that grass-roots power [*à la base*] is not
> enough. I am pretty representative of a generation that has constantly
> oscillated between the two poles.[38]

37. Aron, *Elusive Revolution*, 35.
38. Alain, cited in Giorgini, *Que sont mes amis devenus?* 88–89.

"VIETNAM IS IN OUR FACTORIES"

For the thousands of middle-class French active in '68, the emergence of a new political subjectivity passed by way of the Other, and the figure of the Other in '68 is first and foremost that of the Other who defines political modernity: the worker. But the political subjectivity that pre-existed May for some militants dated back, as we have seen, to Algeria, and was formed along the axis of self and of a different collective alterity, the unresolvable or impossible identification with the colonial Other. "For all of us who entered into politics during that period, the problem of decolonization immediately became the major, if not the exclusive, concern."[39] For others, the "third-worldism" of the early 1960s brought the figures of the militant Cuban or Vietnamese revolutionary in their far-away struggles, gradually into focus: "Other climates: Cuba and Vietnam. How we scrutinized them, Cuba and Vietnam! What we could have known about them, what we could have understood, what we could have done for them, which is to say, what we were unable to do."[40] In its battle with the United States, with the worldwide political and cultural domination the United States had exerted since the end of World War II, Vietnam made possible a merging of the themes of anti-imperialism and anticapitalism; the theoretical justification was loosely provided by Maoism. All revolutionaries are involved in the same struggle (*même combat*): French workers, the North Vietnamese, and even French students have the same enemy, namely imperialist capitalism. Maoism thus initially loosened up the traditional P"C"F (as the Maoists sometimes wrote it) emphasis on the French proletariat by acknowledging the possibility of other political agents—peasants or farmers, for example. The Maoist theoretical current also reinforced the third-worldist geopolitical organization of the world along a North/South axis—the one etched by the international division of labor. Class struggle, only intermittently palpable in the West, was *already there*, already happening, at the international level, in the relations between imperialist and neo-colonial countries. Maoist China exemplified a third-world renewal of the promise of revolutionary socialism that had been betrayed by the Soviet Union. The opening editorial in *Révolution*, an anti-imperialist journal published by Jacques Vergès between 1963 and 1965 whose first issue in September 1963 manifested the earliest stirrings of a Maoist current in France, gives one example of how class struggle was being configured:

39. Terray, *Le troisième jour du communisme*, 15.
40. Peuchmaurd, *Plus vivants que jamais*, 13–14.

The same enterprise of liberation, of an unprecedented scope, is thus being organized. The proletariat no longer assumes the tragic figure of the factory worker, he has triumphed over one third of the globe. He has a bearing today on the destiny of the world: his strength cannot be discounted, and he is recognized from one continent to another. . . . The task of *Révolution* is very clear . . . to assist, in the domain of information, in the consolidation of the largest possible anti-imperialist United Front. . . . We are, in effect, the fellow travelers of all those who struggle. . . .[41]

In the years immediately preceding 1968, as the war accelerated in Vietnam, and especially after December 1966 with the American bombing of Hanoi, it was the North Vietnamese peasant, and not the auto worker at Billancourt, who had become, for many French militants, the figure of the working class. Both chronologically and theoretically, then, the Vietnamese fighter provided the transitional figure, the relay between the "intimate" colonial other, the Algerian of the early 1960s, and the French worker during '68.

A strong identification with Vietnam was common among nearly all of the various French militant camps active in '68, as it was in Germany, Japan, the United States, and elsewhere. As Sartre put it, "The fundamental impact of the war on American or European militants was its extension of the field of the possible."[42] The identification was in part symbolic—external stakes put in the place of interior political stakes that were as yet impossible to define, and in part very pragmatic—a way of getting things started at home. And yet only France and Italy were drawn to make the conceptual leap or relay back to the Other at home, to pass from the figure of the foreign peasant militant to the indigenous worker, to affirm, along with striking Fiat workers in Turin, that "Vietnam is in our factories," or with French watch manufacturing workers in Besançon, "Combat in the *maquis* of the factories of France!"[43] (The term *maquis* had a French connotation: the setting for the activities of the Resistance during World War II. But in the late 1960s the immediate connotation was a third-world one: the national liberation struggles of peasants in Asia, Latin America, and Africa. Make the factories into *maquis:* bring the struggle home.) German student demonstrations, considerably more numerous, violent, and concerted than the French, sparked no reaction or

41. Jacques Vergès, editorial, *Révolution*, no. 1 (Sept. 1963).
42. Jean-Paul Sartre, "Sartre par Sartre," *Situations IX* (Paris: Gallimard, 1972), 127.
43. Slogan cited in *Classe de lutte,* film by the Groupe Medvedkine, SLON-Iskra Production, 1968/69.

simultaneous uprising among German workers. In the case of the French, how did such a relay take place? Or, to ask the same question in the words of historian Jean-Pierre Rioux: "What is meant by the *lien* (link) or *relais* (relay) that joined student May with worker May?"[44]

To answer this question, we must first look to the sites and discourses that allowed the geography of a vast international and distant struggle—the "North/South axis"—to become transposed onto the lived geography, the daily itineraries, of students and intellectuals in Paris in the early 1960s. The nearly twenty-year existence of François Maspero's bookstore La Joie de Lire on the rue Saint Severin, from 1956 to 1975, coincides almost exactly with the roughly twenty-year span—from Dien Bien Phu in 1954 and the Bandung conference the following year to some time in 1975—the period during which the periphery became the center of interest to European, and particularly to French, intellectuals. In these years dominated by the decomposition of the European empires, Maspero's bookstore and press took up the task of representing the image of an exploded world where Europe is no longer the center. And, in so doing, La Joie de Lire became a center of sorts in the lives of many militants, an inevitable stopping place along daily trajectories, a place where, particularly during the Algerian period, any number of censored periodicals, state documents, banned books like Alleg's *La question*, as well as foreign, difficult to locate, or ephemeral political pamphlets, could be found downstairs; a place that was not just a meeting place, nor even, as Maspero himself called it, "the meeting place for all the contradictions of the left,"[45] but, quite simply, "the liveliest bookstore in Paris."[46] It was there that many readers found the tools by which, in the words of Claude Liauzu, "to take into consideration the fact that the West was no longer the measure of everything."[47] "What strikes me the most," commented one frequenter of the store, "is the seriousness with which people look at and touch the books;"[48] Jean-Francis Held, as well, refers to the bookstore's "dense and austere climate."[49] But it was also experienced by many as a welcoming place when the rest of the streets were hostile, a place where

44. Jean-Pierre Rioux, "A propos des célébrations décennales du Mai français," *Vingtième Siècle*, no. 23 (July–Sept. 1989): 57.

45. François Maspero, cited in an interview with Guy Dumur, "Maspero entre tous les feux," *Nouvel Observateur*, Sept. 17–23, 1973, 60.

46. Guy Dumur, in "Maspero entre tous les feux," 58.

47. Claude Liauzu, "Le tier-mondisme des intellectuels en accusation. Le sens d'une trajectoirre," *Vingtième Siècle*, no. 12 (Oct.–Dec. 1986): 75.

48. Cited in Chris Marker film, *On vous parle de Paris: Maspero. Les mots ont un sens*, SLON Production, 1970.

49. Jean-Francis Held, a portrait of François Maspero in *Le Nouvel Observateur*, Aug. 24–30, 1966, 26.

chance meetings and impromptu conversations outside of any determined political framework—be it party or even "groupusculaire"—might occur: across factions, and above all, across nationalities. Militant life circa 1963 was concentrated in a "magic triangle" made up of the Sorbonne (Jussieu then was just a project; Censier and Nanterre were on the drawing board), the new Parisian locale for the UEC on the place Paul Painlevé across the street from the Sorbonne, and the Editions Maspero on the rue Saint-Severin at the bottom of the Boulevard Saint-Michel.[50] Books that couldn't be found at more specialized bookstores like L'Harmattan (the word means "the wind from the South"), located then on the rue des Quatres Vents, or at the Communist Party bookstore on the Rue Racine, might be found at La Joie de Lire, where all revolutionary currents flowed unfiltered. Martine Storti recalls a typical militant trajectory for 1967:

> At the bottom of the Boulevard Saint-Michel, on the rue Saint-Severin, I spent long hours at the bookstore of the Editions Maspero, cultural and political haven for "revolutionaries" . . . farther down, there was the Mutualité for meetings, and on the other side, towards Saint-Germain-des-près, the rue de Rennes with, at number 44, the *Hôtel de la société de l'encouragement pour l'industrie nationale,* where meetings were frequently held. From time to time I walked down toward the Gobelins, to Censier, a sort of annex of the Sorbonne opened in 1965.[51]

Censier, of course, was to be a major laboratory during May for contacts between militant workers and students. And La Joie de Lire would provide a literal haven for wounded and gassed militants who crowded through its doorway in May fleeing the police.[52] But in the early 1960s the Editions Maspero were known primarily as another "wind from the

50. Jean-Paul Dollé, *L'insoumis: Vies et légendes de Pierre Goldman* (Paris: Grasset, 1997), 39.

51. Martine Storti, *Un chagrin politique: De mai 68 aux années 80* (Paris: L'Harmattan, 1996), 70–71.

52. The bookstore itself was regularly a target of bombings, attacks, and surveillance throughout the period: at the hands of the OAS during the Algerian period, and at the hands of the police during '68. A tract signed by Maspero and distributed by the store in September 1968 entitled "In Reference to the Police in Front of Our Bookstore," reads in part:

> Last May new elements intervened: members of the police force in uniform threw gas grenades into our crowded bookstore, preventing people from getting out, beating with clubs [*matraquant*] those who managed to get by, causing several serious injuries. . . . This was the most serious attack that our bookstore has experienced in several years: the laugh is that it was committed by the police themselves.
>
> Today, the same police, wearing the same uniform, have taken up a patrol in front of our shop windows. Against whom?
>
> Let it be very clear that we have nothing to do with this comedy.

South": the press that tracked the ruin and collapse of Empire, that regularly gave voice to South American, African, and Asian political theorists and testimonies, the press that first published Fanon's *Les damnés de la terre* with its preface by Sartre, as well as works by Ben Barka, Giap, Cabral, Che Guevara, Malcolm X, and others. Theory and testimonies were given equal distribution; but readers would also find in La Joie de Lire complex transversals operating between the political and the poetic: Baudelaire piled next to Lenin, Giraudoux with Marx, Michaud and Ché. It was largely because of the Editions Maspero, and because of the editorial direction followed by *Le Monde Diplomatique* and *Les Temps Modernes* during those years—these three publications shared many of the same authors—that one of the great *gauchiste* particularities of the time became palpably evident: theory itself was being generated not from Europe but from the third world. Not only was the figure of action, the militant peasant freedom-fighter a third world phenomenon—this, after all, was to be expected according to a standard international division of labor in which Europe and the West are the thinkers and the rest of the world the doers, the men of action. But "the wretched of the earth"—Mao, Guevara, Fanon, Cabral and others—had become, in this era of *gauchiste* reversal, the thinkers as well.

Maspero's family background—an Egyptologist grandfather, a Sinologist father killed by the Nazis—as well as his own political trajectory that navigated through a break with *la gauche respectueuse* and with the PCF over Algeria, helps explain his attentiveness to developments transpiring in the third world. But in a 1973 interview he recounted a specific event, a great "shock" as he put it, that made him lurch in that direction. A student in the mid-1950s in ethnology and a militant member of the Communist Party, Maspero attended the first festival of ethnological film ever screened in Paris. There he watched a Jean Rouch film about hippopotamus hunting among the Dogon. It was less the film itself that jarred Maspero than the intervention by a number of Africans in the audience critiquing the film's "folkloric" dimensions; they went on to complain about a 1932 law still in place that denied them access to a camera in their own country without the approval of the government.[53] The anecdote is significant in reminding us of one of the most important factors in the development of a third-worldist perspective in postwar France: the sheer number of African, Caribbean, and Asian intellectuals, so many of whom would become loyal clients of La Joie de Lire, living or spending lengthy stays in Paris in those days. For Maspero, it was to this first experience of "meeting" or conjuncture—the film by a French ethnographer and the

53. See "Maspero entre tous les feux," 58–59.

critique it generated among the "people" it sought to represent—that he later attributed what would become his own commitment to diffusing, making available, a range of works in which people engaged in political struggle represented themselves. In his first bookstore, the predecessor to La Joie de Lire on the rue Monsieur-le-Prince, this meant primarily stocking early works published by Présence Africaine; later, with the start of his own publishing company in 1960, it would mean "giving voice" to the FLN during the Algeria years, editing journals like *Partisans* and *Tricontinental* (whose seizures by the government necessitated protracted and expensive legal cases for Maspero), publishing texts that would allow readers to "know with some accuracy what is going on in the head of a Cuban revolutionary or a Black American militant,"[54]—all in the attempt to "open up as widely as possible the possibilities of information and discussion at the heart of left movements in France and in the world,"[55] and thus "to create the instruments for those who wish to use them."[56] Information, for Maspero, was itself an act of militancy, for its sheer existence was an arm in the battle against the inundation of "counter-information" disseminated daily by the bourgeois media—the daily mainstream newspapers, television, and radio.

In the mid-1960s, the third-worldist perspective Maspero had helped make available to French readers became the means, in his view, for reconceptualizing the French national situation. The journal *Partisans*, founded by Maspero in September 1961, shows this trajectory clearly. The opening editorial in its first issue is signed by Vercors, the great underground novelist of the Resistance and one of the founders of *Les Editions de Minuit*, still using his *nom de guerre*. Vercor's editorial situates the journal squarely within an anti-imperialist inception:

> [W]e support, in particular, the Algerian Revolution.
>
> We support it in a much vaster context, of which it is only one element: the emergence of the third world. We think that our era, and probably all the second half of the twentieth century, will be dominated by the gigantic phenomenon brusquely inaugurated in China: the accession of people of color to the political history of the world, and their growing participation in its economic, cultural, and social history.[57]

Largely "third-worldist," then, in its orientation at the outset, *Partisans* in

54. Maspero, cited in Marker, *On vous parle de Paris*.

55. Maspero, cited in Jean-Francis Held interview, *Nouvel Observateur*, Aug. 24–30, 1966, 27.

56. Maspero, cited in an interview, "Le long combat de François Maspero," *Nouvel Observateur*, Sept. 27, 1976, 56.

57. Vercors, Editorial, *Partisans*, no. 1 (Sept. 1961): 5.

the mid-1960s begins to participate in the various cultural debates preceding May; after '68, the journal shows a distinct preference for French social and political issues. Speaking in 1966, Maspero announced his desire to provide in the kinds of books he published more analyses of France and the struggles at home—but only to the extent that these not be considered as local phenomena. France must be viewed through an internationalist lens:

> If I wish, I repeat, to publish more analyses on French social and political life, I still think that "everything is linked," and that one cannot analyze Gaullism, capitalism, or syndicalism in the France of 1966 as though it were a phenomenon isolated from the rest of the world.[58]

Everything that counted in an elaboration of left and far-left thinking, in social, economic, and political studies written within a Marxist vein—including contemporary theoretical texts by Althusser, Rancière, and Macherey, and the "rediscovery" of Paul Nizan, who figures as one of the most widely read authors among French militants of the 1960s and 1970s—would be edited or re-edited in the "Petite Collection Maspero," started in 1967. Published in distinctive pastel covers, and priced at 6.15 francs apiece, the works in this series made up the elements of a shared political culture; by all accounts, people simply bought (or stole) each book in the series as soon as it came out.

During and after May, university professors who castigated the "anti-intellectualism" of student activists, their lack of respect for "bookish culture," failed to see the extent to which students, who may not have been deriving an intellectual culture from the university library and their required course readings, were indeed formulating one from frequenting marginal bookstores like La Joie de Lire and L'Harmattan.[59]

> One has no idea now of the intensity of the intellectual activity of the 1960s, linked to the idea of the critique of Stalinism, to the support for peoples' liberation movements, as we said then. It was the time of *Arguments*, of *Socialisme ou Barbarie* and other journals, not just the *Les Temps Modernes* and *Esprit*. My feeble political culture got renewed, theoretical reflection seemed to me more and more indispensable.[60]

Listening today to the random street conversations of May captured by documentary films like William Klein's *Grands soirs et petits matins*

---

58. Maspero, cited in Held interview, 27. The majority of the volumes focusing on the third world published in the Petite Collection Maspero appear between the years of 1960 and 1968. See Liauzu, *L'enjeu tiersmondiste*, 37.

59. Vladimir Fisera makes a similar point in the BBC Radio 4 documentary program, "Year of Dreams," broadcast on January 20 and 24, 1988, ed. David Caute, prod. David Levy.

60. Denise, cited in Daum, *Des révolutionnaires dans un village parisien*, 143.

11	8088	S

Customer:

Joseph Petrick

May '68 and Its Afterlives

Kristin Ross

W2-S005-87-14

UE-967-251

No CD

Used - Like New

9780226727974

Picker Notes:
M _____ 2 _____
WT _____ 2 _____
CC _____

30463642

1025894792

Print Date: 7/23/2014 12:12:40 AM   Ship. Created: 7/21/2014 10:35:00 AM

quickly dispels any stereotype of the uncouth or ignorant 1960s student. A reading culture—made up of the books and journals of the critical, anti-Stalinist Marxism that flourished from the mid-1950s to the mid-1970s in France, along with the third-worldist texts edited and translated during the same time—seems, on the contrary, to have produced an extremely articulate cross-section of high school and university students, knowledgeable in world affairs, non-xenophobic in their outlook, and capable of mounting an argument.

In the 1970 film documentary by Chris Marker devoted to Maspero, *On vous parle de Paris: Maspero. Les Mots ont un sens*, Maspero is shown giving a three-part breakdown of his definition of an editor. An editor is defined first by his catalog, by the selection of books he has published. More importantly, though, he is defined by the books he has *not* published—in this category Maspero says he is particularly proud of his achievements. And thirdly, he is defined by the books that have been published by other presses because of the existence of Editions Maspero—because that press has established a readership for a certain kind of book that other presses now grab because they don't want him to get it first. This last he calls "my famous catalog of books I published elsewhere."[61] The second category, the books he chose not to publish, included thousands of titles on May '68. French presses were "obscene," "nauseating" after '68, in Maspero's words, publishing "like pigs" about May; for them, 100,000 people on the street equaled 100,000 buyers of books. In an accurate and devastating appraisal of the tide of post-May verbiage that hit the stores only weeks after the insurrection ended, he calls most of the books that came out about May, "kinds of eternal self-glorifications of the student movement": isn't it wonderful what we did, wasn't it great on the barricades? Maspero saw very little in the trend that might be viewed as constructive or informative about future or ongoing struggles, "and you know that future struggles exist."[62]

Editions Maspero published strikingly few titles on May. The press limited itself primarily to works and testimonials about the factory strikes—works that remain among the very few valuable sources for the perspective or voices of individual workers in the May movement to date. In Marker's film, the camera lingers on their titles: *Des Soviets à Saclay?; La grève à Flins; La Commune de Nantes; Notre Arme, c'est la grève.*[63]

---

61. Maspero, cited in "Le long combat de François Maspero," 56.

62. Maspero, cited in Marker, *On vous parle de Paris.*

63. *Des Soviets à Saclay* (1968); *Notre arme c'est la grève* [*travail réalisé par un collectif de militants du comité d'action qui ont participé à la grève de Renault-cléon du 15 mai au 17 juin 1968*] (1968); J.-P. Talbo, ed., *La grève à Flins* (Paris: Maspero, 1968); Yannick Guin, *La Commune de Nantes* (Paris: Maspero, 1969).

"This permanent, precise labor of documentation and denunciation," Maspero said in a 1976 interview, "This molelike activity, this is what interests me."[64]

Maspero's focus by the time May erupted had moved from the figure of the colonial other to that of the French worker; Maspero's career as a publisher and a militant provides one example of a path that allowed such a displacement to take place in the course of the French 1960s. Chris Marker's career provides another. Having worked with a collective of film-makers and workers to produce the *cinétract* on the Rhodiaceta strike in 1967, *A bientôt, j'espère,* Marker and his group chose to premiere the film they had been making virtually simultaneously about Vietnam, *Loin du Vietnam,* to an audience composed of Rhodiaceta workers at Besançon. (Ninety workers had been let go after the end of the strike). In both his choice of screening locale for the Vietnam film and in its actual texture— Marker incorporated clips from the earlier strike film into the footage of *Loin du Vietnam*—the context of anti-imperialism, as Celia Britton points out, was inserted directly into the context of industrial militancy in France.[65] Rhodiaceta worker Georges Maurivard, who introduced the film at the screening, did so with these remarks:

> What questions will be raised on the screen?
> Questions about things happening on the other side of the world?
> About terrible events about which we can do nothing?
> No!
> IT WILL BE ABOUT US.
> About our attitude toward the events, of course, but mostly about
> our attitude toward the world in which we lead our daily lives.
> In Vietnam two powers are in conflict that we know all too well: the
> rich and the poor, force and justice, the rule of money and the hope for
> a new world.[66]

In the discussion between the audience and the filmmakers held after the screening, one of the members of the film collective, Alain Resnais, articulates the desire to "go beyond Vietnam," as he puts it, but in the direction of France, to raise the question, for example, of whether having a refrigerator, for American society, necessarily implies the destruction

64. Maspero, cited in "Le long combat de François Maspero," 56.

65. SLON (Société pour le Lancement des Oeuvres Nouvelles) included Alain Resnais, Joris Ivens, Claude Lelouch, William Klein, Jean-Luc Godard, and Agnes Varda, in addition to Marker. See Celia Britton, "The Representation of Vietnam in French Films Before and After 1968," in *May 68—Coming of Age,* ed. D. L. Hanley and A. P. Kerr (London: Macmillan, 1989), 163–81. See also Sylvia Harvey, *May '68 and Film Culture* (London: BFI Publications, 1978).

66. Cited in "Loin du Vietnam," *Cinéma,* January 1968, 37.

of another country and, after that, one's own destruction. "We start with Vietnam," he says, "in order to get to things that would be almost entirely French . . . to show, in the end, that it is clearly capitalism itself which is at stake."[67]

Culturally militant forms and experiments like Marker's recall that it was above all in terms of class relations that third-world problems were posed in France: global solutions to the problems of the third world could only be found in the radical transformation of the capitalist world system and its replacement by a new economic order. (Anglo-Saxon "third-worldism," according to Yves Lacoste, tended toward a more philanthropic and religious attitude, derived from notions of Christian charity, to the underdeveloped world).[68] Among student militants, a document like the "Political Resolution of the First Session of the First Congress of the UJC (m-l)" (the Maoist group originating in December 1966 among the Althusserians of the rue d'Ulm), reveals the inseparability of the third world situation and that of workers in the West. Here, the common enemy, American imperialism, allows for a passage from "Vietnamese fighter" directly to "French worker"; it attempts to connect the Vietnamese struggle to the internal problems of the West. The principles defended by the group are:

1. A united front of youth against American imperialism, the principal enemy of the peoples of the entire world . . . a powerful support, without reservation, for the popular war that our Vietnamese comrades are victoriously conducting.

2. The formation of revolutionary intellectuals who will join with workers and working people, who will institute new forms of organization that will make possible the realization of such a task.[69]

The relation of French intellectuals to the Vietnamese Other, engaged in their ongoing struggle, is one of "united frontism" and unreserved "support," and could be said to fall under the heading of a fairly straightforward revolutionary unity or solidarity, an interdependence of fronts where solidarity is not charity. France's own colonial history in Vietnam is—surprisingly—not evoked; instead, contemporary American imperialism makes "comrades" of the French and the Vietnamese. The relation of French middle-class students to the "working people" at home in France, on the other hand, is both more complex and more located in the future:

67. Ibid., 48.
68. See Yves Lacoste, *Contre les anti-tiersmondistes et contre certains tiers-mondistes* (Paris: La Découverte, 1986), 17.
69. "Résolution politique de la 1ère session du 1er congrès de l'UJC (m-l), *Cahiers Marxistes-Leninistes* 15 (Jan.–Feb. 1967).

in a process of "formation" and in the invention of entirely new forms that will bring about the joining or linkage with (*se lier à*) the Other as worker. Joining with the worker seems to require something more like the theoretical articulation of the relations between different situations or, better, the invention of forms of practice that would create such an articulation in the first place.

ENTERING THE TIGER'S LAIR

What were those forms? By offering a terrain for practical work, it was Vietnam that would provide them. The UJC (m-l) called for "active solidarity" with the Vietnamese, as opposed to what they saw to be the "purely formal" participation of the PCF in the "Mouvement de la Paix": "the purely formal reality of the Mouvement de la Paix was evident: no action centered in the factories, the neighborhoods, the high schools and the campuses, no agitation, no propaganda, no militant work."[70] The Maoist group set itself off from the PCF through their slogan: "FNL Vaincra" ("Victory for the Vietnamese Liberation Front"); the PCF, concerned mainly with the threat of thermonuclear war, called merely for "Peace in Vietnam" rather than outright victory for the revolution. But more importantly, the Maoist group began to conduct a different kind of political organizing: direct contact, leaving the territory of the university, organizing regularly in workers' housing, outside the gates of factories, in cafés in immigrant suburbs—outside of the Latin Quarter and outside, that is, of the PCF's definition of the way politics was to be conducted.

The role of Vietnam was thus highly overdetermined. Vietnam, quite literally, provided the initial spark that launched the student violence. For May begins when a student breaks a window of the American Express building on rue Scribe in Paris on March 20, 1968. Students protest the arrest of that student and others demonstrating against the Vietnam War in the wake of the Tet offensive; this is how the incidents in Nanterre first erupt:

> In relation to the *Comités de base*, to the *Comité Vietnam National*, to all those operations—the language was new—the "Mouvement du 22 mars" was born then and there. You were a part of the March 22nd Movement if you were anti-imperialist, whether with the CVN or the *comités de base*, pro-Chinese, or whatever faction.[71]

70. Mimeographed account of the activities of the CVB for the militant assembly of October 7, 1967.
71. Mouvement du 22 mars, *Ce n'est qu'un début, continuons le combat* (Paris: Maspero, 1968), 17.

(It is worth remembering that the name of the "Mouvement du 22 mars" was of Cuban inspiration, modeled after Castro's having named their group the "July 26th movement" after their first insurrectional action against Batista, the attack on the Moncada fortress on July 26, 1953.) Vietnam thus both launched the action in the streets as well as brought under one umbrella a number of groups—the CVN was dominated by Trotskyists, the CVB by Maoists—as well as previously unaffiliated militants working together. Groups, that is, that had formerly emphasized "the narcissism of small differences" began to function together as what Jean Chesneaux has called "a confederacy of rebel tribes." As the situation in Vietnam worsened, as more and more numerous American troops replaced advisors, the war served to *reveal* the profound mechanisms of a technologically highly developed capitalist society: it illustrated the monstrous exaggeration of the same forms of oppression that existed in an only latent or occasional state in the West. At the same time, the military and political practices of the Vietnamese Liberation Front, grounded in mass popular anger at home in Vietnam and the growing support of international opinion, became "a model for all the peoples of the world," as the Maoists put it—especially because they were succeeding. When Sartre wrote in 1972 that he continued to be convinced that Vietnam was at the origins of May '68, he did not mean simply that students placed themselves on the side of the FNL in their struggle against the United States. His comment about the effect of Vietnam "extending the field of the possible" for western militants refers to how impossible it seemed then that the Vietnamese could take on the American military machine and succeed, a sentiment echoed in the countless references in Maoist texts to the "exemplarity" of the Vietnamese. "All militants know that the ideas they had in their heads during the May combats came for the most part from the practice of the Vietnamese people."[72] Theoretically, "the struggle of oppressed peoples with, at their head, the heroic Vietnamese people"[73] offered a perspective according to which a number of analogies could be formed between the foreign peasant and the French worker as occupying structurally similar positions in relation to capitalist imperialism, the "principle enemy." Both were struggles initiated "from below": the revolutionary guerrilla struggle of small third-world nations against the American military-industrial empire had its counterpart in the *grèves sauvages* (wildcat strikes) at Rhodiaceta and Caen, brutally or violently initiated "from below," outside of—and increasingly against—the customary trade-union apparatus. As Mao, in the "Letter in Twenty-Five

72. *Cahiers de la Gauche prolétarienne / La Cause du peuple*, no. 5 (April 1969): 24.
73. Ibid.

Points" put it, the "third world" had become the "storm zone" of world Revolution. "A straight path leads from peoples' liberation struggles to the organization of popular insurrection in the imperialist metropoles;" so stated a *Gauche prolétarienne* tract distributed around Vincennes in 1972. As Lin Piao explained in "Long Live the Victorious War of the People," the situation of "the cities encircled by the countryside" would inevitably spark flames in the imperialist capitals. "We believed that the future of the world revolution depended on the victory or the defeat of the Vietnamese. After the 'surprise' victory of the Cuban revolution, American imperialism was determined to block by every means, including massive military intervention, the revolutionary surge elsewhere. World revolution and counterrevolution were fighting it out in Vietnam."[74] The extent to which the working masses of France, preoccupied by their own concerns, came to identify with the Vietnamese peasant and view American imperialism—and not the factory *patron*—as the "principal enemy" was probably very slight indeed. But for militants and intellectuals Vietnam allowed the continuation and development of a transgressional communist position outside of and to the left of the PCF—a positioning that had first come into being, as previously discussed, around Algeria. And, as we saw in our discussion of the emergence of a core of radical student movement at the moment of Algeria, students and other social groups could only become politicized if the forms of organization and political militantism currently available were themselves radically restructured.

Of crucial importance, then, for the question of the link between "student May" and "worker May" were the organizational forms and practices that developed around Vietnam militancy—forms that sought to disengage themselves from a conventional politics of central apparatuses. These were practices that brought students into direct, concrete contact with workers and with others outside the university—a kind of "field-work" or going out "on the terrain," opening up a range of new grassroots (*à la base*) "political fields."

The *Comités Viet-nam "de base"* (CVB), which got started in 1967 and which in many cases formed the basis for the *comités d'action* that later sprang up during May, were the most significant militant organization of the new type, practicing precisely this kind of delocalization and developing a political style in conscious rupture with the heritage.

> We got ahold of what we could use from the Chinese cultural revolution to borrow more contradictory and more unstable forms of organization than those that had been bequeathed to us up until that point

74. Henri Weber, cited in Ronald Fraser, *1968: A Student Generation in Revolt* (London: Chatto and Windus, 1988), 114.

by the tradition of communist movements. As Marxist-Leninists, we thought about radically innovating from the point of view of the theory and practice of the organization. We wanted to build a much more dialectical kind of organization.[75]

Behind their activities lay the recognition that the division between intellectual and manual labor was inseparable from the spatial projection or format of that division: the gap separating city from countryside and even the Latin Quarter from the workers' *foyers* concentrated in Saint-Ouen and beyond. "We had always gravitated to the *banlieues*."[76] But in large part these committees seemed to be the expression of a spontaneous (and by that I mean taking the shape necessitated by what the movement needs at the moment) political sensibility, not fashioned from on high and not produced by apprenticeship within theory but elaborated in common in certain informal "laboratory situations," in Toulouse, in Strasbourg and elsewhere, and largely in the high schools. "It's not true [about May '68] that everything started out of nowhere. In the high schools there was political life: the Comités Vietnam."[77] And within those committees, little by little, a way of working together as a group began to take shape: the idea of allowing as much autonomy as possible at the grass-roots level. Direct contact on the terrain (*à la base*), a certain literalism pushed Maoists in particular to give priority to actions *à la base*, in workers' neighborhoods. Regular *détachements de banlieues*, as they were called, were sent out to work between the factory neighborhoods and the city:

> We called it the style of "mass work" (*travail de masse*). . . . The point of view we had was the following: students were an important part of the composition, but one that must be allied with the masses; if we weren't allied with the masses, we had no future. Allied with the masses in the physical sense of the term."[78]

An early Maoist resolution makes the call for such an alliance:

> Either youth and students will remain within the strict framework of the high schools and the university campuses, cut off from working people and their struggles, and, in this case, their revolt will get bogged down

75. Robert Linhart, "Evolution du procès de travail et luttes de classe," *Critique Communiste*, special issue, *Mai 68–Mai 78* (1978): 105–6.

76. Victor (Benny Levy) in Michéle Manceaux, *Les Maos en France* (Paris: Gallimard, 1972), 217.

77. Yann, cited in Giorgini, *Que sont mes amis devenus?* 120.

78. Victor (Benny Levy) in Manceaux, *Les Maos en France*, 188.

and will not serve the revolutionary cause. Or, on the other hand, youth and students will develop a movement, a concrete solidarity with workers, and, in that case the struggle of students and youth will fuse with that of the working class and working people, and it will be progressive, revolutionary.[79]

Using a combination of discipline and improvisation, assiduous regularity—"implantation" in a particular neighborhood or site—and innovation, the goal on one level was that of trying to integrate the problem of Vietnam into the texture of French everyday life in the manner in which Algeria—because of the draft, because of the significant presence of Algerians in France, because of the OAS attacks—had been experienced as inseparable from French daily life.

> For more than a year, like all the other CVBs, we are patiently popularizing—by all kinds of methods, from explanatory signs and panel boards to posters, not to mention tracts and discussions—the fundamental aspects of national liberation undertaken by the heroic Vietnamese people against the U.S. imperialist aggressors and their lackeys in Saigon.[80]

The committees followed central initiatives but accompanied these with new gestures designed to draw attention, selling the *Courrier du Vietnam,* shouting tracts and slogans out loud, using panel signs, sandwich boards and wall-posters: "It was essential that we not be mistaken for the peaceful people selling "L'Huma-Dimanche" who—a sign of the insipid weakness of the PCF—had long ago renounced any combative energy. Each week, then, we tried to invent a new gimmick to draw attention to ourselves."[81]

A Maoist militant who would later take a job on a factory assembly line recalls:

> I learned how to be a militant in the *Comité Vietnam de base* of the twentieth *arrondissement* where I lived. I sold *Le Courrier du Vietnam,* discovering street militantism. I invented slogans that I yelled very loudly into the ears of passersby doing their shopping; I insisted on not reciting any lessons or stock phrases. That was our politics, at the UJ, to invent slogans ourselves and to design panel-signs that were as striking as possible. It's in the CVB of my neighborhood that I met

79. April 23, 1968, UJC (m-l) resolution, cited in Jean Moreau, "Les 'Maos' de la gauche prolétarienne," *La Nef,* no. 48 (June–Sept. 1972): 77–103.

80. "Une rencontre entre un comité Vietnam de base parisien et une cellule du parti communiste du même quartier," in the CVB journal *Victoire pour le Vietnam* 6 (March 1968).

81. Jean-Pierre Le Dantec, *Les dangers du soleil* (Paris: Les Presses d'Aujourd'hui, 1978), 84.

Jean-Claude, the future father of my son, Fabien. By moving in with him I broke with my parents for the second time.[82]

Maoist practices like the activities of the CVBs bore a clear resemblance to their more notorious experiments in *établissement,* the name given to the practice in the years before and after May '68 of intellectuals taking up positions on factory lines. Both practices were predicated on a necessary displacement, a physical, and not merely textual or theoretical, trajectory outside of one's proper space in the hope of creating new social relations *à la base.* After all, as Mao was fond of asking, how can you catch a tiger cub without entering the tiger's lair? Such displacements—*"se jeter dans le monde"* (throwing oneself into the world) was one slogan; to be *"comme un poisson dans l'eau"* (like a fish in water) was another—were not uniquely Maoist; they were shared by many May militants, including those who began to focus politically for the first time on the figure of the immigrant worker. The *Comité d'action "bidonvilles* (slums)" was one such group:

> Many private and semipublic organizations "are concerned" with the *bidonvilles.* They bring a moral and material aid that, far from contesting the very existence of the *bidonville,* allows the latter to perpetuate itself and to remain a "reserve" of cheap labor.
>
> The *Comité d'action bidonvilles* makes direct contact with the inhabitants of the *bidonvilles,* not only to bring them food but above all to put at their disposition the means of diffusion (posters, group-authored tracts translated into many languages) capable of reinforcing their unity in the face of the exploitation of the capitalist regime.[83]

May '68, in fact, marks the emergence onto the political scene of the *travailleur immigré* (immigrant worker) in French society. Before '68, left parties had been relatively silent about immigration, in part because immigrants could not be mobilized for electoral purposes. The functionalist campus at Nanterre, inaugurated in 1964 and built on the site of the worst immigrant slums outside Paris, provided students with a direct "lived" lesson in uneven development—a daily experience that Henri Lefebvre, for one, never tired of remarking was the foremost "cause" of May '68. Nanterre students had to traverse the slums every day to attend classes on their new campus. But those who made their way back into the immigrant slums surrounding the new campus took a decisive step. Far-left groups in May and June acted as a catalyst for distinctly new forms of expression, representation, and mobilization of immigrant workers; by

82. Danièle Léon, cited in Virginie Linhart, *Volontaires pour l'usine* (Paris: Seuil, 1994), 121.
83. Tract, Comité d'action bidonvilles, June 4, 1968.

1970, rent strikes, hunger strikes, squatting, and other collective struggles unseen before May '68 began to bring immigrants into direct confrontation with the state apparatus.[84] For at least ten years following May, far-left groups provided one of the rare vectors of solidarity with these initiatives.

A peculiar combination of literalism—the insistence on direct contact with workers unobstructed by any theoretical or trade-union mediation, on building understanding through practice—and utopianism, anticipating, particularly for the Maoists, the disappearance of a distinction between intellectual and manual labor, living *as though* that distinction had already been obliterated. Here, the overdetermined figure of the "barefoot doctor" provided by the Chinese Cultural Revolution can be seen to play a role no less important than the figure of the "Vietnamese fighter"—a paradoxical role, perhaps, in that a largely fantasmatic relation, one based on very little empirical knowledge of what was actually transpiring in China, could serve to inspire a set of experiential or reality-based, empirical sets of experiments of "going to the people," voyaging to the "other side" of society, on the part of those who called themselves Maoists in France. Emmanuel Terray has offered the most illuminating account of the desires that crystallized during those days around the figure of the "barefoot doctor" as the embodiment of a lived critique of specialization. His account is all the more unusual and valuable since it departs from the standard narrative paradigm of self-criticism and autodenunciation that began to be invariably adopted by disillusioned Maoists, reflecting, after 1976, on their youthful mystifications with the so-called wisdom of hindsight:

> I was like many others a fervent partisan—from France—of the Cultural Revolution. But I don't consider this to be a regrettable youthful error about which it would be better to be silent today, or, on the other hand, to make an ostentatious confession. I know today, of course, that the Cultural Revolution we dreamt about and that inspired part of our political practice didn't have much in common with the Cultural Revolution as it was lived out in China. And yet I am not ready to put my former admiration into the category of a mental aberration. In fact, the symbolic power of Maoist China operated in Europe at the end of the sixties independently of Chinese reality as such. "Our" Cultural Revolution was very far from that, but it had the weight and the consistency of those collective representations that sociology and anthropology have studied for so long. . . .

84. See tract, "Projet de programme de lutte des travailleurs immigrés" (May 29, 1968); see also Geneviève Dreyfus-Armand, "L'arrivée des immigrés sur la scène politique," CNRS, Institut d'Histoire du Temps Présent, Lettre d'information, no. 30 (June 1998); Yvan Gastaut, *L'immigration et l'opinion en France sous la Ve république* (Paris: Seuil, 2000).

[T]hat "democratic" eruption [in China], unexpected but real, was associated with another "egalitarian" eruption. Intellectuals and managers [*cadres*] had to listen to and put themselves at the service of the masses and to that end share their living conditions. China also knew the particularly deep abyss separating the *cadres* from the mass of the peasantry that is the rule in all third world countries: in the Chinese case that abyss was deepened even more by the cumulative effect of Confucian culture and communist culture, the latter affirming the superiority of the educated class and intellectuals, the former that of the enlightened avant-garde. In these conditions, who could find unreasonable or criminal such a program for rehabilitating those in the scorned social groups? Wasn't it, on the contrary, admirable, in a world largely characterized by arrogance and disdain on the part of the privileged toward "the people"? The "barefoot doctors," those nurses formed by the hundreds, or those medical students leaving the city for the countryside, constituted in some way the paradigm of that egalitarian and populist will. . . . [85]

Terray's remarks suggest to me that French Maoism was perhaps less *about* China than it was about the formation of a set of political desires filtered through a largely imagined China, a filtering that allowed a synthesis of a profoundly French utopian tradition for a new generation. By shifting attention from the forces of production to the relations of production, Mao sought to avoid the bureaucratic hierarchy of the Soviets;

---

85. Terray, *Le troisième jour du communisme*, 19–20. Early influential critiques of French Maoism were mounted by the Situationists; see especially Hector Mandarès, ed., *Révo cul dans la Chine pop: Anthologie de la Presse des Gardes rouges (mai 1966–jan. 1968)* (Paris: Union générale d'éditions, 1974), published in a series edited by Situationist René Viénet. See also Simon Leys, *Les habits neufs du Président Mao* (Paris: Champ Libre, 1971). Self-criticism by former Maoists reached its most elaborate form in Claudie et Jacques Broyelle, *Deuxième retour de Chine* (Paris: Seuil, 1977), and *Le bonheur des pierres, carnets rétrospectifs* (Paris: Seuil, 1978); in *Deuxième retour* Claudie Broyelle attributes the error of her earlier pro-Maoist text on Chinese women, *La moitié du ciel* (Paris: Denoel Conthier, 1973), to an overly rapid first visit to China. Neither book offers a coherent study of the Chinese political system of the 1970s, relying instead on citations taken from Raymond Aron, Simon Leys, and René Viénet to argue that the Chinese experiment was but a poor imitation of the Soviet experience.

Terray is not alone in his refusal to self-criticize for his attraction to Maoist concepts; writing in 1992, Jean Chesnaux affirms the continuing relevance of Maoist ideas to the analysis of global politics: "And yet I continue to think that as tragically as it went astray, Maoism posed fundamental questions the pertinence of which are still shown by the no less tragic situation of the third world today: relations between city and countryside, the impossibility of generalizing western and soviet models of development, the quasi-spontaneous generation of a State neo-bourgeoisie in the under-developed countries, the natural way that intellectuals fall back onto their privileges." See his "Réflexions sur un itinéraire engagé," in *Politiques*, no. 2 (spring 1992): 1–10.

he also brought the division of labor squarely to the forefront of social analysis. Unlike Marx, who saw technology as a release from the division of labor, Maoists saw technology working in conjunction with the division of labor to form the basis for inequality. Technical knowledge was a mystification, a technique to stratify or control workers. The figure of the barefoot doctor hearkens back to a Rousseauist strain, with echoes of the early utopian tradition of Fourier or of an antitechnology contemporary like Jacques Ellul.[86] New ways of critiquing the division of labor at home mattered more than any real knowledge of the political situation in China. French Maoists, for example, appeared to be blissfully ignorant of the complex rivalries between Vietnam, supported by the Soviet Union, and China—rivalries and political circumstances that caused Ho Chi Minh's relations with China to deteriorate drastically once the Cultural Revolution began in August 1966. Such complexities did not prevent French Maoists from remaining friends with both the Chinese and the Vietnamese—"two peoples who are like the lips and the teeth" as one Maoist saying put it. The ability to sustain quite contradictory discourses within one's own utopian discourse—an ability shared by many in those days—allowed them to support the Vietnamese wholeheartedly, while at the same time deriving both an analysis and a project from the Chinese experience. The analysis came from Mao's break with the Soviet Union and his introduction of the concept of "people's war"; now, the successes of the Algerian FLN and the Vietnamese FNL could be thought of in the light of a new revolutionary socialism distinct from the discredited—long before Solzhenitsyn—Soviet experiment, a socialism that could renew the workers movement in France and the West, buried for decades under the Stalinism of the PCF and a long series of social-democratic capitulations. The Chinese revolution presented itself as an alternative both to capitalism and to socialist modernization as represented by Soviet socialism. Mao's fundamental notion of "the people" lent primacy to the political by enlarging the political field of "classes," going beyond their strict economic definition and liberating them from mutual isolation. The project lay in the suppression of the contradictions between manual and intellectual labor, between cities and countryside, and, by extension, the undoing of a whole bourgeois politics founded on the division between those who have knowledge and those who don't, those who command and those who obey—all of the politics of delegation and representation that posit

---

86. See A. Belden Fields, *Trotskyism and Maoism: Theory and Practice in France and the United States* (New York: Autonomedia, 1988); and "French Maoism," in *The 60s without Apology*, ed. Sohnya Sayres et al. (Minneapolis: University of Minnesota Press, 1984), 148–77; in the context of narrating the history of the Maoist groups in France, Fields makes suggestive remarks about the specifically French utopian strains within French Maoism.

a clear distinction between active and passive subjects. The project would be conducted on the one hand through an immersion in the real dynamics of political-economic processes and on the other through an experimental anticipation projected "from the future," as Slavoj Zizek might say, onto concrete lived relations with workers in the present. What one militant called "Maoist aspects, that is to say, a certain relation to reality,"[87] could be detected in this description of the activities of one of the founders of the UJC (m-l), Robert Linhart, long before Linhart would take up a job on the assembly line in Citroën. Speaking about an international communist youth camp that many young French radicals attended in Algeria in the summer of 1963, Tiennot Grumbach writes:

> Of all the young intellectuals who went to Algeria, Linhart was the only one who really tried to understand what was happening. He did fieldwork in the cooperatives, ate with the Algerians, lived with them, tried to help them. He had a very special talent in being able to build theories on the basis of *facts*. A clear understanding of reality. You don't talk about what you don't know, and you only know what you've done, experienced, verified.[88]

Maoist experiments of "going to the people" play a big role in later trivializations of May. Maoists and intellectuals who took up jobs on the assembly line in factories in the years before and after May—the process known as *établissement*—were often caricatured later as the most extreme example of a now obsolete way of life ("militancy"). Figures of populist abjection or masochistic self-denial, the stereotype of the *curé rouge* (militant priest) stands at the opposite end of the pole from that other equally stereotyped figure of May, the libertarian hedonist. The two stereotypes rely on each other to exist, like reflections in a fun-house mirror. At issue in both stereotypes are the related discourses of pleasure and individualism. By separating the two spheres completely, that is, by reinforcing an opposition between, on the one hand, the self-abnegating "reality principle" of the Maoist practicing militant discipline among workers on the factory line—a zone presumed totally pleasure-free—and, on the other, a purely hedonist anarcho-libertarian "thrill-seeker" throwing off the fetters of bourgeois constraint, two paths are opened to an equally hostile rendition of May. In the first case, May was about losing one's self to the masses in a quasi-religious abjection, and losing one's individual voice to the cadences of "militant-speak," the *langue de bois;* in the second

87. Victor (Benny Levy) in Manceaux, *Les Maos en France,* 190.
88. Tiennot Grumbach, cited in Fraser, *1968: A Student Generation in Revolt,* 5–57.

case, as the influential interpretation Gilles Lipovetsky, Alain Renaud, and Luc Ferry would propose in the mid-1980s, May becomes the prefiguration of the possessive individualism of the 1980s, a purely ludic instance of self-expression—in the first case, politics, no pleasure and no self; in the second, festival, only pleasure and only self. Frequently, the split is made along "generational" lines: between older and younger "generations" in the "generation of May": the older students whose formations included the Algeria years versus the younger, more "counter-cultural" types that came after.

But as testimonies like that of Martine Storti make clear, individuality can be completed and not submerged by collectivity, and an experience can be both serious and happy at the same time (in fact, it is most likely in the nature of revolutionary collective experiences to be both serious and happy, or to be remembered as such):

> If I can't assume to communicate the meaning of May, I can tell what I did during the weeks of May and June '68, and say as well that they remain for me the archetype of public happiness. . . . Undoubtedly, each person lived May in his own way. My own May was happy and serious.
>
> I didn't even notice All-of-Paris hurrying to the Sorbonne, the latest "in fashion" place to be. I certainly spent all my days at the Sorbonne or Censier, but I was running from one meeting to another, from one General Assembly to another, and I didn't have time to look at the celebrities doing their turn around the block. The occupied Odeon Theater was an action that didn't concern me, to my mind it even seemed to border on an indecency.
>
> Was I aware of what has been called the "Festival of May"? Yes, if it's a festival to demonstrate every day or almost every day, or to believe it at last possible to change the world, to share with others that hope, and from day to day to live in that kind of lightness of being I described earlier. No, if "festival" is to want "Everything, right away" [Tout, tout de suite], to be invited to "unimpeded bliss" [jouir sans entraves], or to "forbid to forbid" [interdire d'interdire]. To be frank, I attached little importance to those slogans; despite their apparent radicalism, I judged them to be hardly revolutionary. I thought that society could digest those challenges but not the challenge posed by a slogan like "power to the workers."[89]

What is erased from the stereotype of "the festival of May" is the experience Storti chooses to render with the phrase "public happiness": any

89. Storti, *Un chagrin politique*, 88–89.

relation to the collective, or to ways in which pleasure—even the pleasure of self-expression—was not seen or experienced then as the view from the 1980s would have it: as an isolated, individualistic phenomenon. "We could believe that we were carried by the people because there was the general strike, and everyone was in the movement. Everyone was living beyond their intellectual, emotional, and sensorial limits: each person existed above and beyond himself."[90] The "above and beyond" evoked in this description is the formation of a "one" who is not a self but the relation of a self to another, a "one" that holds individual and collective identity and alterity together in an unresolved, unresolvable manner. It is the "we" that emerges when one takes seriously Lucien Goldmann's remark that the personal pronoun "I" does not, in fact, have a plural—"we" is not the plural of "I," but something else altogether. In her vivid analysis of rumor and communication during the insurrection, Evelyne Sullerot evokes that very different relationship between self and other people, the interface of individual and collective, by looking to an unexpected place: the particular phenomenology of the use of the transistor radio during the street demonstrations in May. She discusses the effects of what we might call a purely horizontal, instantaneous, and "parallel" communication that developed some time after television had been discredited, after newspapers had been outstripped by the events, at the moment when only radio, fed by short-wave transmitters operating around the city, remained. "The ubiquity of information by means of the transistors," she notes, "seemed in the view of many of the participants to endow every individual with his own autonomy of judgment without cutting him off from the mass." She cites one student's description:

On May 6, I was at Denfert-Rochereau. From there I went to St.-Germain-des-Prés. Lots of people had transistors. It was wonderful. It was instant information, and everyone could work out his own personal strategy. I felt that the individual was not a sheep in the flock. He was thinking. People clustered around to listen to the transistors. Then they went off again, and everyone made up his own mind after he had listened, sometimes after a quick remark to the people who had listened with him: "Well, that's where they're going! Let's go see whether it's getting hot there. We mustn't leave the guys on their own!" Or: "That's where we can duck out," when one did not feel like getting into the brawl. Basically, it was whatever each one worked out in his own mind in terms of his own temperament and convictions. There was of course a collective spirit, but there were no leaders. Each person was indepen-

90. Adek, cited in Daum, *Des révolutionnaires dans un village parisien,* 18–19.

dent. Listening to the transistor, I had the feeling that I was running the game.[91]

The government shut down the short-wave transmitters on May 23, eliminating direct broadcast. At a more general level, Fredric Jameson has aptly, and sadly, recalled the dynamic between individual and collective in these words:

> In the 1960s many people came to realize that in a truly revolutionary collective experience what comes into being is not a faceless or anonymous crowd or "mass" but, rather, a new level of being . . . in which individuality is not effaced but completed by collectivity. It is an experience that has now slowly been forgotten, its traces systematically effaced by the return of desperate individualisms of all kinds.[92]

By the late 1980s, the dominant version of May as libertarian festival of self-expression had distorted something Storti's remarks render very clearly: that the "festival" or pleasure of the climate of those days was not the residue that remains when politics has been subtracted, but is in fact part and parcel of concrete political action itself. Like Storti, Jean-Franklin Narot links that pleasure directly to the temporal acceleration of those days, to unforeseen spiraling developments that catch up with and ultimately surpass the protagonists.[93] May and June, he insists, had a temporality all their own, made up of sudden accelerations and immediate effects: the sensation that mediations and delays had all disappeared. Not only did time move faster than the frozen time of bureaucracies; it also surpassed the slow, careful temporality that governs strategy or calculation. When the effects of one's actions infinitely supercede one's expectations, or when a local initiative is met with impromptu echoes from a hundred different places all at once, space compresses and time goes faster. Like Storti, Narot evokes a climate of "exaltation and exhaustion": running from one confrontation to the next, wearing oneself out in general assembly after general assembly, being always available and on the alert for whatever might transpire next—a joyous expenditure of self through the transformation of relations with others, through unprogrammed synchronicities, and through the destruction of *things*, rendered suddenly meaningless in the extreme intensity of those social changes. (Indeed, the insignificance, even invisibility of things, of objects, in personal memoirs

91. Sullerot, "Transistors and Barricades," in Labro, *"This Is Only a Beginning,"* 183–84.
92. Fredric Jameson, *Brecht and Method* (London: Verso, 1998), 10.
93. See Jean-Franklin Narot, "Mai 68 raconté aux enfants. Contribution à la critique de l'inintelligence organisée," *Le Débat*, no. 51 (Sept.–Nov. 1988): 179–92.

of those days, is true at a general level). And like Storti, Narot insists
that the joy of self-expenditure and immediacy he recalls experiencing, far
from supplanting the logic of conflict, instead "followed it like a shadow."
Pleasure and conflict were linked. Interpretations from the 1980s of May
as "failed revolution," festival "without finality," or "lacking a project,"
in other words, have an interest, he suggests, in displacing pleasure away
from the place where it actually transpired: in the workings of a different social order that the May movement, temporarily, accomplished, in
the invention of new forms of direct democracy. May's logic of rupture
or conflict worked a kind of *fait accompli:* all the usual mediations and
institutions, be they student unions or the National Assembly, were no
longer forms to be merely critiqued, exposed, or denounced; they would
be treated henceforth *as though they already no longer existed.* All the work
that could then be carried on in spite of those institutions, or outside them,
or in their place, all the work of inventing forms that eliminated representation, that undid the divisions separating directors and subordinates,
that allowed very diverse people to begin to work together to take charge
of their conditions of activity and existence, all the work of producing a
different social organization altogether—this work *was* pleasure.

Stereotyped representations of an abject militant lifestyle erase or ignore an affect that emerges quite vividly as a dominant memory in many
later accounts by activists: namely, the pleasure that was sometimes found
in simply overcoming social boundaries in a deeply compartmentalized
society like France, a society where any kind of communication—let alone
subversive communication—does not pass easily from one sector to another. One of the specific ways in which *things changed* during the insurrection weeks was the frequent occurrence of what Narot calls the *rencontre:* meetings that were neither magical nor mythical but simply the
experience of incessantly running into people that social, cultural, or professional divisions had previously kept one from meeting up with, little
events that produced the sense that those mediations or social compart-
ments had simply withered away. Storti's account does not fail to evoke the
drudgery of militant life, a drudgery that is crystallized for her in the now
obsolete technology of the mimeograph [*ronéotype*], the palpable experience of which overwhelms her years later in all its sensory and emotional
richness (she too is writing from the late 1980s) one day when she finds
the Proustian madeleine of an unused stencil:

And there, folded up in the middle of all those tracts, a relic, that
virgin stencil that must have been thirty years old. It had conserved
its odor, that odor of ink, of carbon paper, a particular odor, at once
acidic and sweet, peppery and sugary, the odor of hours, days, nights

passed mimeographing tracts, with that threat of catastrophe, that fear of seeing the moment arrive when the stencil rips in two, because you have put on too much ink or because the mimeo was turning too fast. After having tried, most often in vain, to glue the torn pieces back together and spin the mimeograph slowly by hand, you had to resign yourself to retyping the text on a new stencil, using two fingers on the old machine.[94]

But a multiform pleasure, one of physical and social transgression, of new friendships or complicities to be gained, emerges in her account and in those of other militants. This is pleasure, as Storti makes clear, not as part of a revolutionary demand or slogan [*jouir sans entraves*]—she is suspicious of just such slogans in May—pleasure not pursued as an end in itself nor even necessarily conceptualized at the time *as* pleasure. The pleasure of overcoming social compartmentalization—both physical and social—exists in proportion to the severity of urban social segregation at the time; dialogues conducted across that segregation transmit a sense of urgent, immediate transformation being lived not as a future reward but at that very moment. Robert Linhart, writing in 1978, recalls: "Fifteen years ago, factories were a closed world, and one had to lie in wait for testimonies;"[95] another militant who worked on a factory assembly line writes that before she and other intellectuals went into the factory "workers labored on the outskirts of Paris, and the factories seemed as far away, as unapproachable, as Algeria or Vietnam."[96] Even Jean-Pierre Thorn, director of the documentary *Oser lutter, oser vaincre* (Dare to Struggle, Dare to Win) on the violent strike at Flins, recalls a childhood and adolescence of pure social segregation. "Until 1968, I was not aware of factories or the working class. At that moment, I began to notice an impressive world that existed around us, with the power to bring the country to a standstill by ceasing to work. Red flags were hanging from the factory gates. I was twenty, it was a shock."[97] Claire, a high school teacher in central Paris in 1968, writing ten years later, expresses the emotion she felt at seeing rules and social barriers, which once seemed insurmountable, overcome:

I met workers for the first time. I had never seen any before. I'm not joking, not even on the metro . . . I had never seen a factory . . . and then, all of a sudden, I was living and working only with workers: the old Party types as well as younger, immigrant guys. The memories, the only

94. Storti, *Un chagrin politique,* 52.
95. R. Linhart, "Evolution du procès de travail," 117.
96. Jenny Chomienne, cited in V. Linhart, *Volontaires pour l'usine,* 102.
97. Jean-Pierre Thorn, cited in V. Linhart, *Volontaires pour l'usine,* 191.

real memories of May '68 that I have aren't of the demonstrations, but rather, of the twice-weekly meetings in workers' homes. The factories were on strike, occupied, and we got together "to do theory." And we did theory, the way we did it in '68. . . . I felt good. And I thought that it was all going to continue. I couldn't imagine, I have to admit, that once again today I would no longer see any workers at all. . . . We were welcomed without any problem into the factory picket line, they brought us into the work-shops with no problem at all. . . . [98]

Another militant recalls similar encounters:

By becoming a militant . . . I entered into contact with a bunch of other people, different from me socially . . . the human warmth that existed between us. When you're a militant, there is something that makes everything worthwhile, it's to find yourself out and about some morning at 4:00 A.M., when it's beautiful out, with a common project that escapes other people, with this happiness of being somewhere where you shouldn't be, this type of complicity. . . . [99]

And a very real "secondary gain" accompanies these transgressive displacements across social boundaries, these voyages to the "other side": the pleasure of leaving behind whatever it is one leaves behind—the whole tissue of congealed expectations and habits that anchor one to one's established place or role. This is another pleasure now frequently forgotten, as Jacques and Danielle Rancière point out, in the post-'68 *miserabiliste* characterizations of militants "going among the workers":

The intellectual must strip his person of everything, in his way of talking or in his way of being, that could recall his origins—everything that in his habits separated him from the people. This was a contradictory ideal that, looked at too simply in retrospect, gets assimilated into a kind of boyscoutism or asceticism. People in those days had no trouble calculating relative pleasure and pain. Leaving old party operators and young careerists behind to jointly take care of managing the universities and painting Marxism up in its latest epistemological and semiological colors, in order to enter into the reality of a factory or the friendly ambiance of immigrant cafes or boarding houses was in no way so dismal (we would feel it at the moment of returning). Serving the people was in one sense just another name for the disgust felt for the pursuit, on either side of the professorial desk, of university exer-

98. Claire, a schoolteacher, cited in *Libération*, May 19, 1978.
99. Anonymous militant, cited in Giorgini, *Que sont mes amis devenus?* 50.

cises. The transformation of the intellectual could thus be lived as a real liberation.[100]

If the pleasure was experienced primarily *après coup*, or after the fact, if it was felt indirectly, laterally, and mostly at the painful moment of the *reprise*, the moment of reintegrating back into one's own habits or milieu, it was no less strong. Among the accounts by *établis*, intellectuals and militants who sometimes spent years working in factories, one finds very little of another aspect of the *misérabiliste* cliché, the one that features militants "going native" or suffering from a kind of *vouloir être ouvrier*, or wanting to actually become a worker. Nor does one find traces of a more Utopian narrative of Deleuzian "becoming"—becoming-animal, becoming-machine, becoming-worker—the desire for metamorphosis. Rather, as one *établi* insists: "The only thing that interested me was to find workers to assure the political relay. Above all I did not want to put myself in their place."[101] "For us *l'établissement* was never a purification measure; it was a political measure."[102] "I felt good in the factory; I hadn't gone there to forget my condition as an intellectual but in order to have people from different origins meet each other. I wanted to work in the interior and above all not burn my bridges as soon as I arrived."[103] And at times, as when May itself erupted, there was the discovery that the distance separating worker from student was not that great at all:

> May '68 happened. The student world was already far away after those few months spent in the factory. After the demonstration on May 13, Renault went on strike; the 15th or the 16th, the occupation of our factory was decided. . . . A real little war on the inside, that lasted six weeks. . . . I was all the more at ease in that atmosphere since in those days workers "were becoming intellectual," and we were meeting up with each other half-way along our respective roads. Young workers from the factory were going out to the barricades and the Sorbonne.[104]

Perhaps, as Daniel Bensaïd has suggested, all of the symbolic accoutrements of early May—the pseudo-insurrectional demonstrations, the forests of black flags, the barricades, the campus occupations—all these transpositions inspired by workers' traditions, should be understood as

100. Danielle and Jacques Rancière, "La légende des philosophes (les intellectuels et la traversée du gauchisme)," *Révoltes Logiques*, special issue, *Les Lauriers de Mai ou les Chemins du Pouvoir, 1968–1978* (1978), 14.
101. Nicole Linhart, cited in V. Linhart, *Volontaires pour l'usine*, 119.
102. Georges, a worker-engineer, cited in Manceaux, *Les Maos en France*, 63.
103. Yves Cohen, cited in V. Linhart, *Volontaires pour l'usine*, 181.
104. Danièle Léon, cited in V. Linhart, *Volontaires pour l'usine*, 123.

a semantic ensemble, a language by which the student movement sought to address itself to workers over the heads of bureaucratic leaders, to create communication between two worlds that had hitherto been closed off from one another, to reach the working class through a long process of concentric circles. Even a slogan like "CRS = SS," chanted by students as early as May 3, when only gendarmes had been called into the Sorbonne and no CRS were as yet in sight, could be read as an act of conjuration. Students in a sense were "borrowing trouble" since the CRS were not yet there—accelerating the situation or bringing it to a head. But they were also interpellating the workers who were also not yet present, and doing so using the workers' own language. For the slogan was not in fact original to the students. It was first used by miners during a strike in 1947–1948 after the initial creation of the CRS by a socialist minister of the interior, who then used the new forces to put down the strike.[105]

Once the general strike began in mid-May, the *Comité d'Action Travailleur/Etudiant* in the neighborhood of Censier gave itself the specific task of shoring up links between the university and the factories. Censier was somewhat off the beaten track of journalists drawn to the great amphitheaters of verbal delirium: the Sorbonne and the Odeon Theater. Documents from the Censier group's steady workings throughout May and June confirm the existence of a cooperation between young workers and students during the strike. But at Censier the displacement worked the other way: students didn't go to the workers, workers came to students. Enormous material possibilities attracted numbers of workers *to* Censier, to the central locations open at any hour, the mimeograph machines, the constantly available work force for liaisons, print runs, discussions. This was a space distinct from the trade-union life within factories where workers might run up against inexplicable interdictions, reticence, controls, surveillance, and maneuvers of all sorts. Collating reports, assigning messengers, providing food and material aid to strikers, Censier became a center of coordination and liaison whose efficacy was sometimes real. Its existence prevents any ironic dismissal of the "workerist" mythology often attributed to May, just as it undermines the view that the strike developed autonomously or purely accidentally at the same time as the students' movement.

Censier's rhetoric marks an evolution in the May movement. In early May, when de Gaulle spoke of the demonstrators as creating a *chienlit* (disorder), a celebrated Beaux-Arts poster responded immediately to the

105. See Michele Zancarini-Fournel, " 'L'Autonomie comme absolu': Une caricature de Mai et des années 68," *Mouvements*, no. 1 (Nov.–Dec. 1968), 138–41. See also Daniel Bensaid and Henri Weber, *Mai 1968: Une répétition générale* (Paris: Maspero, 1968), 142–43.

insult with an image of de Gaulle and the words, "Le chienlit, c'est lui!"—
by throwing back the epithet, in other words, in his face. On May 25,
Minister of the Interior Fouchet escalated the Gaullist rhetoric further,
referring to "the daily more numerous *pègre* [riff-raff, scum, the under-
world], that *pégre* that crawls up out of the lower depths of Paris and that
is truly enraged, that hides behind the students and fights with murderous
madness. . . . I ask that Paris "vomit up" the *pègre* that dishonors it."[106]
The Communist Party paper, *L'Humanité*, quickly adopted an identical
vocabulary: "All night long in various districts in Paris one finds dubious
riff-raff, that organized *pègre* whose presence contaminates those who accept them and, even more, those who solicit them."[107] The vocabulary and
imagery of the Paris Commune, complete with the fetishes of naturalist
representation, comes back to life: the workers, the lower classes are the
savage beasts, the dirty vermin, hiding behind the respectable students,
contaminating them like sordid parasites, responsible for epidemics and
contagion. Censier chose to respond immediately with a tract embracing
the epithet and refusing the social zoology that lay behind it: "If those
in power consider those who were on the barricades with the students
to be *'la pègre,'* then we workers, employees, factory workers, and unemployed, we are *'la pègre.'* "[108] Around the same time, another Action
Committee, one that included Marguerite Duras, Maurice Blanchot, and
Dionys Mascolo, wrote a similar tract: "We who have participated in the
actions attributed to a so-called *pègre*, we affirm that we are all rioters, we
are all *'la pègre.'* "[109] The strategy adopted by both committees is that of
widening the disjuncture between the social being and the constitution
of the political group. As with the slogan "We are all German Jews," by
de-naturalizing *"la pègre,"* by loosening the ties that bind the word to
its sociological connotations, the word—be it German Jews or *pègre*—
becomes available as a new political identity or subjectivity. By embracing
the improper name, the name now stands in for a group that is not sociologically identifiable; the tracts undo the legitimation—be it that of the
ministry or the Communist Party—that distributes place and function.
They propose a non-naturalist definition of politics and conflict. The
pègre becomes the discursive construction of the relation of a self to an
other—what Rancière would call another "impossible identification": political subjects acting in the gap or interval between two identities, neither
of which can be assumed.

106. Christian Fouchet, cited in *Le Monde*, May 25, 1968.
107. Cited in *L'Humanité-Dimanche*, May 26, 1968.
108. The Comité d'Action Travailleurs-Etudiants/Censier, "L'Escalade: Après la CHIEN-
LIT, la PEGRE . . . ," tract, undated but after May 26, 1968.
109. Comité d'Action Ecrivains/Etudiants/Travailleurs, tract, May 26, 1968.

Militant experiments like those conducted at Censier or like the Maoist practice of *établissement,* in their will to leap over or circumvent systems of representation that produced or defined images of the worker for the middle class, show an acute awareness of the domain of representation as one of the determining factors of inequality. Another such practice was the *enquête* (inquiry or investigation), initiated by Maoists in 1967 and conducted with workers and farmers door to door, in market places, in front of metro entrances, and in villages in *la France profonde.* The *enquête* originated in the refusal of one such representation, the mythic or transcendental one that made of "the Working Class" an undifferentiated united block. (François Maspero, too, marked his resistance of any Promethean or transcendental representation of "the third world" by refusing to capitalize the phrase "tiers monde" in any of his publications.) What one did not know about the direct experience of workers—or small tenant farmers, for that matter—one could find out by "going to the people," learning from them—from practical action and close attention to local circumstances, that is, and not from theoretical texts. The Maoist model of Marxism placed greater emphasis on local conditions and historical circumstances—the situation—than on canonical texts. Mao's writings on the necessary link between theory and practice, the need, as he put it, to "get off the horse in order to gather flowers," provided one impetus out of the Latin Quarter, where his writings were read not so much as theoretical doctrine but more frequently as an invitation to leave the books and the city behind:

> We should proceed from the actual conditions inside and outside the country, the province, county or district, and derive from them, as our guide to action, laws which are inherent to them and not imaginary, that is, we should find the internal relations of the events occurring around us. And in order to do that we must rely not on subjective imagination, not on momentary enthusiasm, not on lifeless books, but on facts that exist objectively; we must appropriate the material in detail, and, guided by the general principles of Marxism-Leninism, draw correct conclusions from it.[110]

Another impetus out of the Latin Quarter came perhaps from the pleasure to be had, as one Maoist tract vividly suggests, in simply "leaving behind the vain quarrels of the *groupuscules,* those endless discussions *supported by*

---

110. Mao Tse-tung, "Reform Our Study," May 1941, in *Selected Works of Mao Tse-tung,* vol. 3 (Peking: Foreign Languages Press, 1965), 22–23.

no concrete experience."[111] In their concern with reaching the heterogeneity of the proletarian world, Maoist *enquêtes* appear now like the distorted mirror opposite of that other door-to-door investigation of the working class, the market research survey (*enquête de consommation*), which was being conducted during the same years and immortalized in Georges Perec's 1965 novel *Les choses.* Where the market survey interpellated the worker as consumer, a social category already in the late 1960s quantifiable in subgroups according to spending habits and tastes, the Maoist investigation sought instead "the point of view of the masses" defined by its double opposition to "the point of view of capital" and to that of the PCF-CGT, revisionist in nature. Market research surveys can be seen as the heirs to a whole history of government policy-oriented or sociological studies of workers and their habits, dating back at least to the middle of the nineteenth century. *Enquêtes* undertaken with a view toward regulating insalubrious homes considered "dangerous" to public health, for example, or with studying epidemics acquired a kind of scientific rigor toward the end of the century. But the information garnered in these nineteenth-century investigations of the poor served from the outset the concerns of social regulation, enabling investigators to classify workers or the poor into distinct aggregates and defined social categories. Hygienic observation, as Andrew Aisenberg has shown, served the interests of police regulation.[112] The Maoist *enquête,* on the other hand, laid claim to a Chinese derivation that freed it, at least in theory, from that history; under the same word, they sought a different, subversive practice. Immersing oneself "in the school of the masses," the intellectual's role would not be that of sociologist, hygienist, teacher, or Leninist vanguard leader, but at best that of midwife: drawing out revolutionary aspirations existing in a latent state, encouraging their expression, then synthesizing them and returning them in the form of political propositions. "Sans enquêtes, pas de droit à la parole" [No investigation, no right to speak].[113] Gather the news of the struggle, write it up, give it back in a new form, circulate it, reproduce it, become the vehicle. Theoretical *a prioris* must be set aside, in the pa-

111. "Pour un travail correct parmi les étudiants," mimeographed UJC (m-l) directive, cited in Patrick Kessel, *Le mouvement "Maoiste" en France: Textes et documents, 1968–1969,* vol. 2 (Paris: Union générale d'édition, 1978), 31 (italics in the original).

112. Among the earliest of these sociological *enquêtes* is Eugène Buret's *De la misère des classes laborieuses en Angleterre et en France,* published in 1840, and Honoré Frégier's *Des classes dangereuses dans la population des grandes villes et des moyens de les rendre meilleures,* published in 1850. For the best discussion of this literature and its development in the later part of the century, see Andrew Aisenberg, *Contagion: Disease, Government, and the "Social Question" in Nineteenth-Century France* (Stanford: Stanford University Press, 1999), especially 156–64.

113. Mao Tse-tung, in "Preface and Postscript to *Rural Surveys,*" March and April 1941, in *Selected Works,* III, 13.

tient expectation that a political line will disengage itself directly from workers' representations of their own conditions, problems, aspirations, desires, from their own disparate voices. "Nothing, in effect, can be understood 'spontaneously': to understand, one must investigate [*enquêter*]."[114] Workers who came into contact with Maoists in the factories differed in their assessment of the success of the practice. One worker gives a positive assessment of his meeting with the Maoists in the factory:

> Trotskyists came too. But they were different from the Maoists because the Trotskyists brought a tract: "Workers are exploited because . . . ," with citations to Marx, page numbers, *Capital* etc.—it was all incredibly theoretical, we didn't understand a word! Maoists, on the other hand, took their point of departure from what we told them. They didn't know anything before we talked to them. They didn't arrive with ready-made ideas or tracts. They listened to what we said and then made a tract out of that. We were really struck by that.[115]

Another worker, however, disagreed: "In the factories, there isn't really at this point so much of a difference between Trotskyists and Maoists. In fact, for the guys, all that, that's *gauchiste*."[116] A former *établi* recalls a communicational impasse—but one that did not prevent friendship from developing: "I had started up at Citroën. I kept talking and talking. One of the workers with whom I've remained friends admitted to me two years later that when I was talking back then, he had not understood a word of what I was saying. It must be said that we used a Maoist language, taken straight out of the Little Red Book."[117]

Cahiers de Mai, a journal directed by Daniel Anselme, Jean-Louis Peninou, and Marc Kravetz, which published thirty issues between 1968 and 1973, emerged out of the practice of the *comités d'action* and the *enquête* and sought, particularly after Mai '68, to provide a kind of clearinghouse for new ideas expressed in recent and ongoing struggles in the factories and the countryside. An article published in that journal in 1970, "Le role politique de l'enquête," offers the best analysis of the practice as a potential demonstration or verification of equality, the constitution of a common space. From the outset, the militant *enquête* is defined in opposition to existing forms of "the sociology of workers." The sociologist's gathering of information and compiling of documents constitutes workers as the object of study and places the sociologist on the exterior of the studied

114. *Garde rouge*, no. 5 (April 1967).
115. Georges, a Citroën worker, cited in Manceaux, *Les Maos en France*, 77.
116. Patrick, a Renault worker, cited in Manceaux, *Les Maos en France*, 93.
117. Gerard, cited in Giorgini, *Que sont mes amis devenus?* 50.

situation, a hierarchical distribution of places and functions conforming to what we called earlier, the logic of the police. The *enquête,* on the other hand, places the project under the direction and control of workers, who discuss and elaborate an initial text sentence by sentence. The *enquête* thus serves the political role of *regrouping* workers around a project, the production of the text acting as a unifying force that initiate or sustains the process of self-formation of the group, reinforcing the group's consciousness of its own existence as a group. In its production, then, the *enquête* resembles any number of experiments in collective authorship "from below" that proliferated in those years, from the SLON *cinétracts,* or the Groupe Medvedkine workers film collectives in Besançon, to the production of many anonymous militant pamphlets—experiments that relegated not only the sociologist, but the lone muscular theorist and the film director as *auteur* as well, definitively into the solitary confinement of bourgeois cultural and knowledge production. Once the text of the *enquête* exists, it can be an instrument of propaganda and agitation and, most crucially, it can be an instrument of liaison *between* factories so frequently disparaged if not actively blocked by the "vertical communication" of union leaders. One of the "revelations" of the *enquêtes* in the sense of a need or demand frequently expressed by workers *was* precisely that liaison: communication between workshops in a given factory, between factories in the region, in the same industry. Additionally, the *enquête* diminishes segregation between militants outside the factory and those within. In the words of another militant journalist:

> The *enquêteur* cannot, of course be neutral. There is no neutral instrument. . . . Listen all the way to the end: only then does the *enquête* take on all its meaning. Because all the way to the end means that one is not content with first responses. . . . Then you see better with whom and why you are fighting, you discover the scars and the tumors, you no longer speak about "revolution" with stereotypes, ready-made ideas, triumphalist affirmations, but with all the explosive force that words represent when the imaginary and the real as lived from day to day become the basis for words. . . . [118]

The militant *enquête* sought to differentiate itself as a practice from the discursive representation of workers by any number of people claiming the task—sociologists, trade-union delegates, political theorists, even well-intentioned militant journalists—about whose activities workers frequently used the verb *"parachuter."* (Farmers in the Larzac preferred

118. Philippe Gavi, *Tout,* no. 2 (Oct. 8, 1970).

the term "comet" to refer to those sudden apparitions of brief duration and no follow-up on the part of well-meaning outsiders).[119] Thus, a Citroën worker complains about the PCF delegate who arrives in the factory, "parachute son discours et s'en va" ("parachutes" his speech and leaves).[120] Other workers dispute the representation of their strike in "texts thrown together in haste by militant journalists who come down from Paris," commenting that "when militants are parachuted into a strike, it is doubtful that their work will be a success."[121] Such texts show an absence of "the real movement as it has developed, the manner in which it developed, the problems it posed . . . no concrete reflection on the struggle [which is] relegated to the rear, behind abstract, general analyses." The verb *parachuter*'s military connotations of heroic adventurism—the vertical assault or rescue "from above," the sudden, brief strike—conjure up old associations of the *parachutistes* of colonial wars, many of whom found jobs as security officers in factories. But it also points ahead in time to the humanitarian "parachutistes" of the 1980s, the "Doctors without Borders" (many of whom ex-Maoists), leaping into emergency situations, practicing what some have disparagingly called an "ambulance politics," unaware of the situation in which they have landed. The *enquête* must be the result of "prolonged immersion," not just "dropping in," of the horizontal equality of a shared project rather than vertical communication from on high. It must resist any artificial or arbitrary unities as idealist, just as it must resist the distinction between "the essential" and "the accessory" characteristic of all empiricisms: each person has a say, no one is neglected or taken to be insignificant. It must practice a ratification of and scrupulous respect for diversity.

THE ILLUSIONS OF REPRESENTATION

What becomes of the militant after militancy has waned and the militant must become once again a journalist, a filmmaker, a theorist, or a labor organizer? Must his or her relation to "the people" or "the worker" inevitably become that of the *parachutiste*?

During what Pierre Macherey has called "the particularly agitated and difficult time" of the years immediately following May, the critique of the division of labor and related problems of equality that had been so central

---

119. See Catherine Fabienne and Raphael Fabienne, "Larzac: Lutte contre l'armée et luttes de classes," *Les Cahiers du Forum-Histoire*, no. 5 (Jan. 1977): 14.

120. Worker cited in film *Citroen-Nanterre, Mai-Juin 1968*, Collectif Arc (1968).

121. "Le rôle politique de l'enquête," *Cahiers de Mai*, no. 22 (July 1970): 12.

to the May movement tended, for the most part to get lost, crushed by problems related to the question of "taking power" (both institutional and armed)—but not entirely. In the debates around the division of knowledge in the schools and universities, traces of May's thematics continued to be played out. Referring to his own situation in the university in the 1970s, Macherey recalls a climate of fatiguing and often bitter political discussions, of endless meetings in which young instructors strove to retain or attain some measure of agency amid the massive Giscardian modernization of the university system:

> retrospectively, it is very difficult to remember and, *a fortiori*, to try to make those who did not personally live it understand to what point, on a purely emotional level, those years were confusing and overwhelming. How, despite the powerful return of the reaction in its most direct forms, everything or almost everything still seemed possible, even if the open future of our imagination was in fact engulfed by a mass of uncertainties. For, without knowing which direction to take, we still thought we were going somewhere.[122]

But it was above all in those pursuits that engaged directly with the question of representation, the intellectual's representation of the people—namely journalism and historiography—that new experiments continued to be made in the months and years following May '68. For many militants at that time, the experience of May meant not losing sight of the problem of a direct communication with the exploited and their history, and the continuing effort to construct new means of comprehension (and thus of struggles) between different groups. As militant collectives disbanded, regrouped, and took on new configurations trying to find fresh spaces and direction for struggle, some militants were drawn to the actuality of continuing struggles—and actuality meant revolutionary journalism. Militant journalists schooled in the factory *enquête* like Jean-Louis Peninou, Jean-Marcel Bouguereau, and Françoise Fillinger gravitated from the *Cahiers de Mai* to the new radical daily *Libération*, born shakily in May 1973 and slowly getting going under the auspices of Sartre; they were joined by other militants who had written for *Action*, the daily that ran through May and June and sold for a "minimum price"—as in the case of many militant publications, one could pay more if one could—of 50 centimes, or for the Maoist paper *La Cause du Peuple* whose last issue ran in September 1973.[123] *Libération*, whose initial, Maoist-inflected

---

122. Pierre Macherey, *Histoires de dinosaure: Faire de la philosophie, 1965–1997* (Paris: Presses universitaires de France, 1999), 74.

123. *Action*, which had a detachable front page that could be hung as a street poster, was notable for its slogans and cartoons, frequently by Siné: "Debout les damnés de Nanterre!,"

manifesto proclaimed its utopian purpose to be that of "helping the people seize the word," saw itself, at least initially in the wishes of some of its founders, to be a kind of collective "public writer": "Information comes from the people and returns to the people." To promote the paper, Sartre agreed to go on the radio for the first time since the denigration campaign launched by the government against the Manifesto of the 121 during the Algerian War. In the broadcast, he described the paper's aspiration to direct democracy: "We want the *actors* of an event to be those whom we consult, we want them to be the ones to speak."[124] Michel Foucault, who was involved in the early *Libération* discussions about new journalistic forms to be invented that would elicit the voice of the people, wanted to experiment personally with "a chronicle of workers' memory."[125] Direct democracy would pertain as well to the daily workings of the paper: editorial decisions were to be debated and shared as a collective; everyone working at the paper was to be paid the same salary—1500 francs a month in 1974, barely more than the minimum wage—and everyone was to share equally in the tasks of writing and physical production. In the months and years that followed, *Libération* would become a kind of way station or halfway house for literally hundreds of militants who worked for varying lengths of time at its office in a working-class neighborhood in the nineteenth *arrondissement*. It was, as one of these described it, "a way of not returning back into the ranks . . . of being in a place where you could, every day, help advance a certain number of ideas, give testimony about struggles, defend causes."[126] While some, like director Serge July, have stayed with the paper until this day, many others departed in disagreement with the compromises and turns taken by the management over the years; still others, like Sartre, simply lost interest in the paper as it became more established and conventional.

But regardless of what the paper later became, for readers of its early issues, particularly those in the provinces who felt isolated or stranded in the quite terrifying political climate of post-May and who often experienced great difficulty getting their hands on an issue, *Libé* provided a continuity, a connection to the recent events; it was a tangible sign that something had indeed happened in May '68.

"Les chiens de garde aboient toujours de la même façon"; "La rue vaincra!" During May and June, when other journals and newspapers were paralyzed by the strike, *Action* was read for daily information, along with the twelve issues of *L'Enragé*, the "official bulletin" of the events. (The second issue of *L'Enragé* featured a cover by Siné that simply read "Crève général"). During the second half of 1968, *Action* was one of the outlawed publications particularly pursued by the government, in part because of its rapid growth from 100,000 printings of each issue to 550,000.

124. Jean Paul Sartre, radio show, "Radioscopie," Feb. 7, 1973.
125. See Didier Eribon, *Michel Foucault* (Paris:Flammarion, 1989), 267–68.
126. Storti, *Un chagrin politique*, 132.

The story of *Libération* is well known; its rise from humble Maoist origins to become what one of its own journalists called "the Pravda of the new bourgeoisie"[127] follows the familiar path of the mainstreaming of a counter-cultural institution.[128] *Libération* would play a central role in producing and circulating the tropes and images through which May came progressively to be transcoded. But for many other militants coming out of the experience of May and its aftermath, the problem of the relation between the intellectual and "the people," the question of popular memory and the voice of the people, could be best engaged at a theoretical and practical level elsewhere, within the field of history and historiography. By returning to the past and to a new examination of workers' speech, experience, and practices, the Utopian aspects of May could be prolonged, and the disappointments of May and its aftermath could be examined and assessed. A new renegade historical practice could continue the desire of '68 to give voice to the "voiceless," to contest the domain of the experts. While the theories that would come to dominate the 1970s—structuralism and post-structuralism—carried out what Fredric Jameson has called their "relentless search-and-destroy mission against the diachronic," another kind of work, deriving directly from the experience of '68, was being carried on within and on the outskirts of the discipline of "official history." It is here that we should look, rather than to the sociologists, or to the philosophers of Desire like Lyotard or Deleuze frequently summoned up to embody the legacy of May within intellectual production, to find some of the most interesting and radical political experiments around the question of equality.

The conjuncture was rich in the works of individual historians such as Michelle Perrot, who was completing her long study of *Les ouvriers en grève* as the events of May erupted; years later, she would write:

> My decision to do workers' history is rooted in that conjuncture . . . to take the working class as the object of my research seemed like a way to join with it, or to serve it, by contributing to its knowledge and its recognition . . . to write that history for a University that ignored it, that even, obscurely, held it in contempt. . . .
>
> [It seemed] an enterprise worth the effort and a form of solidarity.[129]

Alain Faure submitted his *mémoire de maîtrise* at Nanterre's Faculty of Letters in 1970; published later as *La Parole ouvrière*, its subject was work-

127. The phrase is Guy Hocquengheim's. *Lettre ouverte*, 15.

128. See especially François-Marie Samuelson, *Il était une fois "Libération"* (Paris: Seuil, 1979); and Jean-Claude Perrier, *Le roman vrai de Libération* (Paris: Julliard, 1994).

129. See Michelle Perrot, "L'Air du temps," in *Essais d'ego-histoire*, ed. Pierre Nora (Paris: Gallimard, 1987), 286. See also her *Les ouvriers en grève*, 2 vols. (Paris: Mouton, 1974).

ing class and popular movement during the early 1830s. In a series started by Maspero called "Actes et mémoires du peuple," Alain Cottereau published a new edition of an 1870 text by Denis Poulot, *Le sublime ou le travailleur comme il est en 1870 et ce qu'il peut être*, with a *gauchiste*-inflected preface that, according to Cottereau, "could be read not just by the usual public, but also by militant workers";[130] the preface analyzed Poulot's text in terms of workers' resistance and counter-strategies against exploitation. But three journals that sprang up after May, simply by virtue of their being collective efforts, rooted in the practice, alien to the academy, of joint research, authorship, and decision making, are perhaps more intimately tied to the political events of '68 than even the works of individual scholars. For each of these journals—*Le Peuple Français, Les Cahiers du Forum-Histoire*, and *Les Révoltes Logiques*—"revolt" or contestation was put forward as the central premise from which historians should begin their investigations. Each in quite distinct ways attempted to break with a certain tradition of academic elitism, individual research, and political institutional history to create a different history generated out of a left politics. And though the three journals occasionally ran advertisements for one of the others in their pages, and interacted with each other from time to time in interviews and debates,[131] the very real differences that separated these three interventions into the writing of history are more revealing than any similarities they might share. The differences arose around three broad themes: the figure of the worker or "the people," the role of the historian, and the relation between past and present.

Le Peuple Français, a review of popular history, was started in 1971 by some former members of the Nanterre *comité d'action*, a group dominated mostly by people on the lower end of the academic hierarchy: *maîtres-auxiliaires* (substitute teachers) and *lycée* instructors. Its populism ("We write for the people"), anchored in a readable, highly accessible style ("which means first of all that we force ourselves to write simply"), [132] was overt; its readership—between 5000 and 7000 subscribers—reached a high level in part because its staff's dedication to efficiency and to working hard, without secretary or professional staff, kept the price of each issue low (4 francs). The journal counted a significant number of workers (20 to 25 percent) and agricultural laborers (10 percent) among its readers.

130. Alain Cottereau, cited in "Au sublime ouvrier: Entretien avec Alain Cottereau," *Révoltes Logiques*, no. 12 (summer 1980): 32.

131. See, for example, "Le Peuple Français," a critical analysis of that journal in *Les Cahiers du Forum-Histoire*, no. 7 (Oct. 1977): 41–46.

132. Editorial, *Le Peuple Français*, no. 24 (Oct.–Dec. 1976): 3. The two names on the masthead of the journal are Gilles Ragache and Alain Delale.

But despite its origins, *Le Peuple Français* showed few signs of the ongoing *gauchiste* upheaval beyond its questioning of the idea that "the historian" must be someone professionally certified as such: "We are in our own way 'researchers,' but this is work that anyone can do."[133] If the collective questioned the assumptions of competence made about the historian outside the academy, it left solidly in place all of the assumptions prevailing around the object of its research: "le peuple français." The very title of the journal reflected the collective's faith in a homogenous French "people," the product of an unquestioned, centralizing process of national integration. (The *Peuple Français*, as such, showed no interest in *le peuple breton* or *le peuple flamand*, for example). Rather, this was the People with a capital "P": immutable in its heroism and represented in the journal's articles in a small set of familiar poses: undergoing brutal oppression or, by contrast, the hero of a glorious epic: emerging from mine, factory, or hovel under the banner of a collective flag. At times, the people appeared in a more anthropological guise, engaged in repetitive, folkloric, daily activities. *Le Peuple Français* actively resisted any theoretical rethinking of this notion of the people, a category so ambiguous and yet monolithic that everyone from Pétain, through the PCF and Gaullist deployment of the mythic image forged in the Resistance, all the way up to Giscard, could lay claim to it and use it as a secure and legitimizing support for their political discourse. In this area, for *Le Peuple Français*, May '68 had made little difference; the only difference between their mode of representation and the traditional one could be detected in the slight tinges of Maoist sentimentality, left over from *La Cause du Peuple*, that sometimes hovered on its edges.

Nor did *Le Peuple Français* make any attempt to avoid the natural propensity of historians to "nest" or settle into territories of the past as though they were distinct, autonomous zones with little or no bearing on present concerns. If anything, nesting was encouraged. Thus, while the journal covered an extremely wide range of subjects and historical periods, it stopped short of venturing into the Fourth or Fifth Republics, and only rarely proposed some connection or relation between past events and present concerns. One didn't need to be a specialist to write history, but one very quickly became, reading the pages of *Le Peuple Français*, a specialist of the past, that is, of historical knowledge about the past as a closed circuit or end in itself. A strict division of labor, in other words, subsisted, separating the technical and ultimately highly pedagogical role of the historian—gathering and furnishing information about the past—

133. Ibid., 4.

from that of the militant, engaged in current political reflection and analysis. "There is no good theory without a good knowledge of the facts,"[134]
the collective argued, but the never-ending process of getting at the facts,
it seems, makes the horizon of theory recede indefinitely.

The *Forum-Histoire* collective grew out of the anti-Vietnam war and
anti-imperialist groups (the CVB and CVN) based in the departments
of history and geography at Jussieu; unlike the other two collectives,
then, it was formed within the university milieu of professional historians. Though the journal, whose first issue was published in January 1976,
functioned as a collective—participants organized themselves into work
groups around topics like "Algeria" or "History and the Environment"—
only one name, that of then Sinologist and sometime Maoist, Jean Chesnaux, appears on the masthead as director of publication. The subtitle
adorning the journal's cover, "L'histoire pour quoi faire?" (Why write
history?) announces the collective's intention of performing, as historians,
an ideological critique of their own function, according, as they put it, "to
a Chinese inspiration."[135] Their first editorial announced the line they
would follow: "Forum-Histoire is constituted as a political action group
on the terrain of history . . . to aid in the transformation of the relation
to the past."[136] Less explicitly concerned than the *Peuple Français* group
with the question of who gets to write history, *Forum-Histoire* centered
their investigation on the function of history writing itself: why study
the past?

The answer they came up with was that the study of the past was perfectly meaningless unless it was conducted as a response to the demands
of the present:

> The division of labor (when I need to know the past, I ask a qualified
> historian) that seems evident to a good number of intellectuals, appears
> dangerous to us in most cases: it creates and maintains a factual separa-
> tion between those who, by means of their profession, can have access to
> knowledge and those who truly need this knowledge today at the level
> of their daily lives. This separation is instituted because what motivates
> intellectual knowledge is totally foreign to people's real life: historians
> write books because they have completed a thesis, because they are re-
> searchers, because they need money, or because they enjoy it: at best,
> historians on the left write the history of the workers' movement, but

134. *Le Peuple Français* collective, cited in "Une société sans mémoire?" *Vendredi,* Nov. 23–
Dec. 6, 1979, 11.

135. Jean Chesnaux, cited in"Une société sans mémoire?" 11.

136. Editorial, *Les Cahiers du Forum-Histoire,* no. 1 (Jan. 1976): 2.

the course they take derives from themselves more than from the current needs of workers' struggle.[137]

In an interview, Chesnaux commented, "The way in which historians accept to bracket off their own divergences from contemporary society in the service, say, of their research into the eighteenth century . . . [shows that they] accept as normal a radical separation between past and present."[138]

The *Forum-Histoire* group showed complete disdain for debates *within* historical discourse conceived of as a science—those merely technical polemics about categories like the *longue* or *moyenne durée*, for example. Instead they strove to critique the social practice of those who, like themselves, write history. The question was not *how* to write history, but rather which past for which future? Unless that question was addressed at the outset, history in their view could aspire to being nothing more than a commodity produced by specialists and then made available to different consumers, the latter interpellated according to varying levels of passivity and incompetence.

The *Forum-Histoire* group, then, set out to undo the following three separations that they saw defining traditional historical practice: the past and the present, the study of the past and political practice in the present, and historians and those who are the objects (or subjects) of their history. The past must serve to nourish political action and analysis today—not by forming a mechanical or continuous link with the present but rather by helping clarify precisely what is *not* continuous, what is available only now for the new. Studying the past should help us see the contingency of the present in all its immediacy and not in the light of repetitive schemas or epistemological categories whose certainty can never be demonstrated. "Think the past politically in order to think the present historically"[139]— i.e. to think the present as something that can change. *Forum-Histoire* had little use for the revivalism of the folk practiced by *Le Peuple Français*, nor for their monolithic construction of "the people," nor for their channeling of heroic moments from the past as a means, at best, of "morale-building" in the present.

Like *Révoltes Logiques* and most other radical publications, *Forum-Histoire* (priced at 8 francs an issue) had a hard time staying afloat; eventually, François Maspero took over the journal's publication and distribution. About four thousand copies of each issue were published. But more severe problems arising out of the group's own practice began to make it

137. Editorial, *Les Cahiers du Forum-Histoire*, no. 5 (Jan. 1977): 2.
138. Jean Chesnaux, cited in Christian Descamp, "Jean Chesneaux, historien du présent et de l'avenir," *Le Monde Dimanche*, Sept. 4, 1983, 4.
139. Ibid.

clear that while they had succeeded in putting the three separations into question and in getting out from under the dead weight of certain historiographical traditions, they had, by their own evaluation, failed in providing "another history." Their encounter with the farmers and workers of the Larzac in the mid-1970s, then engaged in what was materializing as one of the most significant popular uprisings of the time, was a case in point.

In 1971 the French government decided to expand a military camp in the relatively poor, isolated, and depopulated agricultural region of the Larzac in the Sud-Aveyron *département* on the grounds that it would both contribute to commercial activity in the region and contribute to the defense of Europe. The farmers of the plateau revolted, and a confrontation began between the army and farmers—including both the extremely poor, traditional farmers who operated subsistence farms and the larger, landholding "modernist" farmers. The confrontation would last for ten years. Soon a third group, "paysans installés" or *établis* of sorts, transplants to the region from other walks of life who took up the activity of farming, began to arrive to support the movement by occupying—often illegally by squatting—the land the army wished to annex for its purposes and by moving into buildings owned by the army. José Bové, one such *paysan installé*, arrived on the plateau in July 1976 and never left. In 1973, the first of several immense gatherings of supporters of the movement convened; as one participant observed, this was probably the first time ever that more than 100,000 people from all over France got up and came to a precise place, for whatever reason. Meanwhile, the movement carried out what the Maoists liked to call a "protracted war," ten years of obstinate and inventive legal battles designed to throw a wrench into the army's projects. At one point, in 1978, a group of farmers made their way by foot from the Larzac to Paris along with sheep which they brought with them into the courtroom. The force of the movement lay in the diversity of people and disparate ideologies it brought together: antimilitary activists and pacifists (conscientious objectors); regional Occitan separatists; supporters of nonviolence; revolutionaries aiming to overthrow the bourgeois state, anticapitalists, anarchists, and other *gauchistes*, as well as ecologists. When Mitterrand was elected in 1981, he felt called upon to make a gesture toward the radical left who had worked so hard to save the Larzac, and kept the promise he himself had made standing on the Larzac plateau in 1974: the army was obliged to abandon the extension project.

Among the various efforts to counteract the military's ruling assumption that the extension was justified because the plateau was a dead, underpopulated region, was the establishment of Larzac-Université, a site where locals, militants, and farmers, and Parisians and other outsiders could come together to organize seminars and other cultural and educational projects. In 1976, a group from *Forum-Histoire* joined with historians from the region and nonhistorians—local workers and farmers—to undertake a seminar on local history, that of the farmers and of workers in nearby Millau. From the outset, differences in expectation divided the participating groups: regional historians, for example, of a traditionalist bent, saw the seminar as an effort to better understand the Sud-Aveyron region; *Forum-Histoire* historians, on the other hand, came with a more theoretical goal of using the ongoing struggle in the Larzac as a means of thinking the past politically and enabling the popular masses to reappropriate that history themselves without being dependent on professional historians. In a frank series of articles published in their journal, *Les Cahiers du Forum-Histoire*, the collective analyzed the uncertainties, deceptions and fantasies that collided before and during the seminar.[140] The Parisians, for example, strangers to the region, tended to stick to themselves; nonhistorians didn't talk much to historians. The group from Millau, very active in preparing the seminar, receded as it got underway. Indeed, the Larzac farmers and the Millau workers, who were supposed to be at the heart of the endeavor, allowed themselves to be interviewed for *enquêtes*, but participated only rarely in the seminar itself, perhaps because of conflicts with their work schedules.

In the end, it seemed, the Parisians had over-idealized both their own theoretical ideas and the Larzac movement itself. They had arrived with a conception of the movement, then five years old, derived from books, films, and articles; in this version, 103 farmers, united into a model of democratic organization, had broken with a reactionary past to undertake a prolonged and radical combat against the authority of the State, in order that they might continue living much as they had been living all along. Their battle with the army was the mythic struggle of life against death. They were open to newcomers, to all those marginal people who, attracted to their struggle, had pulled up stakes and had come to live on the plateau; they welcomed the immense gatherings of thousands and thousands of people who came to lend them support; and they actively allied with other peoples in struggle, notably with the Lip factory workers then engaged in a protracted strike in Besançon, with the Irish, and with other native peoples' self-determination efforts.

What the Parisians were stupefied to find instead, when they actually came to the Larzac, was a group of farmers who were hesitant, deeply worn out and fatigued by their years of battle, tempted by compromise,

---

140. See the articles grouped under the title "Le Stage d'histoire de Larzac-Université," *Les Cahiers du Forum-Histoire*, no. 5 (Jan. 1977): 3–27; and "'Faire de l'histoire' . . . avec les paysans du Larzac. II," *Les Cahiers du Forum-Histoire*, no. 6 (May 1977): 50–54; my discussion of the encounter between historians and farmers in this section relies on the reports in these issues.

dominated by the big farmers of the area—those farmer "notables" of the plateau who had become the self-appointed spokesmen of the movement. They found a group of farmers, that is, gravely divided among themselves. If the Larzac farmers welcomed the counter-cultural types, the marginals who made their way to the plateau, they were less welcoming to those like themselves, other agricultural laborers seeking to move there; if they allied with other struggles, it tended to be with those that weren't next door: workers on strike in nearby Millau complained that they had garnered little enthusiastic support from their farmer neighbors.

As for the intellectuals, farmers tended to look upon them as suppliers of the only kind of political participation their "métier" allowed them: that of unconditional support for what they—the farmers—alone decided. This was precisely the kind of support farmers themselves seemed reluctant to give to workers in Millau. That is, while they welcomed the support and liveliness the outsiders brought, they showed little or no interest in the history seminar or its subject: their own past. Given the immediate urgencies of their struggle with the army and the divisions among themselves, the farmers weren't overly concerned with "getting a handle on" their past nor with linking that past to the present political battle. They spoke for the most part only about the present or about the five years that had transpired since their battle had begun. They were preoccupied with whether or not to negotiate with the army.

The *Forum-Histoire* people found themselves increasingly confused about their own role. In effect, the Larzac experiment insisted on keeping separate what their theory sought to bring together: a local, living history of the past and the contemporary, essentially political stakes of the struggle in the Larzac; professional history and living practice. They found what they could do more and more dominated by the concerns of the present and turned to producing a series of *enquêtes* based on conversations, in an attempt to understand the evolving situation at hand. They made no attempt to be sociological, devised no so-called representative samples, and adopted no mask of pseudoscientific objectivity in conducting their interviews. From these *enquêtes* emerged a set of themes or problems related to the division between traditional farmers and modernizing farmers— those who had significant investments in the area, large holdings, and who ran farms with agricultural employees. These problems in turn led the collective to widen their analysis of the Larzac and to see it not simply as a defensive fight against the army, but rather as a place where far-reaching questions about the capitalist development of agriculture were being posed and debated.

History, as such, had dropped out of the picture. Not only was the present the point of departure for their endeavor, but, they found, they were increasingly ending up there as well. They had stopped "working on" and had begun "working with": history had dissolved entirely into political practice. They had certainly succeeded in refusing historical erudition as an end in itself. "But we stayed at that point; we didn't know how to define an alternative historical research, nourished by the present, and yet exigent and rigorous."[141] And their attempt to combine a radical critique of dominant history with the voices of grassroots history "from the people" had largely failed.

> The contribution by "savage historians" was very important in feeding our critique of dominant history and its professional elitism, in showing that the division between history and the present—political struggle— wasn't ineluctable. But it was we who called them "different historians"; it wasn't of any interest at all to them to define themselves in that way.[142]

To a certain extent, the encounter between the *Forum-Histoire* group and the farmers of the Larzac, an encounter beset with misplaced expectations, surprises, disappointments, and readjustments on each side, produced the kind of lived complexities that the third—and most theoretically ambitious—of the history collectives, *Les Révoltes Logiques*, set out to investigate as their chosen subject. Coming primarily from a training in philosophy rather than history—the group evolved in part out of a philosophy seminar taught by Jacques Rancière at Vincennes on workers' practices—the members of the *Révoltes Logiques* collective did not wish, as *Forum-Histoire* was failing by their own estimation to do, to write "another history."[143] They wanted rather to disrupt or interrogate the epistemological categories and representations that serve to ground historical discourse, particularly the discourse which, like that of social history, sets out to tell the story of the privileged "other" of political modernity: the worker. Where do the representations of labor and laborers generated by social historians come from, and what do they obscure?

The collective took their name from a line in a prose poem by Arthur Rimbaud, "Démocratie," written soon after the end of the Paris Com-

141. Chesnaux, cited in Descamp, "Jean Chesnaux, historien du présent et de l'avenir," 4.

142. Jean Ahmad and Jean-Michel Dominique, "Pourquoi cessons-nous de publier *Les Cahiers du forum-histoire?*" *Les Cahiers*, no. 10 (Nov. 1978): 57.

143. The initial membership of the collective included Jean Borreil, Geneviève Fraisse, Jacques Rancière, Pierre Saint-Germain, Michel Souletie, Patrick Vauday, and Patrice Vermeren. About 2500 copies of each issue were published. When the last issue of the journal was published in 1981, the collective had been joined by Serge Cosseron, Stéphane Douailler, Christiane Dufrancatel, Arlette Farge, Philippe Hoyau, Daniel Lindenberg, and Danièle Rancière.

mune. In that poem, Rimbaud parodies the speech of a mobile and im-
perialistic bourgeois class, expanding out from the metropolis into the
"languid, scented lands," "feeding," as the poem says, "the most cyni-
cal whoring," and "destroying all logical revolt." After the Commune's
bloody defeat, faced now with the "swamp," as Rimbaud called it elsewhere, of the French middle class consolidating the colonial impetus that
would propel it through the next several decades, how could a different
future be imagined? Like many of the *Illuminations*, "Démocratie" evokes
the wrenching emotional aftermath of the repression of revolution, the
lived experience of political possibilities shutting down, the dismantling or
dimming of utopian conceptions of change—a set of perceptions and experiences undoubtedly shared by the *Révoltes Logiques* collective when, in
the wake of May '68, they turned to Rimbaud for a title.[144] The "révoltes"
of the title announces the journal's overtly political (as opposed to historical or philosophical) aims, its attempt to prolong in other ways the
revolutionary and democratic energies of the recent revolt they had participated in, and to counteract the ongoing post-May reabsorption of politics
into sociology that was then dominating the intellectual scene. This was a
reabsorption, in the view of the collective, that could only result in something like a "radical" critique of an unchangeable or immutable situation.
The journal's title also echoed the slogan of the Maoist group, the *Gauche
prolétarienne*, with whom some of the collective's members had been associated: "On a raison de se révolter" (literally, one is right to revolt)—a
slogan in which the indeterminacy of the French pronoun "on" indicates
the extent to which the process of revolutionary subjectivation had been
opened up, made available to any collectivity—even a virtual one. That
slogan had, of course, also been taken up by Sartre, Philippe Gavi, and
Benny Levy (aka Pierre Victor) as the title of their 1974 book-length conversation published by Gallimard in its collection "La France sauvage,"
a new collection launched that year with a manifesto stating "we mean
to base ourselves on facts and perpetually return to them . . . as a path by
which a possible philosophy of freedom may be reached."[145] Sartre's share
of the profits of the sales of the book (some 30,000 francs) were channeled
by him into funding the financially strapped *Libération*.[146] And *Révoltes*

144. Rimbaud's own title, "Démocratie," alludes to the ideological slippage of the term in
his own time: it had undergone a profound modification during the Second Empire when it
was appropriated by the imperial regime in opposition to the bourgeois regime—the emperor
claiming to have given back to the people its sovereignty. See my *Emergence of Social Space:
Rimbaud and the Paris Commune* (Minneapolis: University of Minnesota Press, 1988), 152–53.

145. Cited in Simone de Beauvoir, *Adieux: A Farewell to Sartre*, trans. Patrick O'Brien (New
York: Random House, 1984), 68.

146. See Annie Cohen-Solal, *Sartre: A Life*, trans. Anna Canagni (New York: Pantheon,
1987), 486.

Logiques, both the title and the project itself, bears some trace of a ghostly "non-event" of the mid-1970s, a television series, "The Meaning of Revolt in the Twentieth Century," that was to be produced using the intellectual itinerary of Sartre as a focus. Rancière, Philippe Gavi, Simone de Beauvoir, and some eighty other researchers and historians worked for about a year on the initial stages of the project, to be directed by Roger Louis, a television reporter who was among those who had resigned from the ORTF during its long strike in May and June 1968. Small teams of historians, militants, and scholars organized, and got underway researching particular topics like feminist revolt or workers' revolt. Daniel Lindenberg, who would later join the *Révoltes Logiques* editorial collective in the 1980s, was in charge of preparing a study on Paul Nizan for the television series: "We immediately put in a considerable amount of work," he recounts, "sure as we were that the project would be carried through."[147] Ultimately, though, the series, to which Chirac had been overtly hostile from the outset, must have appeared too controversial for state-run television. Under pretence of technical and financial difficulties—the government even tried to suggest that Sartre was attempting to personally profit financially from the series—the project was cancelled, prompting Sartre and others to conduct a press conference entitled "A television censorship problem."

The nervousness with which the state viewed the "History of Revolt" television project and its featured philosopher, Sartre, contrasts sharply with television's enthusiastic showcasing, beginning in those same years, of the faces and discourse of the New Philosophers. The contrast gives some sense of what kinds of *gauchistes* were acceptable in the Giscard years and what kind were not. But if the television project ultimately failed, it helped nurture the group of mostly Maoists who founded the Centre de Recherche sur les Idéologies de la Révolte; it was this Center that in turn published *Révoltes Logiques.* The journal's aim, as the collective wrote in the first issue, was that of "interrogating history beginning with revolt and revolt beginning with history." But the adjective "logiques" in the journal's title calls attention to another set of problems: those that arise in the interaction in historical writing between two interdependent logics: the logic of the historian and the logic of his or her object of study. According to the logic of the historian, truth lies in data about the past turned into knowledge, and in knowledge then turned into lessons ("the lessons of history") for today. According to the logic of the object (which is really just another version of the logic of the historian), truth lies in an authentic "working class culture" believed in by Marxists and

147. Daniel Lindenberg, cited in Cohen-Solal, *Sartre: A Life,* 504–5.

empiricists alike (or by both groups together, as in *Le Peuple Français*), a truth embedded in workers who cannot themselves know or articulate this truth any more than they can avoid embodying it and manifesting it to the trained eye of the historian. What, asked *Révoltes Logiques*, is wrong with this picture?

In their opening statement, the collective expressed a kind of utopian desire, resonant with an earlier Maoism, of ascertaining "another memory," a popular memory or "thought from below" unencumbered by mediation and linked to the people's capacity to, in effect, represent themselves or write their own history. This was a capacity that all the conventions of historicism and all the social, anthropological, and economic "types" through which the working class has been identified and classified, praised or denigrated, serve only to obscure. But first *Révoltes Logiques* set out to enumerate all of the kinds of historical enterprises or excavations of popular memory that they would *not* resemble or perform themselves. State or official history merely affirms the heroic capacity of the masters: "[It] knows neither worker nor peasant revolt. Nor that of women or national minorities." Fashionable—i.e. *Annales*-school—history is castigated for its vision of an immobile history and an equally immobile "people" who are content to leave to the elite the task of historical change in history. *"Gauchiste"* or Party history offers a mere "metaphysics" of revolt; in a prescient characterizing of the New Philosopher phenomenon only then getting under way, *gauchistes* who have freed themselves from Marx are viewed by the collective as having toppled over into the metaphysics of Desire or Religion. "Popular literature"—the kind of popular memory encoded in folkloric songs and legends and presided over by custodians of folk memory busy proclaiming the purity, authenticity, and impermeability of the folk to outside influence—is viewed as nothing but a repository of the representations and stereotypes of the people *Révoltes Logiques* was seeking to undo. Nor did they see their project reflected in the kind of "discourse history" practiced by the contemporary perhaps closest to their own aims, Michel Foucault. They did not want to write discourse history, they said, but instead to analyze the articulation *between* discourses and practices. For Foucault, whom the collective interviewed in one of their issues, discursive practices were always those of power; as such, Foucault (and even more so, his followers like Michel de Certeau) remained locked in a mechanistic schema made up of the seesaw of power and popular resistance. In their interview, the collective formulated a critique of Foucault around the following questions: Doesn't the analysis of techniques of power make power absolute by presupposing it as always already there, persevering in the face of the equally persevering guerrilla action and resistance tactics of the masses? And doesn't this serve to avoid the real question posed by power, namely whom it serves and to what purpose?[148]

Having dispensed with the reigning modes of history writing, the collective defined its own project in these terms:

> *Révoltes Logiques* wishes simply to listen again to what social history has shown, and resituate, in its debates and what it has at stake, the thought from below. The gap between the official genealogies of subversion—for example, "the history of the workers' movement"—and its real forms of elaboration, circulation, reappropriation, resurgence.
>
> The disparity in forms of revolt.
>
> Its contradictory characteristics.
>
> Its internal phenomena of micro-powers.
>
> What is unexpected about it.
>
> With the simple idea that class struggle doesn't cease to exist, just because it doesn't conform to what one learns about it in school (or from the State, the Party, or the *groupuscule*) . . .
>
> *Révoltes Logiques* . . . will try to follow the transversal paths of revolt, its contradictions, its lived experience and its dreams.[149]

As such, the past would be approached transversally from the present to find the prehistory of a certain number of contemporary problems perceptible in the gap between the organized workers' movement and the actual speech and form of their struggle. Was it the role of the past, then, to provide lessons for the present? *Révoltes Logiques* rejected any pedagogical relation between past and present, any conception of the past as a knowledge that can be extracted in the form of lessons or edifying stories. They did not seek to perform historical reconstitution in the form of a story. Nor were they drawn to systems or lessons as a mode of expression. The past teaches nothing. "Leave lessons to those who make a profession out of revolution or a commerce out of its impossibility."[150] If the past does not give lessons to the present, then why study it? The "lesson" of history at best, is to "recognize the moment of a choice, of the unforeseeable, to draw from history neither lessons nor, exactly, explanations, but the principle of a vigilance toward what there is that is singular in each call to order and in each confrontation."[151] The past allows a certain vigilance in the present,

148. See "Pouvoirs et stratégies: entretien avec Michel Foucault," *Révoltes Logiques*, no. 4 (1977): 89–97. The critique of Foucault made by the Révoltes Logiques collective resembles one mounted by Nicos Poulantzas a year later. See his chapter "Towards a Relational Theory of Power," in *State, Power, Socialism* (London: Verso, 2000), 146–53.

149. Editorial, *Révoltes Logiques*, no. 1 (winter 1975).

150. Ibid.

151. Editorial, *Révoltes Logiques*, no. 5 (spring–summer 1977): 6.

the ability to know when a choice must be made, a choice that is contingent
and singular, and not the product of repetitive structures or determinations. Ruptures rather than continuities, singular individuals rather than
statistical agglomerations, what people said rather than what was said in
their name: "What interests us . . . is that history be at all times a break,
to be interrogated only *here,* only politically."[152] *Révoltes Logiques* set out
to write the particularity of revolt, its "other memory."

What then is this "other memory," and where can it be found? For
Révoltes Logiques, unlike, say, for the *Forum-Histoire* collective, it was located in the archives and specifically in the words, the speech, of particular
men and women—words that can be heard or listened to only to the extent
that one takes the notion of the worker as subject literally. How is what
workers say and do active, conducive to liberty? Words themselves are
part of the struggle—not the words of people speaking "for" the masses,
but simply people speaking at all. This is the chatter that social historians
wade through to get at the statistical truth of workers or that they ignore
because it doesn't conform to any of the various essential natures of the
worker: love of trade, hatred of trade, solidarity, community, and so forth.
Encountering people of the past as equals means according their chatter, their texts, and their actions with as much attention that one would
accord the words of bourgeois intellectuals, those of yesterday or today.
And it means paying particular attention to the rhetoric of those voices
in the archives that don't "sound like" workers, that throw a wrench into
the assumptions we have about workers, the voices of those that might, in
their mimicking of bourgeois speech, for example, be relegated by other
historians to the status of "class traitor."

> The worker who, without knowing how to spell, attempts to make
> rhymes according to the fashion of the day is perhaps more danger-
> ous to the existing ideological order than one who recites revolutionary
> songs. . . . With the introduction—however limited, however ambigu-
> ous—of aesthetic sentiment into the workers' universe, the very foun-
> dation of the whole political order is placed in question.[153]

Too much attention had been paid to workers' collectivities and not
enough to their divisions; too much focus had been placed on workers'

152. *Révoltes Logiques* collective, "Deux ou trois choses que l'historien social ne veut pas
savoir," *Le Mouvement Social,* no. 100 (July–Sept. 1977): 30.

153. Jacques Rancière, "Le bon temps ou la barrière des plaisirs," *Révoltes Logiques* 7 (spring–
summer 1978): 30. This essay, as well as another early *Révoltes Logiques* essay on the Universal
Expositions and the Cottereau preface to Poulot's "Le Sublime," have been included in a volume
edited by John Moore, Adrian Rifkin and Roger Thomas entitled *Voices of the People: The Social
Life of "La Sociale" at the End of the Second Empire* (London: Routledge and Kegan Paul, 1988);
the book contains a very informative general introduction by Thomas.

culture and not enough on their encounters with other cultures, with their displacements and meetings across class lines. These moments of encounter, not unlike the complex meeting of workers and intellectuals during '68, or of historians and farmers in the Larzac, were instances of what others might be tempted to conceptualize as cultural "contamination" or "the infiltration of bourgeois values." But it was encounters with people different from themselves—and not the glow of shared identity—that allowed a dream of change to flourish. In their search for contradiction and singular destinies, it is not surprising that the place and speech of nineteenth-century women—both workers and intellectuals—would emerge in the journal's pages as a privileged topic, nor that an important feminist theorist like Geneviève Fraisse would begin her writing about women and feminism as a member of the collective.

At the center of *Révoltes Logiques'* critique would thus be the entire enterprise represented by a journal like *Le Peuple Français*—a journal which they viewed as embodying all the empiricist and positivist tendencies on the left they were seeking to dismantle. *Le Peuple Français*'s project was nothing more than the accumulation of detail, seeking to know more about what we already know. In the end, historians of social conditions— sociologists of the past—filter out the idea that things could be radically different. Their homage to the working class veils another, quite different message: stick to your collective identity, stay in your place, act like workers—which is to say, act the way we think workers act.

But to pay the kind of attention that *Révoltes Logiques* proposed to the particularities of workers' speech meant an inordinately patient and time-consuming combing of the archives in the search for specificity, and a careful close reading of often obscure texts. If *Forum-Histoire* ultimately lost its grasp on the past and dissolved into present-day activism, *Révoltes Logiques,* on the other hand, risked getting lost in the archives. Their task demanded a deep and prolonged immersion in highly specific archives of nineteenth-century French workers—frequently archives previously unexamined. Not only must one be an alert and patient archivist to find the voices overlooked because they don't conform to standard representations of workers—one must almost be a better historian than the historians. Though their own theoretical ambitions prevented them from taking the empiricist's route of facts for facts' sake, the same theoretical ambitions seemed to call for a kind of hyper-empiricism: the refusal to conceptualize or generalize. The journal remained for the most part anchored in the radical specificity of singular destinies, unusual, rarefied, or hidden moments—the asides of workers' struggles. Theoretical stakes so radical and far-reaching that might be expected to exceed a specific locale remain rooted in that locale by virtue of the archives, risking, in the journal's limiting of comparability or its reluctance to extend the search outside of France, for example, a kind of exceptionality.

To the extent that they did depart from nineteenth-century workers' archives, they did so in the direction of the present. In that writing, history appears less as an archive than as a laboratory that enables the exploration and critique of contemporary political discourse and practice. When in 1978 the group turned to an analysis of the remnants and memory of May in French life, to the activities of many of their own comrades and former comrades, and to tracing the fate of a certain idea of politics "from below" associated with May and once shared in common, the special issue of *Révoltes Logiques* that resulted, *Les Lauriers de Mai*, became perhaps the most serious writing we have on the memory of May on the occasion of its tenth anniversary.

Les Lauriers de Mai is a moving document in part because its authors refuse to claim for themselves the role of those who know the truth about '68—the genuine revolutionary doctrine, say, or the real political desires of the masses—and yet by the same measure they refuse to see themselves in the emerging hegemonic version of their history propagated, primarily, by reformed ex-*gauchistes*, New Philosophers, busy reencoding the anti-Stalinist elements of *gauchisme* into celebrations of liberal capitalism. The thoroughness with which the memory of the events of May '68 had been distorted had initially provided the impetus for the collective's decision to work at recovering other lost "interruptions" in the past. It had led them, as Donald Reid has suggested, to combat a reading of history that would relegate such utopian "interruptions" or attempts to live or think in a different world to a list of so many failures or deviations—with the effect, if not the purpose, of berating anyone who would try to do something similar.[154] Having immersed themselves in nineteenth-century interruptions, they turned now to writing the aftermath of the interruption that was May; their own recent history would be another kind of "alternative historical memory." Tracing the various *gauchiste* paths taken in the ten years since May, from the New Philosophers to the Parti Socialiste, from *Libération* to the CFDT, meant inevitably, for the *Révoltes Logiques* collective, performing a kind of self-analysis as well, "an interrogation of ourselves . . . on the reasons for our intolerance of certain discourses and

154. Donald Reid made these remarks about the work of Jacques Rancière, the writer most closely associated with *Les Révoltes Logiques*, in a round-table he, Linda Orr, Lloyd Kramer, and I participated in on Rancière at the French Historian's conference in Vancouver in 1995. See Reid's excellent introduction to the English translation of Rancière's *La Nuit des prolétaires*, *The Nights of Labor* (Philadephia: Temple University Press, 1989). See also my introduction to my translation of Rancière's *Le maître ignorant*, *The Ignorant Schoolmaster* (Stanford: Stanford University Press, 1991).

practices." Without claiming scientific objectivity or a superior truth, the collective sought to distance itself from those fellow *gauchistes* on whom May had conferred a new political legitimacy—be it syndical, intellectual, or journalistic—constituting them now, ten years later, as the managers of a patrimony.

The collective's attempt to allude to or keep alive "another memory" of May ran immediately into trouble, even before publication. *Les Lauriers de Mai* was originally supposed to have been published as a special issue of *Les Temps Modernes.* However, the lead article, a highly controversial reading of the newly emergent New Philosopher phenomenon that situated the latter's effort to enthrone itself as the new post-'68 intelligentsia in the practices of the Maoist *Gauche prolétarienne* and the disappointments of post-May, was deemed unacceptable by the *Temps Modernes* editorial board—a board that then contained some former *Gauche prolétarienne* members (notably Benny Levy) for whom that reading of their shared history must have seemed controversial if not offensive.

The difficulty of laying claim to a version of one's own recent history is alluded to as well in an article in *Les Lauriers de Mai* analyzing the trajectory of *Libération,* that daily whose origins ("*Libération,* which was not a Maoist paper but which had been launched by Maoists")[155] and initial aspirations to elicit the voice of the people so closely resembled those of the *Révoltes Logiques* collective. Entitled "*Libération* mon amour?" the article sets out not only to read *Libé*'s own institutional history according to the transformations of the slogan *"on a raison de se révolter,"* but to read the paper as itself actively engaged in a history-writing project. "We could not remain indifferent to the representation *Libé* makes of that history [of *gauchisme*], which is to a great extent our own."[156] If the newspaper is a vital part of the history of the movement and of post-'68, it was rapidly becoming no less a—if not the—principal vehicle in producing the popular representation of that history.

To avoid writing from the perspective of the disgruntled consumer, the *Révolte Logique* collective conducted an *enquête* with five *Libé* workers, including director Serge July, a former typesetter and writer, B. Mei, and one of the co-authors, with Sartre, of *On a raison de se révolter,* Philippe Gavi. The article, based on their remarks, begins by quickly rendering the verdict that the *gauchiste*-populist aims of the paper to be, as one of the newspaper's earliest issues proclaimed, the voice of anonymous people, of "France from below, the France of the housing projects, the fields

155. Jean Paul Sartre, cited in Beauvoir, *Adieu: A Farewell to Sartre,* 373.

156. Pierre Saint-Germain, "*Libération,* mon amour?" *Révoltes Logiques,* special issue, *Les Lauriers de Mai* (1978): 59.

and the factories, of the metro and the tramway,"—these aims have, by 1977, completely failed. *Libé* is then analyzed in terms of the three things it has instead become: a journalistic enterprise, a cultural institution, and an ideological apparatus. Where once one became a journalist by being a militant, now one becomes a journalist by profession. The pressures of getting an issue out every day have contributed to a situation where tasks shared by all in the early days of the newspaper are now clearly demarcated and assigned: now, a clear break between editing (performed during the day, largely by men) and production (night work, almost entirely performed by women) has been reasserted, along with other traditional aspects of the division of labor. An anecdote "from below," that is, from the former typesetter, gives a clear picture :

> One day we wanted to put four pages about the production process of the paper into an issue. . . . They couldn't stand that we would simply tell how that happens in the paper: we had to fight, some of them even threatened to quit if it was published. . . . What pissed them off was the idea of a perspective onto the paper that wasn't theirs. For them, this wasn't a political analysis of the paper.[157]

The turning point or emblematic moment in this process of market–driven professionalization was, for Gavi, the entry of director Serge July into the *Club de la Presse* of *Europe 1* sometime in 1976. Former *Libé* journalist Martine Storti concurs. Although it is impossible for her to fix a precise date in what was in fact a progressive slippage on the part of the paper from militancy into journalism, she too singles out the importance of the day when July announced he had been invited to sit in on the Sunday press conferences that brought together the "cream" of the French press. Up until that point, the paper had had little to do with "politician's politics." And if one person represented or incarnated *Libé* to the outside world, Storti and others worried at the time that this might be opening the door to the star system and other insidious aspects of personalization.[158] Wouldn't *Libé* then become attached in people's minds to a particular face, the face of the "boss" or "owner" who is commonly thought to be a necessity at the head of every company? Around this time, July began as well to publish his own signed editorials in the paper; Gavi comments: "To put an editorial on the front page of *Libé* that isn't signed by the paper

157. Saint-Germain, *Libération*, 61.
158. See Martine Storti, *Un chagrin politique*, 128–64. Storti recounts that when staff members suggested that they take turns with July attending the Sunday meetings of the Club, he insisted that the Club's rules were that the same person had to attend every week. Later, staff members learned this was not true.

but instead by the paper's director, is to retreat to a form that is itself that of the politicians."

The reasons for *Libé*'s evolution, in Storti's view, were clear: the fatigue of living on the margins, the desire to put an end to militantism, the desire for social recognition, the need to create a newspaper that would sell better. But the evolution itself was being hidden behind various alibis by people managing to appear all the while the guardians of the temple that they were busy dismantling. By the end of the 1970s, when Storti left the paper, "faithfulness to a cause was taken for ideological blindness, militant action for imbecile activism, while reconciliation with society passed as a liberation from political taboos."[159]

The invitation extended to July by professional journalists was itself an indication that *Libé* had entered the ranks of the serious newspapers, that it was recognized, as the authors of *"Libération*, mon amour?" point out, by other institutions to the point of being expected to play the particular role, the particular musical instrument assigned it in the orchestra of the French mainstream press. Each paper that aspires to being a good product must fulfill its task in the division of competencies; to *Libé* would go the task of specializing in the off-beat, the marginal, the work of creating a kind of cultural enclave for the left. Their job would be to chart all the contradictory fragments and individual paths taken in the disintegration of *gauchisme* into the various social movements of the 1970 and beyond, the rise of the "liberal-libertarian"—July's prescient 1978 description of the paper's ideology—consensus of the 1980s. And because it had become purely a newspaper of "information," one that described the contradictory reality it sees rather than analyzing it in view of transformation, the *équipe* had become less a collective working toward producing a minimum of common thought, than a group of somewhat random individuals. Thus, the role played by the "Mail from readers" page had become, in the view of the *Révoltes Logiques* authors, that of an alibi for the earlier goal of "giving the people a voice": *Libé* threw open its pages to its readers mostly at the precise moments when the paper didn't want to take a stand itself, when a particular topic like rape had become too controversial, or when the death of members of the Baader-Meinhoff group in Germany elicited queasiness in *Libé*'s editorial staff about their own former left militancy. Topics that might be thought to have elicited an opinion on the part of the paper are dealt with instead, according to B. Mei, by bowing to "popular opinion":

> When they have to take a position, they pass the ball to the reader. For the Baader affair, it was significant: in order to take a certain distance

159. Storti, *Un chagrin politique*, 163.

and not appear too allied with them, we neither criticized nor supported them. A pile of angry letters came in: suddenly, it's decided to do a double page of letters from readers to re-establish the balance. That way we would be saying: emotionally, *Libé* supports the Baader group, while criticizing them politically.

Around the same moment that *Révoltes Logiques* published *Les Lauriers de Mai,* Serge July wrote a famous editorial in *Libération* on May 3, 1978, called "Ras l'mai" ("I'm sick of May"); in an interview, he made comments to the effect that journalism had become the major mode of expression of the age, replacing literature and philosophy, and that the journalist had become the new intellectual.[160] *Libération*'s founding director, Jean-Paul Sartre, felt called upon to respond, characterizing July's view of the journalist as absurd. In the same 1979 interview, Sartre also marked a considerable reserve toward what the paper had become, suggesting that the commonly held reason for his own departure from an active role in the paper in 1974, namely his health, was not the full story. "I thought that *Libération* could be part of my work, that is to say that I would work on it and that it would be better. Today *Libération* is still going. It's a paper that's not bad. . . ." As for its style, which Sartre had once wanted to see develop into a new "written/spoken" language, the written translation of popular speech, that of the cleaning lady, the worker, or the student—the style of the paper as it stands is, in his view, merely "infantile." "*Libération* tells leftist truth. But one no longer feels the truth behind it. There's good work, but one no longer feels the revolt."[161]

*L*ibération is, of course, still going. The life-span of the three radical history journals, however, proved to be much shorter. All three collectives published their final issues between the late 1970s and the early 1980s, succumbing in part to the financial difficulties of keeping a small journal afloat at a moment of shifting intellectual and political perspectives.[162] In its penultimate issue, *Révoltes Logiques* published an urgent SOS, a plea for subscriptions, from the failing *Peuple Français,* whose determination to maintain a low price in the face of rising production costs had wreaked havoc in their finances. For ten years, fewer than

160. See Paul Thibaud's interview with July, "De la politique au journalisme: *Libération* et le génération de 68," *Esprit* 5 (May 1978): 2–24.

161. Jean-Paul Sartre, interview with François-Marie Samuelson, *Les Nouvelles littéraires,* Nov. 15–22, 1979. Cited in Perrier, *Le roman vrai de Libération,* 161.

162. *Les Cahiers du Forum-Histoire* ended in 1978, *Le Peuple Français* in 1980 (with some of the collective spinning off into another, similar journal, called *Gavroche*), and *Les Révoltes Logiques* in 1981.

ten people had carried out the editing, printing, and circulation of the journal, with no secretarial help, nor support from the media, political parties, or financial institutions, relying essentially on a network of friends to keep going. "Today we have debts instead of salaries."[163] On the very next page of the same issue, *Les Révoltes Logiques* printed its own call for help, their own plea for subscriptions in the form of an auto-itinerary. The journal, they reminded their readers, had been born in 1975 "out of the illusions and disillusions of post-'68" and out of a refusal of the different forms of returning to traditions that those disillusions frequently induced. The sense of an enormous temporal and political chasm separating the ideological climate of 1981 from the moment of the journal's inception a mere six years earlier is palpable in the editorial. In 1975, political, artistic, and historical research was flourishing; innovative new venues for creative thought were springing up almost daily. Perhaps, the collective notes, these research efforts were already in 1975 living under the threat of being overcome by the new "theoretical and commercial imperialisms." But to the extent that this was known at the time, it hadn't mattered; it hadn't prevented the collective from taking up their work at the margins of official historical discourse, interrogating the certitudes of that discourse. "After five years of groping along that path, we have received signs of interest and encouragement that have sometimes calmed our own uncertainties. But we have also felt that the 'other side' of the contradiction was moving much faster than we were." Now, in 1981, the signs were all too clear. "Present ideological and commercial conditions leave very little room for the circulation of work whose fragmentary nature and interrogative form places it outside of the profit-making arena. Competent journalists no longer find the time to remind readers of the existence of "small" journals, and fewer and fewer bookstores are willing to stock them."

The *Cahiers du Forum-Histoire* group had reached a similar impasse two years earlier. In their tenth and final issue, the group discussed their reasons for ceasing the publication of the journal. As in the case of the other two journals, the subscription level had not grown significantly. And the group was reluctant to adopt any of the solutions or accommodations they saw other radical journals making. They did not, for instance, wish to follow the example of *Hérodote*, the radical journal founded by Jean Dresch and a number of militant geographers soon after 1968. After a few hesitant issues, *Hérodote* had deliberately oriented itself toward addressing a readership of professional geographers, setting itself up as the successful rival professional journal to the *Annales de Géographie*. (*Hérodote* is still going today.) The *Cahiers* did not want to confine itself to a readership of historians or other knowledge professionals. And given the self-proclaimed and cultivated lack of ideological cohesion within their group, they could not claim to be the expression of a precise ideological tendency, as journals like *Dialectique* sought to be. Nor did their commitment to the anonymous collective authorship of articles allow them to go in the direction of what they saw *Révoltes Logiques* becoming, a "revue d'auteurs."[164] They were drawn as much as ever to a critique of specialization—their own and that of their presumed readership—but after ten issues they had not managed to reach a broad audience nor to extend their initial working group in any significant way beyond the confines of the Jussieu university "ghetto."

Collective endeavors whose inception was so intimately tied to a particular political history, and to a climate of expansiveness and possibility, could not, it seems, escape from history when that climate receded or disappeared. None of the journals, in their subject matter, "reflected" their own moment directly; they were, after all, concerned with history and the question of the past. But by their nature, they proved extremely vulnerable to the vicissitudes of their times. The ephemeral but real existence of such projects shows them to be, in every sense of the word, situational—that is, implicated in the present, tied to the immediate demands and constraints of the moment, without access to any of the institutional protection that can sometimes keep those demands and constraints at bay. An enormous sadness and confusion accompanied the attempt in the final issues of the journals to come to terms with the problem of their own *duration*, with the problem, that is, of the duration or continuity of spontaneous political practices and collectives created in a moment that now, it seems, had passed. But there are also indications that, for some of the militants, the difficult process of displacing energy to a new site, a new endeavor, was already underway.

> At the risk of displeasing the paleo-Leninists among us, is the permanence of an "organized" structure really the principal objective and primary condition for political pertinence? Maybe it's the opposite. Shouldn't a "structure" give way as soon as possible, as soon as it has ceased to fulfill a positive function and risks becoming an end in itself, devouring people and their energy? . . . To know when to stop is not necessarily admitting failure or powerlessness—quite the contrary![165]

164. Ahmad, "Pourquoi cessons-nous," 57.
165. Ibid., 58.

3

DIFFERENT WINDOWS, SAME FACES

REPRISALS AND TRIALS

At the edge of the factory esplanade, at the point where the factory merges with the street and where economic struggle is transformed into political struggle, a young woman worker at the Wonder Battery Factory in St. Ouen cries out that she won't "go back into that prison," that she won't take up the rhythm of the line again, that the vote to end the strike has been rigged. We are in mid-June 1968, just after the Grenelle Accords have been signed, just before the end of the strikes, just before everything returns to normal again—the last moment between uncertainty and the certainty of deception. The woman wears a thin white cardigan; her arms are folded tightly in front of her. Other figures, mostly men, surround her: the CGT delegate, the factory owner, the Maoist lycéen, the head of personnel. Several of the men try to reason with her, telling her "that it's important to know when to end a strike," that significant gains have been made or would be made, soon, sometime in the future. The woman continues her cries of refusal; other workers can be seen in the background, slowly filing into the factory entrance. What could she have possibly been dreaming of?

La reprise du travail aux usines Wonder (The Return to Work at the Wonder Factory), ten minutes or so of documentary footage shot by two film students who strapped a camera to the hood of their *deux-chevaux*, students whose own institution, l'IDHEC, was out on strike and who could thus take off on an *enquête* of sorts out to the industrial periphery of Paris in mid-June. Their footage is perhaps the most striking document from the '68 years.[1] It is the result of a purely contingent meeting of the world of film and the world of work: it is only

---

1. Willemont and Bonneau, *La reprise du travail aux usines Wonder*.

138

because the workers are outdoors, on the factory esplanade, that they can be filmed—the space of production, of workers working, has always been largely ruled off limits to the camera by factory management. Only when they are not working can workers be filmed. In 1995, a young filmmaker, Hervé Le Roux, had the idea of using that brief documentary footage from 1968 for a *reprise*, as he titled his own film—a second take. *Reprise* depicts Le Roux's efforts to locate the woman in the original footage now, some thirty years later—unnamed, unknown, a flickering, powerful but ephemeral figure at the center of some black and white images from the 1960s. Using the goal of finding the woman as an excuse to enter, armed with a camera, into the daily lives of people, he meets up with and talks to the other characters that appear in the footage—co-workers in the factory for the most part, but also the union leaders, the Maoist *établi*—after showing each the footage again as a way of mobilizing their memories. His film consists of the stories and associations each recounts about what the images provoke.

Why do so many of the more interesting recent attempts to consider the history of the 1960s and its relation to the present make use of the detective genre? I am thinking here not only of Le Roux, but of more obvious examples from the detective novel genre itself: Jean-François Vilar, Didier Daeninckx, and Francis Zamponi, whose texts have already figured in this study, as well as some of those by Jean-Patrick Manchette.[2] Le Roux explains his choice of forms in this way:

> The investigation [*enquête*] was the guiding thread that amused me and allowed me to play with the spectator . . . to play with codes of the detective film that lighten a rather heavy material made up of the experiences that people brought to the film: their life conditions, work conditions were difficult . . . thus, the investigation as a means of lightening the material. What allowed me to avoid sociology, was to spend time with the people. . . .[3]

What interests Le Roux—as much, it seems, as the past—is the here and now of daily life in the *banlieues* in the 1990s, the contemporary repre-

---

2. See in particular, Jean-François Vilar, *Bastille tango* (Paris: Presses de la Renaissance, 1986), and *C'est toujours les autres qui meurent* (Paris: Actes Sud, 1997); Didier Daeninckx, *Meurtres pour mémoire* (Paris: Gallimard, 1984), and *Le bourreau et son double* (Paris: Gallimard, 1986); Francis Zamponi, *Mon colonel* (Paris: Actes Sud, 1999), and *In nominé patris* (Paris: Actes Sud, 2000); Jean-Patrick Manchette, *Nada* (Paris: Gallimard, 1972). See also a highly uneven 1988 collection of short fiction pieces about May-June 1968, *Black Exit to 68*, which includes works by Daeninckx and Vilar, as well as other *polar* authors like Jean-Bernard Pouy and Thierry Jonquet; only Vilar's story, "Karl R. est de retour," is worth reading.

3. Hervé Le Roux, cited in an interview with Serge Toubiana, *Cahiers du Cinéma*, Feb. 1997, 51.

sentation of which is almost entirely limited to sensational sound bites on the evening news. His gamble is that Parisian middle-class viewers, who rarely if ever see that way of life, can be tricked, so to speak, into encountering the intolerable effects of uneven development in their own immediate surroundings (immediate, yes, yet as far away now, historically *and* geographically, as Algeria or Vietnam) by the allure of the most traditional, tried and true, of investigation plot devices: *chercher la femme.* "The film had to be the investigation, and that's what it was."[4]

But in setting out to make one kind of *enquête*, a detective story, Le Roux in fact ends up with something in the lineage of the old Maoist *enquête*: the dream of giving voice to the people. His film is one more attempt to confront the ongoing problem of a direct communication with the exploited and their history. The detective structure itself is a red herring; the fiction of locating the woman is the device that allows him to gain access to people now, to create a shared project of sorts. Its most important effect is that of allowing the filmmaker to virtually disappear, to block any overriding interpretive narrative—whether as voice-over or as *a priori* thesis—from structuring the material he obtains. Even the montage, Le Roux insists, is not designed to produce "truth" from the juxtaposition of two conflicting descriptions, say, of the same situation: the end of the strike or the conditions of work at Wonder. "My goal was not to establish the truth in a contradictory manner but to give people a chance to speak. I didn't have any objective thesis to prove."[5] The stories he collects take the place of any sociological representation—numbers, facts, statistics—that would structure the lives recounted: lives that emerge in the course of the film as those of girls taken at the age of fourteen by their mothers to work without interruption on the assembly line until the time came when they could retire.

In November 1995, in the midst of his filming, large-scale strikes on the part of transport and other workers brought France to a halt once again. The distance could not be greater between Le Roux's project and the representation of the strike on daily French television, in which workers' voices are heard for just a few seconds, if at all, while a chorus of the same "experts" appear, interviewed at length every night on the evening news, assessing the strike as "fantasmatic," "irrational," or "archaic."

In Le Roux's film, we watch again and again bits and pieces of the earlier film footage: the young woman as pure refusal, as the impossi-

---

4. Le Roux, interview, 50. I've argued something similar about Daeninckx's work; see my "Watching the Detectives" in *Postmodernism and the Re-reading of Modernity*, ed. Francis Barker et al. (Manchester: University of Manchester Press, 1992), 46–65; reprinted in *Postmodern Literary Theory*, ed. Niall Lucy (London: Blackwell Press, 1999).

5. Le Roux, cited in Toubiana interview, 51.

bility of tolerating the moment *after* experiencing revolutionary ferment. When life has been lived differently, and when it seems as though it just might continue to be lived differently, when all this is fading and existence threatens to lapse once again into the dreary routine—"la bonne ornière," as Rimbaud, who would know, once called it, "the good old rut"—how can this possibly be tolerated? Novelist Leslie Kaplan who worked in a factory during and after 1968, evokes the sordid aftermath of the end of the strike, when workers returned to work amid general dissatisfaction, in an image that goes far in capturing the atmosphere and experience of that highly variable segment of time—a few months? five years? thirty years?—known as "post-May":

> That impression of a cadaver impossible to kill off, a rotting cadaver that keeps returning, this is what we could feel after the strike about society as a whole—everything appeared under this sinister form.[6]

By repeating the original footage, in slow motion, in short extracts, in freeze shots, far more frequently than is actually needed for the transmission of information, the intolerability of that earlier *reprise*—*reprise* in its most habitual sense of picking up and doing the same things again after an interruption—insinuates itself into our memory. In that *reprise* we are led to come to terms with the second, quite violent, meaning of the word: something initially seized or experienced by workers during the interruption from work that was the strike (a *prise de pouvoir?* a *prise de parole?* a *prise de conscience?*) is being now forcibly taken back by the forces of order, being lost, perhaps irretrievably.

Earlier in her novel, Kaplan evokes the way in which the suspended moment of the general strike allows, if only for an instant, the perception of other possible lives, a vast unexplored territory of possibility:

> Something ungraspable, something difficult to grasp, that was there during the strike and the occupation. Something is in the midst of happening, something is happening: just that, the feeling of that. . . . That something should come from outside, to meet you, to surprise you, to take you away, to raise you up, to undo you, it's there, it's now, we are beside it, we are with it, we feel the pressure and we create it, everything is happening, everything can happen, it's the present, and the world empties itself and fills up again, and the walls pull back, they are transparent and they pull back, they separate, they fade away, they leave room, and it's now and now and now. . . . Love can create this feeling, or art; it is rare to feel it in society, where one is almost always

6. Leslie Kaplan, *Depuis maintenant: Miss Nobody Knows* (Paris: P.O.L., 1996), 83.

confronted with a kind of obligatory inertia, where the activity one pursues, the activity that one can pursue, goes almost always hand in hand with the painful feeling of its limitations.

But during the strike we could touch it with our fingers, rub our hands across its back.[7]

That the woman in the '68 film footage herself should prove lost, difficult to trace, is explained in the course of LeRoux's film: she worked, it seems, in the most sordid of the workshops at Wonder, where the work—with tar and chemicals—was so intolerable that people didn't stay long; they moved on to other factories. But the ghostly presence of the woman as pure refusal, momentarily at the center of our gaze, suggests a kind of historical condemnation whereby '68 itself becomes spectral, partaking of the peculiar spectrality and ungraspability of the recent past in the minds of those whose past it is. Preserved and floating, like the woman, in a state of proximity, but at the same time very far distant in time, '68 appears always (especially in visual documentation, so much more powerful than the written texts) to be happening in another world, another distinct era. Did it occur in our own lifetime or during the nineteenth century of Zola? ("Zola-esque" and "nineteenth-century" are words that recur in the testimonies in Le Roux's film to describe the working conditions at Wonder in the 1960s.) The original Wonder footage—so brief, barely a narrative—does not tell the story of a pre-existing "anthropological" people, the "working class," who, in the course of their oppressed existence, rise up together and come to say no. Rather, it shows the woman, "the people" if you will, coming into existence in the pure actuality of her refusal. And it is that version of the people that is difficult now to locate—resurfacing like a ghost in Le Roux's film to unsettle the present, to disturb its forgetfulness. For it is only in their "actualization" that "the people" appear—disrupting all the various narratives and representations that anthropologists, social historians, and sociologists mobilize to categorize such an event.

Reprise is in some ways more interesting than its director's stated intentions. In an interview, Le Roux suggests that he was trying to create continuities in workers' social memory disrupted by the vast industrial restructuring that drove jobs out of areas like St. Ouen, where some 40,000 metallurgists alone once lived and worked in the late 1960s.[8] If so, his endeavor incorporates yet another sense of the word *reprise:* the repairing or reweaving of a fabric, filling in the holes to make the tissue whole again.

7. Kaplan, *Depuis maintenant*, 61–63.

8. See Toubiana's interview with Le Roux, 50–55. See also Emmanuel Burdeau's article about the film in the same issue, "Lettre à une inconnue," 47–49.

This is a fairly traditional metaphor for the goals of a fairly traditional notion of memory within social history. But even within this model of dutifully "reinjecting memory" into the anthropological social group in question so as to firm up its vacillating identity—the *reprise* as reweaving the threads that have been severed between generations—certain problems emerge, for the historian as well as the seamstress. The repair always shows. Le Roux's film is at its best in showing the discontinuities between past and present, in creating a palimpsest or layering of the two temporal moments where neither is given priority, where each is given equal validity, where neither moment is elevated to the position of judging or critiquing the other. Certainly, the past in the film is not mobilized as a solution to present *malaise*—and none of the characters watching their former selves responds in this way. But neither is the present constructed, as it invariably is in the dominant media depictions of the post-war period, particularly those of the 1980s, to be "the consummation of all times."

As an exercise in writing a possible history of the 1960s, *Reprise* resembles the best of recent attempts to document the May movement as a mass movement: Elisabeth Salvaresi's *Mai en héritage* and Nicolas Daum's *Des révolutionnaires dans un village parisien*. Both books were published in 1988 in time for the twentieth anniversary of May, both by obscure small presses; both, at the moment they appeared, seeming almost iconoclastic in the context of the habitual literary production about May of those years, which was concerned above all with exorcising any militant past. Daum's experiment bears the most formal resemblance to Le Roux's. Like the filmmaker, his ethnography has been originally circumscribed by an organization: not a factory, in Daum's case, but the decentralized structure of the membership of the *comité d'action* that sprang up in mid-May in the 3rd and 4th *arrondissements* in Paris, and that continued its operations in various forms until 1972. Daum, who had been a member of the *comité*, located about twenty of its original members—workers, artists, teachers, engineers, of widely varying ages—and records his interviews with them. In the final chapter, several of his interviewees then interview Daum in turn. Anonymous militants, neither celebrities nor martyrs, people embedded at the time in the texture of everyday neighborhood grassroots activity—these are voices that by the mid-1980s had all but disappeared from any version of '68, eclipsed by those who had become the post facto stars, leaders, and spokesmen for the movement. Was all that was left of '68 a knowledge about '68 on which some, and only some, are authorized to become experts? That Daum was conscious of his method as a deliberate assault on or intervention at the generic level on the strategies of personalization, recuperation, and spectacularization that had come to govern May's representation is apparent in his introductory remarks:

I fear I might frustrate some readers . . . by my inability to cap these
interviews with something along the lines of: "A sparkling forty-year
old, she receives me surrounded by her cats in a loft near the old Halles
neighborhood, watering her collection of cacti. She has not changed a
bit, with her laughing eyes and curly hair." Or: "Married, a father, he
works in administration where he is in charge of recruiting." This kind
of reductive and insignificant detail will remain an insignificant mystery,
because Adek is not only a painter, J.-P. is not only a physician, etc.; they
say it themselves, they are many other things *as well*. Besides, they are
private people; none of them has occupied the forefront of the media
scene, there was no leader, they made themselves known (and how!) in
their neighborhood, but they remained anonymous.[9]

They are many other things *as well*. Just as in the 1960s they had never
been Protagonists with a capital "P," never on the front page, never symbols of their generation (in fact, by their widely varying ages giving the
lie to the very notion of a "generation"—that privileged mainstay of representations of the 1960s, firmly in place by the mid-1980s), never professional militants, never "exemplary." The people Daum interviews are
part of that mass of comrades that made up the structure of general assemblies, that worked in front of factory gates and in any number of decentralized initiatives and *comités d'action*. Le Roux, too, in his film followed
a similar representational strategy with the people he interviewed: "trying to respect their words, allowing each enough time to appear in their
complexity, their contradictions, never reducing a protagonist to a social
label (foreman, worker) or to a politico-syndical one (the Trotskyite, the
Maoist, the CFDTist, the CGTist, the communist). . . ."[10] But Daum has
more success than Le Roux in showing people who are *something else as
well*—not surprisingly perhaps, given the relatively aleatory way in which
people from various walks of life adhered to and drifted away from the
comité d'action compared to the determination of factory and métier. Le
Roux's syndicalists, for example, for the most part speak the *discours syndical;* the workers he interviews speak, for the most part, as workers; the
factory assigns them their roles—except during the strike of course, but
the strike is ending. The people included in Daum's volume by contrast
are the result of a quite contingent meeting twenty years earlier; even the
spatial "origin" of the neighborhood they share does not subsequently naturalize them into anything resembling "the voice of the Marais." Though
their terrain of action was the Marais, what brought them together or what

---

9. Daum, *Des révolutionnaires dans un village parisien*, 15.
10. Hervé Le Roux, *Reprise: Récit* (Paris: Calmann-Lévy, 1998), 151.

made them drift apart was much more chancy; Antoine, for example, follows a girl in the rain who he thinks is going to a certain political meeting he is trying to find, ends up at the *comité d'action* instead, and stays—for years. As another of the people interviewed by Daum remarks, "The cohesion was independent of the individuals that made it up: when someone arrived, he was integrated, if someone else left, it wasn't important, because what was important was the cultural mix."[11]

Against the dominant image of the professional militant (or rather the professional ex-militant) prevalent in the 1980s, Daum offers this reminder of a collective experience:

> But as much as we felt all together to be in the general current in May '68, I have just as much the impression now to be totally in the counter-current of the dominant ideology. That's the only nostalgia I have about May '68: what we were doing wasn't really militantism, it was a way of life, there was no difference between life and militantism, there was no break between them. At home there were friends over almost every evening. There was a relative harmony between what one said and what one did.[12]

These evocative remarks provide the best description I have found of what is experienced when the political imaginary becomes the everyday fabric of peoples' lives. They give precision to the notion of praxis as an experience of the quotidian relieved of its various miseries and restored to richness—everydayness fused with politics as the place where the divisions caused by alienation can be repaired, where the slow and profound rupture between the everyday and the nonquotidian, between the public and the private, between militant life and ordinary life, is lived as abolished. What can be gleaned in these few sentences is what Henri Lefebvre meant when he spoke of "transformed everydayness": the creation of a

---

11. Adek, cited in Daum, *Des révolutionnaires dans un village parisien*, 24. The fluid membership of the "action committees" is captured in an internal report from another such committee, the Students-Writers Action Committee, published originally in 1969 as a collective text, but later attributed to Marguerite Duras:

> Sometimes someone comes whom we've never seen before; comes back eight days running, then never again.
> Sometimes someone comes whome we've never seen before, and keeps coming back.
> Sometimes someone comes whom we've never seen before—where does he think he's come?—reads the newspaper, and disappears forever.
> Sometime someone comes whom we've never seen before, comes back a few days later, then at intervals less and less far apart, then, suddenly, stays. . . .

"20 May 1968: Description of the Birth of the Student-Writers Action Committee," in Marguerite Duras, *Green Eyes* (New York: Columbia University Press, 1990), 55.

12. Adek, cited in Daum, *Des révolutionnaires dans un village parisien*, 27.

culture that is not an institution but a way of life, reproducing for a time its own conditions in the activity of a group taking its role and its social life in hand. Political activity no longer appears as a distinct and separate sphere isolated from social life: each person may, there where he or she lives and works, prepare the birth of another future. Specialization—the "natural" domain of experts—is based on the separation of spheres; here, the social has been reconfigured to eliminate such a separation, to refuse naturalized categories of expertise.

No unifying principle beyond their activism in May '68 governs the people included for interviews in Elisabeth Salvaresi's book. Unlike Daum or Le Roux, she interviews some well-known people—Guy Hocquenghem, Christine Fauré, Serge July—as well as anonymous people and herself in the form of an "auto-itinerary." Her goal is a palimpsest made up of "their dreams and nightmares of today . . . confronted less with their ideas from the past, than with the phantom of their twenty-year-old selves."[13] Like Le Roux, Salvaresi characterizes her work as an *enquête* in the sense of a detective investigation, though, again, what emerges is perhaps closer to the *gauchiste* impulse of arriving at "the voice from below," the unmediated testimony:

> Reading the *enquête* may thus resemble the investigation itself, something that consisted in hours and days spent interrogating some people about their memories of others: and so-and-so? Do you remember her? Do you still see her? Have you had news from her? The quest began to take the form of a detective's labor, scrambling from one scrap of information to another in order to find so-and-so, whose name, sometimes incomplete, sometimes just a last name, had emerged on the peripheries of an interview, accompanied by an image, a scene of an episode from '68. This kind of *enquête*, which proceeds by cross-checking, is at once fastidious and fascinating. I took pleasure in it, and there again, I hope this pleasure will be shared.[14]

Nevertheless, one reason for the recurrent use of the detective trope or genre by writers concerned with the 1960s like Vilar, Salvaresi, or Le Roux can now be proposed: the recent past, it seems, has been lost or concealed, perhaps even confiscated. The crime consists of that confiscation, the crime of excluding, or of having one group—the experts—to stand in for a mass movement. And it is a crime that allows the hygiene of the contemporary national fiction, the present social order, to prevail. The goal of uncovering what has been lost, or of naming the criminals or forces

---

13. Elisabeth Salvaresi, *Mai en héritage* (Paris: Editions Syros/Alternatives, 1988), 18.
14. Ibid., 219–20.

responsible for the concealment, is less to give the French a rival "image" or different version of their past, an alternative version of '68, than to defamiliarize and restructure their experience of their own present.

The mainstream media, preoccupied by its own commemorative reconstructions—of '68, and, more importantly, of the bicentennial of the French Revolution the following year—took little if any notice of Salvaresi's or Daum's books when they appeared in 1988. And pleasure, of the kind evoked by Salvaresi—her own as well as the reader's—is an affect missing from the predominately morbid tone of those "organized events" that are television commemorations, even when "pleasure" or "the imagination" is heavily thematized as a major demand, if not the only demand of May. [15] Consider, for example, "Le procès de Mai," screened in 1988, hosted by former UEC militant, co-founder of Doctors Without Borders, ubiquitous media personality and organizer, most recently, of the United Nations mission in Kosovo, Bernard Kouchner.[16]

As its title makes clear, "Le procès de Mai" was organized loosely in the format of a trial, complete with an accused, prosecution and defense arguments, and a jury. Dispensing with even the minimal festivity that a "festival-with-a-fixed-date" like a commemoration might be supposed to resuscitate in its viewers, the show adopted the much more somber mode of the trial: judging May '68. Judging and sentencing? In any case, having the last word—something that is impossible for a historian but not for a judge—the final evaluation, passing ethical judgement according to the eternal division of good and evil on an event recast now as a crime and then drawing lessons from that history, in the form of maxims or morals to live by. It is not enough that May be an "elusive" (Aron) or impossible revolution; it must now become a crime. Here, of course, it is not the confiscation or the concealment of May that constitutes the crime, but May itself. Assembled in the studio audience is a group of young people interpellated as "jury": it is they—the generation of '88 presumably— who are being called upon to judge the generation of '68, personified by Kouchner in the now familiar posture of "self-critic," playing the roles of both prosecutor and accused in the trial of his past and those of countless

15. This is particularly true of a show like "68 dans le monde," an episode of the television series "Les Dossiers de l'écran," screened on Antenne 2 on May 2, 1978. Within the context of an international survey of insurrections in the 1960s, the French section focuses entirely on "verbal delirium," the demand for the imagination figured by poetic graffiti; French May is characterized as a "revolt in the pure state," "a revolution without a project." This show takes the TV commemoration format's general tendency of occulting the workers in favor of the students and the Latin Quarter to its most extreme point, making absolutely no mention of the strike at all.

16. "Le procès de Mai," hosted by Bernard Kouchner, prod. Roland Portiche and Henri Weber, screened on Antenne 1, May 22, 1988.

others that he presumably embodies. Introductory visuals and voice-over set the scene for the event of '68: a "dynamic and prosperous" France—shots of the Concorde, big boats, and automobiles—with a "prestigious leader," peaceful and wealthy, with very little unemployment. Cut to shots of overturned, burnt automobiles in the Latin Quarter. What happened? "Quelle mouche a piqué la jeunesse française?"

Taken idiomatically, the question as phrased merely suggests an inexplicable touchiness on the part of privileged or spoiled students living in the lap of prosperity. What could possibly have been bugging French youth? But it also hearkens back to students' activities as inexplicable except when seen as the result of the transmission of an external virus: politics as an airborne or insectborne fever that contaminates from abroad, a return of the tropes widely used by the mainstream media in the 1960s: "Fever has seized the Latin Quarter" (*France-Soir*, May 11, 1968); the "Cohn-Bendit virus" (*Aurore*, June 13, 1968). The first answer to the question is proposed by Kouchner himself, the host (and, fortunately, a doctor). Kouchner offers a strictly culturalist or "lifestyle" interpretation, reminding the "jury" about the France of the 1960s' archaic dimensions; his examples are the dress codes in place in the high schools and the lack of access to birth control. "Life," he says, "was going too fast." France was being industrialized too quickly, and "we forgot to speak to each other." "We had to stop for a moment, even if it was over a barricade, in order to speak to each other." The distance separating the old Maoist dictum that "The revolution is not a dinner party" from this image of a peaceful, conciliatory conversation could not be greater. Here, the barricade, far from figuring contestation or division, appears to be what *enables* therapeutic dialogue to take place.

In the following section of the show, "The Excesses of May," the heavy prices paid by France for the revolt are depicted and analyzed by experts. Indeed, the notion of "excess" itself points to the need for an expert knowledge that can assess such "excess" in the light of the movement's goals. The first of these "excesses" deals with the disorganization suffered by the university, and is presided over by Annie Kriegel, a former professor of history at Nanterre, and ex-communist turned anti-communist. Kriegel argues that May '68's discourse disqualifying knowledge and schooling slowed down the modernization of the French university by "fifteen to twenty years." Accompanied by a musical track indistinguishable from a funeral dirge, shots of an upended Nanterre classroom appear; the camera zooms in on a single phrase of graffiti written on the chalkboard: "Je rêve d'être un imbécile." Are we in Peking or Paris? Kriegel makes the comparison explicit: "Something happened here that resembled the Chinese Cultural Revolution," she states. People have forgotten excruciating scenes of humiliation, the horrible moments at Nanterre when "men of learning" were literally dragged through the mud.

Turning to the next excess, "ultrafeminism," a *former*, as she repeatedly emphasizes, militant feminist, and now journalist at *Libération*, Annette Lévy-Willard is brought on to describe the early days of the women's movement as a time when women decided they didn't need men to live, when they decided they would be *like them* instead, and "show that they had balls." From the vantage point of her maturity in the late 1980s, Ms. Lévy-Willard goes on to regret those excesses that have led, as she recounts it, to countless women suffering because they didn't have children, women who were divorced or now find themselves alone and unhappy. She holds up a copy of the new book she has just published; zoom-in on the title: *Moi Jane, cherche Tarzan.*

Feminism clearly poses problems for the show's ideological grasp, since a certain kind of loosening of rigid family roles and morés restricting sexual behavior has to be made to play the role of a significant positive gain or result of May, and presumably women must have had something to do with that change. In fact, the great majority of the images on the show as a whole deal with men and women, the life of the married couple, the sexual relations of adolescents in high schools. To this end, another *ancien combattant,* Trotskyist-turned-Socialist Party representative Henri Weber appears later in the show to dispute Lévy-Willard's depiction of feminism. In support of his interpretation of May as a great libertarian and democratic movement, Weber claims sexual liberty and the MLF (Mouvement de Libération des Femmes) not only as results of '68 but as its greatest achievements, leading to "a society modified for the better." (A woman doctor is called on to certify that now, thanks to '68, family members recognize each other as sexual beings.) But the logic of the show's exposition is quite clear. The libertarian Weber, speaking with the voice of the Socialist Party's claim to be the inheritors of the spirit of May, takes credit for the Women's Movement at the same time that the "radical feminist" disavows and apologizes for her former radicalism. In fact, the woman's apology precedes the male ex-militant's recuperation of and recasting of that political history, not as politics but as "a necessary modification of society." Necessary, presumably, because it happened, because it was part of the mechanical, evolutionary unfolding of social destiny. Politics must be excised to allow the great (and inevitable) forward movement of cultural modernization to be celebrated: May is a continuity, not a rupture. For the commemoration, the past is not other, but is in a necessary continuum with the present.

Violence, another "excess of May," presents even thornier problems than does feminism; the show chooses to deal with these quite hurriedly.

The section on violence is very brief; in fact, the only images of violence shown are close-ups of headlines from the Maoist newspaper, *La Cause du Peuple*, and photographs of sequestered or confined factory bosses in occupied factories during the early 1970s. Violence is situated entirely on the side of the insurgents and is shown occurring only during the *gauchiste* period of post-May. No visuals appear depicting police or state violence, the colonial pre-history of May, violence on the part of imperial powers like the United States, or the brutal showdowns between CRS and workers at Flins and Sochaux where workers and a high-school student activist died at the hands of the police. The show even avoids any depiction of the street violence during May. The state, as such, is depicted as eternally passive, bereft of agency—as though agency belongs only to those who act against authority. The forms of state violence I just mentioned actually constituted the major part of the visuals of tenth-anniversary commemorations like André Frossard's "Histoire de Mai." But by the time of the twentieth anniversary, at the peak of the great liberal counterreformation of the 1980s, the agency of the state has disappeared, and violence has become simply a minority or extremist "fringe" deviation of the early 1970s.

The voice-over that introduces the brief section on violence is a good illustration of the way in which the twenty-year commemoration, or rather trial, of May is being called upon to do double duty as a prelude to the bicentennial commemoration of the French Revolution the following year. The voice-over phrase "Terror finds its beginnings in virtue" situates the political violence of 1970s *gauchisme*—the kidnapping and sequestering of factory owners, the various peoples' tribunals, factory sabotage, bombings, and other reprisals that proliferated throughout the early 1970s—as the regrettable "terrorist deviation" taken after a good start. The "joli mois de Mai"—that happy conversation evoked by Kouchner—thus skidded outside of and beyond itself into these unfortunate deviations. The narrative model has, of course, been borrowed from one of François Furet's various interpretations of the French Revolution—each of which, despite their contradictory and sometimes confusing relations with each other, finds expression in some form during the show. The problem of commemorating revolution is this: as anodyne a format as the commemoration is—evoking nothing so much as the carefully ironed and scented souvenir stored carefully away in a drawer—it is nevertheless a conjuring up of memory, and as such, even a heavily orchestrated and controlled time capsule, such as a commemoration of 1968 in the 1980s, runs the risk of escaping its management and waking demons, simply by its formal acknowledgement that something happened, that an event took place. If nothing took place, how could there be a commemoration? But if an event took place, then presumably sometime somewhere someone decided to throw a stone, someone somewhere chose to stop working. Commemorations of the recent past, particularly when they are dominated by former (even if repentant) activists, cannot rely entirely on a sociological overview that sweeps the event up into a post facto cultural modernization narrative such that it—the event being commemorated—disappears entirely into a smooth and fractureless transition to modernity. Once they have been purged of their "extremist" elements, cleansed of their various utopias— their counter-family, counter-couple aspirations—and cordoned off safely in their preserve of a newly reinforced, bourgeois private life, sexual liberty and the women's movement can be harnessed to such a narrative as simply being supportive trends in the unfolding of peaceful transformation. Violence, it seems, cannot be handled in this way. At times, the show presents the *gauchiste* violence of the 1970s as that which must be repudiated in order to save a good-natured, virtuous May, just as Furet at various moments in his interpretations of the French Revolution is drawn to repudiating 1793, Jacobin rule, and the Terror, in order to praise the 1789 of the Déclaration des Droits de l'Homme. But even this strategy is sometimes not sufficient, and the show's unfolding ultimately suggests that the late 1980s is one of those times. In his 1978 text, *Penser la révolution française,* Furet presented an interpretation of the French Revolution wherein the rule of Terror was analyzed as the necessary and inevitable fate of any revolutionary politics. According to this more totalizing vision, terror always already seeps *backward* into any impulse for systemic social change. Thus "terror finds its beginnings in virtue": the very *thought* of change leads directly, inexorably, to a series of totalitarianisms. Just as the Terror was the necessary destiny of 1789, so Soviet totalitarianism and the Gulag centuries later—and eventually Pol Pot!—were the necessary destiny of the French Revolution; Stalin was already alive in Robespierre. And *gauchiste* violence of the 1970s was the necessary outcome of the May insurrection.

Still later in his career, Furet would present a further revision of his analysis of the French Revolution. In the final version, the Revolution is reframed as the invention not of socialist revolution, but of modern democratic political culture.[17] But the section on violence in "Le procès de Mai" owes more to Furet's late 1970s discourse, according to which the Gulag is envisioned as the inevitable essence or outcome of revolutionary politics. Furet's aggressive reinterpretation of the French Revolution in the realm of academic historiography gave, in the words of Sunil Khilnani, "a crucial

17. See Sunil Khilnani, *Arguing Revolution: The Intellectual Left in Postwar France* (New Haven: Yale University Press, 1993), particularly chapters 5 and 6, for an excellent analysis of Furet's various versions of the French Revolution and the political and intellectual context of their production.

historical imprimatur"[18] to the ex-*gauchistes* known as New Philosophers, who were then involved in proclaiming a more histrionic discourse of the Gulag at the level of the mass media. Furet and the New Philosophers, in effect, worked together to co-produce and disseminate the new critical vocabulary centered around the term "totalitarianism," a ready-made doxa according to which the "excesses" of the French Revolution are named as the territory where totalitarian discourses and practices take root. Furet's close journalistic affiliation in the late 1970s was with the mass weekly, the *Nouvel Observateur,* the magazine that championed Solzhenitsyn and allowed the New Philosophers to first reach a mass readership. It was also the weekly that became in the course of the 1970s the magazine of choice for "distance-taking" toward one's revolutionary past. But other, more academic journals played a role in disseminating the new discourse. The journal *Esprit,* for example, devoted two special issues around the same time to establishing, under the title of "the return of politics," the equation that revolution = communism = totalitarianism.[19]

Near the end of the show an economist, Michel Albert, is brought on to offer an expert diagnosis of French industry, one that is remarkably similar to Annie Kriegel's diagnosis of the state of the university, and one which relies heavily on an implicit evocation of the scenario of the Chinese Cultural Revolution. In Albert's schema, French industrial decline is a result of and begins with '68; May '68 set French industry back "ten years or more." According to what baseline? Apparently the one provided by the Japanese experience—the visuals show images of clean, efficient Japanese assembly lines, exemplary of a correct and successful economic modernization. These visuals are juxtaposed with shots of the French Usinor factory in the 1970s, occupied by workers and draped with strike-related banners. Robots, not workers, are seen manning the Japanese assembly lines—the image of the good worker, one that can labor night and day without complaining: the perfect form of rationality.

"Le procès de Mai" is actually more concerned with post-May, and with mobilizing the gains of the Women's Movement of the 1970s to discredit *gauchiste* or worker-related violence that was also very much a part of the same years. To this "violence" is credited a general retardation or lag in development of the university and industry—issues of vital interest, it could be presumed, to the generation of '88 facing a high level of unemployment. Like the French Revolution in one interpretation by Furet, May '68 is a violence done to the natural, evolutionary course of the progress toward liberalism from which French society emerges deformed,

18. Khilnani, *Arguing Revolution,* 124.
19. See *Esprit,* July–Aug. 1976 and Sept. 1976.

running to catch up with its own missed modernization. Thus, *anciens combattants* like Kouchner and Weber who still need to salvage a partially positive version of May, claim a version of the women's movement, conceived of essentially as a rehabilitation of the private against the excesses of the public that helped put the flowering of the individual back on track. On this basis, as well as on the basis of the "friendly chat over the barricade," the show can maintain that May furthered cultural modernization and the liberal agenda in a salutary way. In this narrative, May must bear absolutely no traces of a political, Marxist, or utopian dimension. Kriegel and Albert, on the other hand, who have less personal stakes, argue that May set France back, created handicaps or disabilities that slowed down the restructurings needed after 1973 when the beginning of the economic crisis set in. Ironically, perhaps, more damage is done to the memory of May by those who, concerned with pushing a sociocultural interpretation at the price of a political one, claim to be May's advocates.

And what is the young people's verdict? It is extremely difficult to ascertain, since the show opts for the most part for listening to an "expert" on 1980s youth, rather than to the youth assembled for that purpose themselves.[20] This is not too surprising, since the show's main purpose is less any assessment of May than the creation and certification of "experts" who are specialized in such a task. Laurent Joffrin, author of a book, *La génération de '86*, written in the wake of the 1986 mass demonstrations by students regarding education, tells the jury that they, today's youth, are pragmatic and conservative, distrustful of politics and ideology. The students in the "jury" respond accordingly, to the effect that 1960s activists, in their judgment, "broke all the barriers"; they themselves, on the other hand, will be intelligent and look for harmony. From the point of view of youth today, '68 looks "too ideological"; young people today, Joffrin concludes, make up a "*moral* generation," concerned with classical, democratic, and, above all, moral values like "the right to education."

It is difficult to imagine what the youth called upon to be members of the jury—they have been chosen, presumably, because they are Joffrin's "ethical" generation—or the run of the mill TV viewer at home, for that matter, could think and feel. They have already been at once bludgeoned

---

20. The producers of "Le procès de Mai" seem to have learned a lesson from an earlier talk show/commemoration, André Campana's 1983 "Mai: Connais Pas," which also brought in students onto the set but in a much less controlled, more improvisatory way. The problem Campana confronted was that the students, from technical high schools, were far too curious and asked too many questions about the '68 events, questions that for the most part went unanswered as Campana appears to lose control of the show. Campana's is one of the only TV shows to screen the "Wonder factory" film footage. It also features Daniel Cohn-Bendit arguing that 1968 was a worldwide "sexual revolution."

with and rendered inadequate by the past. Kouchner, in particular, is given to adopting a sentimental-heroic, yet at the same time pedagogical, tone. At one point, he tells the jury: "Every twenty years, pursuing a dream is necessary! *Everything* changed in '68!" At the same time, the younger generation is praised for possessing a moral sensibility and pragmatism lacking in their reckless elders. "Judgment," which the show was supposed to elicit, is in fact anesthetized. A battle of memories is not an exchange of arguments, a discussion whose stake would be to tease out reflection on the part of a public; it is rather one voice drowning out others. To that end, the show uses heightened volume and telling silences rather than reasoned arguments; its strong images conjure up affects and emotions rather than understanding. Youth of the 1980s are inferior or superior (and sometimes both) to the twenty-year-olds of the past—but they are never equal. Anxieties about unemployment and education, high in the late 1980s, are fed by the show's discourse of the "lag": '68 caused France to fall off the track of economic development and university modernization, and the result is that young people today will not find a job. Radical politics (embodied by Lévy-Willard) leads to personal misery or (embodied by Kouchner) to a lucrative career as a highly visible media pundit and advisor to the state. Resentment, envy, inadequacy, gratitude, contempt, pity, boredom: an array of elicited emotions predicated on a hierarchical relation (inferior and/or superior) to the past, not one of which (with the possible exception of boredom) is a political emotion. May and its viewers have the right to just about anything, it seems, except politics.

If I have lingered so long over "Le procès de Mai," it is because it offers a staggeringly rich inventory of the doxa, narrative strategies, rhetorical devices, and personalities at work in the dominant revisionist rendering of '68—one whose slow sedimentation had been accruing since the mid-1970s but whose form only reaches perfection in the political ambiance of the late 1980s. Many of the narrative strategies and tropes— "self-criticism," for example, or the very concept of "generation," which undergirds the entire structure of the broadcast—became ubiquitous first in written genres: essays and print journalism, primarily. Indeed, "self-criticism" and "generation" tend to work hand in hand: "generation" is only mobilized as a concept at the moment when the self-appointed custodians of the memory of May *need it* to generalize their own repudiation of May in any number of collective self-critical narratives recounting the transition from blind enthusiasm to systematic denigration. But the format of the television documentary/commemoration undoubtedly facilitates their perfect formal achievement. Nowhere else, to take one obvious example, could the "incarnation of truth" provided by the body of the aging ex-*gauchiste*, as spokesman and relic of '68 history, be so fully realized—certainly not in the written text. And nowhere else could the interests and opinions of those who had by that point become the official memory functionaries and custodians so exactly coincide with the interests and opinions of the government elites and corporations that own the media. Television requires that ideas be expressed concisely, and "Je rêve d'être un imbécile," and "Moi Jane, cherche Tarzan" are concise ideas. Ideas or phrases like these that are too readable, too elementary, betray the intense activity of a social imaginary aggressively installing ostensible symbols of the desired orthodoxy. Much of television's power resides, as Noam Chomsky never tires of pointing out, in simple acts like the initial selection of topics and the way certain topics within those chosen are emphasized and framed. Why, for example, are middle-class women emphasized and workers represented only negatively?[21] The showcasing of women and gender in "Le procès de Mai" is completely new in the history of '68 on television, but this does not mean in any way that "women's perspectives" or women themselves are controlling the production in the 1980s, any more than it means that "gender" was a conscious or explicit concern in '68. None of the 1978 television productions, for example, focus on or even mention women or gender in any form, despite being chronologically much closer to the upheavals of the MLF in the early 1970s.[22] In my own reading of the documents from May–June '68 specifically, women activists in the Comités d'Action, in the streets, or in the factories tend to self-identify as any number of things—as workers, as members of different groupuscules or political tendencies, as German Jews, as the "pègre," as activists or citizens—rather than as women per se. In the repertory of the approximately 350 posters produced by the Atelier Populaire des Beaux-Arts during May and June, only one bears a representation of a female figure—and it is Marianne, the Republic![23] During the May–June movement, in other words, gender difference does not seem to have been experienced in a conscious fashion. And once the Women's Movement gets started in the early 1970s and women begin to make demands predicated on gender in a new way, it is not clear that those demands were viewed by male militants at the time as at all compatible with "the movement of '68." (Many women, of course, saw such

21. Except for photographs of occupied factories and sequestered factory bosses incorporated into a narrative of France's economic retardation, the subject of workers is addressed only briefly, not by workers themselves but by another expert, a CFDT union leader, René Bonety, who had helped negotiate the Grenelle Accords. Bonéty characterizes '68 as a "useful explosion."

22. I'm referring here to commemoration screenings like *Mai 68 5 ans après* (Claude Lebrun, 1973), "68 dans le monde" (Les Dossiers de l'écran, A2, May 1978), or "Histoire de Mai" (André Frossard and Pierre-André Boutang, 1978), as well as to serious documentaries like Michel Andrieu's *Le droit à la parole* (1978).

23. See Jean-François Vilar, "Les murs ont la parole," *Rouge*, May 9, 1978, 8–9.

demands as completely compatible, "in line with" '68).[24] All this suggests once again that for a 1980s narrative intent on making '68 an originary moment in the "conquest of autonomy," a certain highly sanitized version of the women's movement, narrated as part and parcel of a return to "private life," is more compatible with those aims or can be harnessed to them more effectively than could the thematics of class struggle or anti-imperialism. Nonviolence is made to characterize the women's liberation movement as essentially as violence characterizes the insurrection movements against bourgeois property or against colonization. Struggles by women and homosexuals in the 1970s that only in fact became mass struggles to the extent that they succeeded in rendering "political" questions that had previously been held to be "private" (abortion, sexuality) are recuperated back into the service of the dominant bourgeois ideology against which those struggles were engaged in the first place.

Certain topics are not merely neglected but actively targeted for amnesia, erased from the record. This is the case in one of "Le procès de Mai's" most striking manipulations, one that occurs quite early in the broadcast. Kouchner, who has just praised the '68 generation's "daring to dream" in a tone of high self-satisfaction, switches abruptly, and briefly, into the posture of self-criticism. "But we were navel-gazing, we forgot the outside world, we didn't see what was happening in the rest of the world, we were folded in on ourselves." He continues, much more triumphantly: "We didn't know what we would discover only in the following years: the third world, misery."

In one fell swoop, Kouchner assumes the power to clear away an entire dimension of the movement: its relation to anticolonial and anti-imperialist struggles in places like Vietnam, Algeria, Palestine, and Cuba, where Kouchner himself traveled in the early 1960s to interview Castro for the Communist student journal *Clarté*. Kouchner has conducted a massive clearing of the terrain so that he and his friends can "discover" the third world ten years later, like the first colonial explorers of virgin lands . A whole world disappears—the war in Vietnam, the iconography of Che, Mao, and Ho Chi Minh, the efforts of editors like Maspero—which is to say a militant or combative third world, so that another can be hero-

---

24. For a discussion of the early moments of the women's movement and its relationship to *gauchisme* and the political atmosphere of '68, see Geneviève Fraisse, "La solitude volontaire (à propos d'une politique des femmes)," *Révoltes Logiques, Les Lauriers de Mai*, 49–58. Historian Robert Frank concurs with my sense that gender is absent as a category during May–June 1968: "A new such combat, that of women for example, generated by the large evolutions of pre-'68, is virtually absent from the scene in 1968, only to reappear later in a frame modified by '68." In Michelle Zancarini-Fournel et al., eds., *Les années 68. Le temps de la contestation* (Brussels: Edition Complexe, 2000), 16.

ically "discovered" years later: the third world as figured in the Human Rights discourse, of which Kouchner has by that time emerged as one of the principal spokesmen. Fanon's "wretched of the earth" as the name for an emergent political agency has been essentially reinvented: the new third world is still wretched, but its agency has disappeared, leaving only the misery of a collective victim of famine, flood, or authoritarian state apparatuses.[25] The whole political subjectivation that took shape among some French over the War in Algeria is annihilated.

Such is the danger of a situation in which a few of a mass event's actors have been granted the authority, on the basis of that activism, to deny or repudiate aspects of the event according to the needs of the present moment. The danger is compounded, of course, when those same few voices have been allowed to become, in the process, the most listened-to interpreters of the event as well. To view '68 through the frame of the television commemorations that are produced every ten years is to confront the fact that old *gauchiste* principles like "la base doit emmener la tête" (literally, the base should lead the head) or "Don't let the loudspeakers speak for you"—principles that governed the movement—hold no sway in its commemoration, as again and again the same "spokesmen for a generation" reappear. Nor are the attempts on the part of students to "flee the student ghetto" in May reflected in the virtually uniform concentration by the commemorations on "student May" and the Latin Quarter, at the expense of the general strike or events taking place outside of Paris. As the designated spokesmen age, changing their ideological clothes according to the spirit of the age, "what happened," and not just the evaluation of the event's effects, changes as well. The very nature of the event—its contours, aims, and aspirations—become subject to revision. Whatever Bernard Kouchner, André Glucksmann, or Daniel Cohn-Bendit think at any given moment becomes proleptically ascribed to '68, "what the movement really meant." Whatever they become throughout their lives can be then projected retrospectively back onto May, where the seeds, at least, for their current transformation can, amazingly, now be found. "It is not inconsequential that someone like André Glucksmann, whose political path is not 'solitary' but rather in solidarity with a generation, take this posi-

25. This is one of the areas in which a show like "Le procès de Mai" registers a distinct political distance from 1978 television productions like "68 dans le monde," with its opening shots of Algeria, Palestine, Biafra, and Vietnam. But even those shows that do not adopt an internationalist perspective assert a clear connection between third world events and the uprising in Paris: an early Belgian production from 1973, Claude Lebrun's *Mai 68 5 ans après*, maintains, correctly, that a demonstration against the War in Vietnam initiated everything. Similarly, André Frossard and Pierre-André Boutang's lengthy documentary, "Histoire de Mai," first screened in 1978, gives Vietnam a causal role in the narrative of French events.

tion. . . ."[26] *Libération* in particular made a specialty out of this type of phrase whereby the self-confessed "errors" or the newfound enthusiasms of some are allowed to bleed out of their contours to become those of an entire generation. In Kouchner's phrase, "We didn't know then what we would only discover later on," the membership of the "we," presumably, has remained constant: a congealed and cumbersome "generation," lurching forward from the same blindness and ignorance to the same revelations, from the same naïvetés to an equally monolithic lucidity: thousands and thousands of people whose political passions, injuries, achievements and disappointments Kouchner can confidently speak for and embody—throughout all time, it would seem. This is his "we," the generational "we": a trajectory presented in the form of a once lived drama that has become destiny. We didn't know then what we know now. Or maybe "we" did know then what "we've" forgotten now: Let no one speak in your place.

ANTI-THIRD-WORLDISM AND HUMAN RIGHTS

For ex-leftists during the late 1970s and early 1980s seeking to realign themselves to the values of the market, the problem represented by "third-worldism" is roughly this: what is to be done about a twenty-year period—from the mid-1950s to the mid-1970s—to which the name "third-world-ism" can be given to signify a focus informed by the international division of labor and the long tradition of colonialism? How can we understand a twenty-year period (the North/South axis) that doesn't fit into the now dominant Aronist-Furetist or Cold War historical narrative of France's inevitable march to liberalism? How can the vocabulary and building blocks of that narrative ("totalitarianism," "Gulag"), wielded like terminological bludgeons from 1975 onward by ex-*gauchistes*, be used to mold or tether those recalcitrant twenty years during which it appeared as if *something else was happening*, back into the disciplinary constraints of the master narrative? Are the years of colonial upheaval and the accession to political subjectivity by "the wretched of the earth"—what Sartre, writing in 1964, called "the most significant event of the second half of this century: the birth of nationalism among the peoples of Africa and Asia"[27]—are these developments now just a parenthesis in that narrative? A mistake? A footnote? A delusion? A deviation? Is the attempt to link the stakes of Algerian independence—through the radical anticolonialism associ-

26. Cited in *Libération*, Nov. 24, 1983.

27. Jean-Paul Sartre, "Les grenouilles qui demandent un roi," *Situations V* (Paris: Gallimard, 1964), 155.

ated with French and Francophone thinkers like Sartre, Vergès, Debray, Fanon, Memmi, and Maspero—to a leftist alternative in France of mere archeological or historic interest at this point? Is the effect of the block of time represented by the years of decolonization on the "master historical narrative" something akin to what Annie Kriegel says about the effect of '68 on the French university? That is, a delay factor, something that "delayed" the "realizations" about totalitarianism, realizations that *should have* occurred for the French at the moment of the Soviet Invasion of Hungary in 1956, but which get deferred until 1975, until Solzhenitsyn is translated and the New Philosophers first begin to speak out from their garage of lost illusions? Does "third-worldism" simply represent another set-back or delay, the loss of crucial years when totalitarianism could have been confronted?

Contemporary French problems like the rise of various forms of neo-racism focusing on the figure of the immigrant, the nebulous status of the inhabitants of French territories like New Caledonia and Guadeloupe, not to mention that of some of the inhabitants of the outskirts of large French cities, suggest that the page on Algeria and the 1960s has not yet been closed. But the effort mounted by that part of the left eager to shed an identity based largely on its rejection of capitalism—the effort to have done with the whole question, to inflict a death sentence on their past all the while retaining whatever vaguely leftist auras of that past that would allow them to best inflict that death sentence—all this shows what an obstacle third-worldism represented.

Kouchner's remarks on the television show in effect claim victory in an ideological battle he and other former *gauchistes* had been waging in the popular press for the previous ten years to dismantle the "third-worldism" of the '68 years. Their efforts constituted a veritable media *matraquage*. The critique of *"tiersmondisme"* was initiated originally by Jacques Jul-liard, Kouchner, and a few others as a noisy polemic in the pages of the *Nouvel Observateur* in 1978 and was published as a volume, *Le tiers monde et la gauche*, by Le Seuil the following year. "Anti-third-worldism" received its most concerted and lengthy expression in ex-*gauchiste* Pas-cal Bruckner's *Le sanglot de l'homme blanc* (1983), published in a series edited by an ex-Maoist, Jean-Claude Guillebaud. In 1985, Doctors With-out Borders organized a big conference devoted to the debate; by the time that *Paris-Match* jumped in, deciding to devote extensive coverage to the conference with a splashy article entitled "Les impostures du tiers-mondisme" ("We knew that third-worldism, the doctrine that claims that wealth in the West was constituted at the expense of the poor countries, was weak and vulnerable. But we didn't expect that the *coup de grâce* would come from 'Doctors Without Borders')"[28] some observers began to suggest that the readership *Paris-Match* addressed was made up primarily of those French people who thought there were far too many Arabs, Asians, and Africans living in France.[29]

Though the debate, transpiring for the most part in the popular media, was highly sensationalized and represented in and of itself the latest stage in the post-'68 construction of the "media intellectual" out of the shards of his previous militancy, it was, nevertheless, to a certain extent, a debate. And though it could be viewed as just another melancholic rendition of the ex-*gauchiste*'s tune, "the God that failed"—as another step, in other words, along the painful road bringing the "lost generation" of May back into the embrace of the society it once condemned—at least there appeared to be two sides. On one side were the anti-third-worldists: Jacques Julliard, a former advocate of Algerian independence, editor of the *Nouvel Observateur*, and future member of the Fondation Saint-Simon,[30] Bernard Kouchner and other doctors from *Medecins sans frontière*, Pascal Bruckner, other reformed *gauchistes* like Jean-Pierre Le Dantec, the former editor of *La Cause du Peuple* and activist for Breton autonomy, and assorted anti-Communists like Emmanuel Leroy-Ladurie. Representing an opposing position, one that could be characterized as affirming the continuing validity of an analysis based on imperialism, were foreign correspondents like Guy Sitbon; geographer Yves Lacoste; a specialist in Islamic culture, Claude Liauzu; and economist Samir Amin.

Jacques Julliard, who invented the debate at the level of the mass media, simply continues in his own essay an agenda made familiar by the New Philosophers: he extends the map of the Gulag to incorporate the entire "third world." "In Africa there will be no socialism except a totalitarian socialism."[31] On one side lives the West with its freedom and

28. Patrick Forestier, "Les impostures du tiers-mondisme," *Paris-Match*, Feb. 22, 1985, 3.

29. See Yves Lacoste, *Contre les anti-tiers-mondiste et contre certains tiers-mondistes* (Paris: La Découverte, 1985), 6.

30. The Fondation Saint-Simon, founded in 1982, was a cross between a British-style "gentleman's club" (though not restricted to men) and a research institute. Presided over by François Furet until his death, the club served as a meeting place for intellectuals, and government "decision makers." Its seventy to eighty members included notables from the media, big business, and the various social science disciplines; indeed, the existence of the "club" is indicative of the intricate mesh that had developed between these three realms in the new ideological context of the 1980s. Like the journal *Le Débat*, it helped facilitate a rehabilitated image of the intellectual as "expert" and advisor to policy making. Its membership included many of the authors responsible for producing the revisionist line on May '68, including Gilles Lipovetsky, Luc Ferry, Alain Minc (treasurer of the foundation), and Serge July. The club came to an end in 1999.

31. See Jacques Julliard, "Le tiers monde et la gauche," *Nouvel Observateur*, June 5, 1978; reprinted in *Le tiers monde et la gauche*, ed. Jean Daniel and André Burgière (Paris: Seuil, 1979), 36–40. Julliard also published a collective book entitled *Regards froids sur la Chine* (1976) that

civilization; and, on the other, everyone else who doesn't live like us: i.e., the Gulag. Julliard also adopts the prophetic voice favored by the New Philosophers, the one that confidently predicts the "end" (of various "old dogmas") at the same time as the "return" (to "democracy," "the market," "ethics"—or in this case, "human rights"). The prophetic tone has the advantage of remaining suspended between the constative and the performative, thus providing both a description of the new world and a prescription for making the world conform to what the proposed description says. African and (by extension!) all of third-world socialism, writes Julliard, is and *can never be anything other than* "totalitarian" (if not "tyrannical" or "bloodthirsty.") Given this gloomy inevitability—New Philosopher discourse was never known for its lightheartedness—the European left can do nothing but denounce "power" in the third world, with the aim of supporting people as individuals oppressed by the totalitarian nation-state, and adhere to the Internationale of Human Rights. "It is true that there are two opposing sides in the third world. But they aren't the American and the Soviet sides. They are those of the torturing State and the martyred people."[32] The time for political actions or analyses, it seems, is now past; we can do nothing but aid the victims of human and natural disaster.

In his critical response to Julliard, journalist Guy Sitbon notes that the vocabulary Julliard marshals to describe third world regimes bears an uncanny resemblance—almost word for word—to the terms that the old colonialists habitually used during the national liberation struggles to describe what the future independent governments would look like were independence to take place. In the wake of decolonization, the former colonies, for Julliard, have reverted back to their former precolonial state of misery, savagery, and barbarism. In fact, the pre- and post-independence third world seems to elicit the same imperialist shibboleths; the rhetoric of "human rights," whether from the mouth of Jimmy Carter in the United States or Jacques Julliard in France, bore an uncanny resemblance to tired old songs about the moral mission of colonialism, the old imperial myths of uninhabited lands (uninhabited, at least, by speaking, articulate beings) awaiting the salutary arrival of the West. Was Julliard suggesting that colonialism was better for colonized people than independence? If so, Sitbon says, he'll have to try and look up the OAS guy who

---

was one of the earliest signals of the rupture of many French intellectuals with Maoism. More recently, Julliard has been an enthusiastic supporter of the Gulf War, Maastricht, and the Juppé plan that provoked the strikes of November–December 1995.

32. Julliard, "Le tiers monde et la gauche," 38.

used to beat him up in the Latin Quarter in the early 1960s to congratulate him on his clairvoyance.[33]

It was Pascal Bruckner's *Le sanglot de l'homme blanc* that provided a kind of text book of anti-third-worldism. Turning to psychology, Bruckner excavated what he saw as European guilt and abjection in the face of the suffering world poor, a set of misplaced affects and responses he sums up succinctly as "the imbecilic masochism of third-worldism." Europeans should throw off the shackles of their guilt complex and self-hatred, he counsels, and return to both a fortified self and a fortified Europe of values: "Europe is our destiny, our lot. More than ever, we develop as individuals through the respect of its borders, its traditions, and its territorial integrity."[34] He continues:

> The ridiculous plea of Frantz Fanon was to "go beyond" Europe. . . . It is impossible to "go beyond" democracy. If the peoples of the third world are to become themselves, they must become more Western. . . . [Europe] is the only culture that has been capable of seeing itself through others' eyes (even though its perceptions may be mistaken). Because there has been no doubt about its identity, it has been able to grant a great deal to other cultures.[35]

If Fanon is ridiculous, how much more so must be Fanon's preface-writer, Jean-Paul Sartre, the old third-worldist, ally, and fellow-traveler of students like Bruckner in '68? Sartre's preface to *Les damnés de la terre* in 1961, along with his preface to Nizan's *Aden Arabie* the year before, both published by Maspero, constitute the "manifestos" of third-worldism in France. (Maspero sold over twenty-four thousand copies of *Aden Arabie*.) The frantic ambivalence shown by Bruckner and other ex-*gauchistes* toward Sartre suggests that one of the motivations for the concerted assault on "third-worldism" might well be in part the standard "generational" claim to destroying older intellectual systems in order to install themselves in the empty place, for it was with Sartre, of course, that the whole utopian *élan* of May and post-May had been lived through and shared.

Geographer Yves Lacoste uses history to undo the psychologizing discourse of Bruckner, recalling a prehistory absent from Bruckner's account. The "third-worldism" of the 1960s, he reminds us, arose in part as a critical response to the massive aid campaigns launched by the United

33. See Guy Sitbon, "Le temps des méprises," *Nouvel Observateur,* July 10, 1978; reprinted in Daniel and Burgière, *Le tiers monde et la gauche,* 73–76.

34. Pascal Bruckner, *The Tears of the White Man: Compassion as Contempt* (New York: Free Press, 1986), 156.

35. Bruckner, *Tears of the White Man,* 142–43 (translation modified).

States at the end of World War II to "underdeveloped"—a term invented by those aid campaigns—countries it saw as in danger of becoming communist after having achieved independence.[36] Aid campaigns to poor countries were one of the direct consequences of the Cold War that began in 1947. Third-worldist discourse, far from being masochistic or self-hating in its attention to the unevenness and disequilibrium between rich and poor nations, was an aggressive new way of accusing the capitalist system—multinational firms, aid programs from the United States or Western Europe—the whole neo-imperialist apparatus, culminating in Vietnam. Third-worldists did not feel "personally" responsible for third-world misery as Bruckner asserts; rather, they were actively pointing a finger at those—the military, state leaders, big business—who they thought indeed were responsible.

The arguments made by anti-third-worldists Jean-Pierre Le Dantec and Kouchner are substantively indistinguishable from Julliard's. But they are of rhetorical interest, since both adopt the genre of "generational," collective autobiographies to condemn the illusions of what Kouchner calls "our third-worldist generation,"[37] to castigate that moment when, according to Le Dantec, "we believed naively. . . ." "we were blinded . . ." and "we invented the third world"[38] (!) Theirs is the chorus of the formerly blind who now can see the real as horror, those who have shed the dream or delusion in the harsh light of reality. It is, of course, difficult to imagine how a new authority can be founded on a former blindness—why should anyone trust the present judgment of someone susceptible to being so inordinately duped in the past? Guy Hocquenghem, activist during '68 and gay theorist, offered the first and the best analysis of what he rightly saw to be the stylistic or ritualistic dimension to the conversion narratives and chronicles of disenchantment then springing up in clusters among his former comrades—those who, beginning in the mid-1970s, rushed to sell at a high price the confession of their errors. While pretending to be the man who has seen the horrors of the politics of his century and courageously renounced his illusions, the convert is in fact participating in a rite or ceremony marking his own social reaggregation. The "lessons of history," the content of the ideas expressed, Hocquenghem points out, are alibis for what is in fact an initiation. Thus, the gesturing toward self-criticism (a Maoist genre revisited) and self-flagellation is inevitably combined with a heavy dose of self-

36. See Lacoste, *Contre les anti-tiers-mondistes et contre certains tiers-mondistes*, 25–28.

37. Bernard Kouchner, "Les bons et les mauvais morts," *Nouvel Observateur*, July 3, 1978; reprinted in Daniel and Burgière, *Le tiers monde et la gauche*, 44–51.

38. Jean-Pierre Le Dantec, "Une barbarie peut en cacher une autre," *Nouvel Observateur*, July 22, 1978; reprinted in Daniel and Burgière, *Le tiers monde et la gauche*, 40–44.

congratulation ("We invented the third world!"—Le Dantec; "We discovered the third world!"—Kouchner). The point of departure must be ceaselessly recalled in order to deny it, for it is the heroism of the point of departure that will guarantee a non-mediocre—even perhaps starring—role in the post-*gauchiste* world. Self-criticism becomes the best kind of advertisement for oneself. And the "we" that makes of the conversion trajectory an inevitable, collective fate makes this renegade, supposedly "dissident," show of free thought into a foreclosure of anyone else's deviation from the narrative, rendering him or her not much more than the remnant of some prehistoric age, still, as it were, "blind." It eliminates the experience of all those individuals, to take just one example, for whom the difficulty and pain of post-May were lived not as a conversion, but rather as a displacement or a sequencing of displacements necessitated by the inertia of the real: those who parted with militancy without either disowning or repudiating it. And it of course eliminates those who remained, in whatever fashion, militants. As Jean-François Vilar remarked already in 1978, when the first wave of commemorations were getting underway, "those for whom May was neither a divine surprise nor an extreme menace but simply a stage in a long struggle are not invited to the commemorations."[39]

It is the horror of being ineluctably caught up himself, against his will, into the generational "we" of the grave-diggers and *poseurs* that fuels Hocquenghem's 1985 assault on some of his former comrades, *Lettre ouverte à ceux qui sont passés du col Mao au Rotary* (An Open Letter to Those Who Traded in Their Mao Collars to Become Rotarians):

> "Generation"—for years I swore to myself not to pronounce that word; I find it, instinctively, repugnant. I do not like the idea of belonging to that coagulated block of deceptions and cronyisms, something that only comes to be realized and felt as such at the moment of the massive betrayal of maturity. One only becomes a generation after one has retracted, like a snail into its shell or the confessed prisoner into his cell; the failure of a dream, the strata of rancor and bitterness, the undissolved remainder of a former uprising is called a "generation." Those who, today, are going from their delayed thirties to their precocious fifties are the sediment, the bitter salt of disillusion.[40]

Hocquenghem must adopt the word "generation" because this is what his former comrades have in fact become now in the mid-1980s—not,

---

39. Jean-François Vilar, "Le temps des fossoyeurs," *Rouge*, May 11, 1978, 10.
40. Guy Hocquenghem, *Lettre ouverte à ceux qui sont passés du col Mao au Rotary* (Paris: Albin Michel, 1986), 15–16.

that is, in their contestation during the 1960s, but only afterward, in their joint *effacement* of a contestatory dimension, their erasure of any difference between ideologies, and their telling of that particular story. Becoming a "generation" is part and parcel of the act of renunciation and the act of retrospective narration: creating oneself as the star of one's own story. Hocquenghem points out that by simply switching a few letters, the word "generation" becomes "rénégation," something that for him is less a question of facts or ideas, than a question of form, of *ethos*. Already by the late 1970s, the disillusionment of post-May had, in other words, with the appearance (or fabrication) of the "lost generation," become a literary genre, with all its requisite figures and rhetorical tropes. The post-May conversion narrative as form is but an extreme version of the retrospective bourgeois narration of the nineteenth-century novel described by Sartre. A narrator looks back from a great distance on the turbulent events of his youth. "There was difficulty to be sure, but this difficulty ended long ago . . . the adventure was a brief disturbance that is over with. It is told from the viewpoint of experience and wisdom; it is listened to from the viewpoint of order."[41] Neither the author—Sartre's example is Maupassant—nor the reader of these novels is running any risks. At the end of the century the event is past, catalogued, understood, and recounted by a stabilized bourgeoisie who have lived through 1848 and the Commune and who are confident, like the ex-*gauchistes* of the 1980s, (writing, it must be said, from a much briefer chronological distance than Sartre's narrators!) that "nothing else will happen." Hocquenghem's newly formed "generation" is made up of the men who have helped each other spin their disillusionment into gold, who have become newspaper directors, champions of nuclear power, recent capitalists, "professional ideologues of realism," and "supporters of what exists." Hocquenghem offers their composite portrait: "He has Glucksmann's nose, July's cigar, Coluche's round glasses, Bizot's long hair, Debray's moustache, BHL's open shirt, and Kouchner's voice."[42] A single corporate body, whose physical characteristics have assumed a certain grotesque quality by way of ubiquitous media exposure. It was the left, he points out, and not the right, that was responsible for a generalized devaluation of utopia. In their eagerness to not only shed past illusions but to hold the past itself in contempt, he suggests, one can only conclude that it is not errors, illusions or mystifications they revile but rather the desire for radical systemic change.

41. Jean-Paul Sartre, *What Is Literature?* trans. Bernard Frechtman (New York: Braziller, 1965), 134.

42. Hocquenghem, *Lettre ouverte*, 17.

"Third-worldism" was one name for that desire. Reading the anti-third-worldist arguments disseminated throughout the 1980s, it is difficult to remember the reality at the center of third-worldism, a reality nowhere mentioned by Julliard, Bruckner, or Kouchner: the three thousand tons of bombs dropped every minute on Vietnam by the United States for three years.[43] Were the struggles that rose up against Western aggression in those years an error? Should the French empire have been defended? Bruckner's call for a return to Europe and the values of Europe, in which human rights merge with the West and find asylum there, was quickly echoed by two other ex-*gauchistes* in 1985 books: Alain Finkielkraut's *La défaite de la pensée* and André Glucksmann's *La bêtise*, followed quickly by a third, Michel Henry's 1987 *La barbarie*. Henry's title states succinctly what the world beyond Euro-America had become in these works, an invading force against which it is now the vocation of a small elite group, namely Western intellectuals, to remain vigilant. For Finkielkraut the battle has already been lost: "Barbarism has thus ended up conquering culture," while Glucksmann launches a vigorous argument for the need to rearm Europe in defense of "civilization."[44] The term of "barbarism" favored by this group of writers was used first in this guise by Bernard-Henri Lévy in his 1977 *La barbarie à visage humain*. Its reiteration conjures up the evolutionary anthropology of Gustave Le Bon for whom the "barbarian" constitutes a stage that while not precisely qualified as inhuman, is, nevertheless, distinctly morally underdeveloped. In each of these books, the remedies proposed for the identity in crisis are those that were once proposed for individual nations: Europe must return to itself, to its values, its tradition, its borders, and reunite its essence. All the ethnocentrism of the colonizers returns in an elitism that disqualifies the non-West once again under the guise of a Manichean opposition between barbarism and culture. To the Western intellectual falls the task of safeguarding the ineffable difference between the two, a role not at all incompatible with a construction of "the barbarian" or the inhabitant of any place outside the West as an object of pity or compassion, in need of humanitarian aid from the West.

Of course, one does not have to hearken all the way back to Le Bon for the figure of "the barbarian" as absolute alterity. A much more recent manifestation appears in the figure of insurgent students and workers dur-

43. Statistic taken from the *Washington Post*, cited in *Le Monde*, April 12, 1972.

44. See Alain Finkielkraut, *La défaite de la pensée* (Paris: Gallimard, 1985), 165; and André Glucksmann, *La bêtise* (Paris: Grasset, 1985). Recently the rhetoric of the need for Europe to provide a bastion of civilization against barbary was utilized by Daniel Cohn-Bendit in television debates to justify the bombing of Kosovo.

ing 1968 as characterized by Raymond Aron: "an outburst by barbarians who are unaware of their barbarity."[45]

At work then in the anti-third-worldist discourse of the early 1980s is a three-part transformation. First, by trading in (and trading on) their former expertise in contestation, ex-*gauchistes* are allowed to re-emerge in the imperial guise of the "official dissident-intellectual," a term first used by Jacques Rancière in his analysis of the earliest manifestation of this maneuver, the one performed with great fanfare and success by the self-proclaimed New Philosophers in the mid-1970s. (Their discourse might sound something like this: "We are only individuals, lending our voice to the oppressed, the excluded, we can do nothing but speak for those deprived of speech. We ourselves are a persecuted and censored minority"— this last, despite their privileged access to and complete exploitation of every form of the bourgeois media: journalism, publishing houses, television, radio). Secondly, the colonial or third-world other of the 1960s is refigured and transformed from militant and articulate fighter and thinker to "victim" by a defense of human rights strictly identified as the rights of the victim, the rights of those who do not have the means to argue their rights or to create a political solution to their own problems. The interest awakened by the third world in the West is thus now in inverse proportion to its political force, to its capacity to construct its own future or to have any remote bearing upon our own. The pathos of the victim rivets attention onto the effects of the crisis immediately at hand, blocking any analysis of the processes that led to such a crisis; a rhetoric of emergency reinforces the paralysis of thought. The patient and painstaking work of documenting the historical and political context of the oppressed and of creating the means by which their voices could be heard analyzing their own context and expressing their political aspirations—the narrative labor associated with Maspero and others—that work is now very far in the past. The new figuration of the victim occurs in a regime of pure actuality created by the rhetoric of emergency, an eternal present that not only dispossesses the victim of her own history, but removes her from history itself. In the new politics of emotion, subject and object are described in different, indeed invidious terms, with the objects of the relationship—the victims—bearing distinctive, and distinctively less equal, qualities than the subjects from the West. In fact, to call it a politics of emotion is something of a misnomer. For to what extent can the figure of suffering—the new generic figure of alterity in the 1980s and 1990s appearing nightly on television screens in the West—lead in and of itself to a politics? Are pity and moral indignation political emotions?

45. Aron, *Elusive Revolution,* 4.

At stake then is a third transformation, a change in the relation of French intellectual to third-world "other," one that takes the form of a retreat from politics into ethics. The third-worldism of the early 1960s resulted in a political relation to "the other" to the extent that such engagement—being open to absorbing the ideas and aspirations of the other—was predicated on dis-identifying or breaking with the systems and patterns of allegiance that had once grounded one's identity—with the French state, for example, or with the Communist Party. The new, ethical relation to alterity is grounded instead in a fortification, even a hypertrophy of identity—of the West, its values, of the intellectual as professional spokesperson for the suffering—the suffering who now, within the contemporary regime of the representation of the humanitarian victim, by definition *cannot* speak and can only attain visibility within highly overdetermined logics of esthetics and marketing. The new relation involves quasi-military acts of rescue and the emergency landing of doctors—"commandos in white coats" in the words of Claude Liauzu[46]—into perilous situations. Liauzu's phrase underlines the way in which parachuting doctors were frequently indistinguishable from their colonial *parachutiste* predecessors, the way in which humanitarian pretexts sometimes masked the deceptively colonial character of rescue interventions into third world "hot spots." It is only a short step from reasserting Eurocentric moralism to justifying such neocolonial adventures as the expansion of capital might require—perhaps no step at all,[47] for only a difference of degree and not one of essence separates a military from a humanitarian intervention. The moral imperative used to plead the right to humanitarian interference quickly transmutes that right into an obligation and then, even more quickly, into an obligation that must be given all the force of an armed intervention. By rehabilitating values of "freedom," human rights, and a frantic antistatism, France once again has the right (and the duty) to intervene in Chad, as it did in 1983 with the full support of Kouchner and André Glucksmann.[48] Similarly, Reagan and the United States must be urged, as in a petition signed by Bernard-Henri Lévy along with converted Maoists, Jacques and Claudie Broyelle, in *Le Monde* on March 21,

46. See Claude Liauzu, *L'enjeu tiersmondiste: Débats et combats* (Paris: L'Harmattan, 1988), as well as his "Le tiersmondisme des intellectuels en accusation," *Vingtième Siècle*, no. 12 (Oct.–Dec. 1986): 73–80, for the best summary and critique of the "anti-third-worldism" *matraquage.*

47. This is the thesis of Jean-Pierre Garnier and Roland Lew, elaborated in their essay, "From the Wretched of the Earth to the Defence of the West: An Essay on Left Disenchantment in France," *The Socialist Register* (1984): 299–323.

48. See "Tchad, l'engagement à reculons," in *Libération*, Aug. 12, 1983. *Libé*'s issues in August and September 1983 are filled with headlines ("French *paras* on the Front Lines"; "Handsome as a new *para*" [Beau comme un para nouveau]), and photo-spreads celebrating the return of the French *parachutiste.*

1985, to maintain and increase its aid to the Contras in Nicaragua. Hocquenghem, in his *Lettre ouverte,* focuses much of his scathing attack on his former '68 comrades against what he calls the new "warrior moralism" and militaristic fantasies of the ex-*gauchistes.* The emergence of doctors like Kouchner, prescribing the correct dosage of human rights and bombs, could be ascribed, he suggests, to unresolved masculinity crises left over from post-May. Through the adventures that emergency situations offered, a supplement of rough-hewn, virile masculinity, a new aura, was being added to the physical image of the intellectual. (Again, the physical image of Sartre provides the best contrast.) It was the same intelligentsia, Hocquenghem notes, who rallied around the installation of Cruise missiles in Western Europe in the early 1980s and France's sinking of the Rainbow Warrior in 1985.

PHILOSOPHERS ON TELEVISION

Anti-third-worldism is in one sense just a *reprise* and a continuation of the New Philosopher episode that made such an impact in the mid-1970s on the very composition of the French political landscape. Best known for their radical anti-Marxism and their ushering of the "Gulag" down what Peter Dews has called its rapid degenerative slide from terrible historical reality to pseudoconcept to slogan,[49] the significance of the New Philosophers for us lies in their successful manufacturing of a certain representation of themselves as the emergence, ten years after the event, of the first "true voice of May '68." It is through them that the watchword of '68, namely "equality," is definitively changed to "liberty." Thus, in the words of Michel Le Bris, former editor of *La Cause du Peuple* and subsequently a minor New Philosopher, a new experience of freedom and liberty had been "lived" during May '68, but it could not be "thought" at the same time. Now, a decade later, "consciousness has returned to itself"—an efficient way to dispense with the political ambiguities, disappointments, and developments of the 1970s—and the thought of that freedom can emerge— in the works of none other than the New Philosophers.[50] The "generation," as described by Hocquenghem, the disabused "we" that does not have to specify whom it includes, is born, then, just in time for the tenth

49. See Peter Dews, "The *Nouvelle Philosophie* and Foucault," *Economy and Society* 8, no. 2 (May 1979): 127–71. This essay, along with another by Dews, "The 'New Philosophers' and the End of Leftism," in *Radical Philosophy Reader,* ed. Roy Edgley and Richard Osborne (London: Verso, 1985), 361–84, are the best critical analyses of the "New Philosopher" phenomenon available in English.

50. Michel le Bris, interview in *Génération perdue,* ed. J. Paugham (Paris: Robert Laffont, 1977), 93–94.

anniversary to confiscate the memory of May; it would consolidate itself in time for the twentieth.

In the mid-to-late 1970s, when the New Philosophers began to occupy center stage of the French media-intellectual scene, it was difficult to see that their target for liquidation was actually May and the memory of May. After all, May was not their alleged target, it was rather an item on their resume, although an important one, for it was their past as militants that guaranteed their legitimacy as social analysts and gave them the moral authority they needed to assert their present political pronouncements. Their confessed political errors of May—even if in some cases, notably that of Bernard-Henri Lévy, the errors had first to be invented in order to be confessed[51]—were just the supplement of truth and virtue, as well as a recertification of the "effet de réel" in the present. Their explicit target, in fact, seemed to be much bigger and ambitious than May: the Gulag—"discovered" by the French, with the help of a French translation of Solzhenitsyn, in 1974. Claiming the role of prophets and prosecutors of Marxism, they proceeded to mount a critique of Marxism by way of a semi-hysterical use of the terminological bludgeon "totalitarianism." This analytically shapeless and elastic term was willfully confused in their discourse with the theoretical category of "totality," a concept with a rich philosophical past. For Lukacs, for example, "totality" meant simply that there is a framework of contemporary reality provided by the commodity economy that cannot be relativized, even if it isn't always experienced in exactly the same way by every individual or group at all times. Sartre used the philosophical term of "totality" to refer to the way in which "perceptions, instruments and raw materials were linked up and set in relation to each other by the unifying perspective of a project."[52] By conflating "totality" with "totalitarianism," the New Philosophers were able to assert that any "totalizing" or systemic analysis, or even any vaguely Utopian thought, carries within it congenitally the seeds of the Gulag. And since any tentative social change produces the Gulag, there is nothing better that can possibly be imagined than the way we are right now.

Why did the publication of Solzhenitsyn's book in France take on such a powerful resonance? Before 1974, the Stalinist Camps were not unknown; testimonies from Trotsky, Victor Serge and others were available and read in France.[53] The camps were known, but they had not taken on

51. "The young Bernard-Henri Lévy was a brilliant subject about whom I can testify that he was never either a Marxist or a Maoist." Lecourt, *Les piètres penseurs*, 76.

52. See Fredric Jameson, "On Cultural Studies," in *The Identity in Question*, ed. John Rajchman (New York: Routledge, 1995), 267.

53. See the discussion by Daniel Bensaïd and Alain Krivine of what they call the "Gulag effect" in *Mai si!* (Paris: PEC-La Brèche, 1988), 74–80.

the emblematic status of the Gulag. Why did that which had already been revealed in 1936, and in 1947 when David Rousset denounced the universe of the camps, and again in 1956 at the moment of the Khrushchev report, now acquire the status of a shocking revelation in 1974—a revelation so shocking that a veritable chorus of the formerly blind arose—Glucksmann, Lévy, Le Roy Ladurie—proclaiming their sight miraculously restored by Solzhenitsyn's book? The difference in impact, Solzhenitsyn's champions maintained, was attributable to the difference in genre. Because it was, as its subtitle indicated, "an essay of literary investigation," and not a treatise or a politician's report, Solzhenitsyn's *Gulag Archipelago* could be proclaimed as offering something that abstract statistics and dry analyses could not show: the representation of the individual victim of human suffering. Articles by tormented leftists in *Les Temps Modernes*, wrote Bernard-Henri Lévy in 1978, can't have the same effect on popular political consciousness as the *Gulag Archipelago*, and this, to his mind, was not surprising. Such articles "lack that aspect of myth, of fiction, of the symbolic that makes it possible that Evil, which cannot be thought, can be represented."[54] For the New Philosophers, the figure of the suffering individual could then be mobilized to show the primacy of the ethical or moral dimension over the political, the superiority of insight over cognition, as well as the superior value of aesthetic modes of representation over the scientism or rationality of the social sciences. It was that blanket of cold rationality—all the facts and figures about the camps, all the information that existed before Solzhenitsyn—that had in fact helped to stifle the cries of the victims. The figure of individual suffering, baptized "the pleb" in the writings of André Glucksmann, would quickly evolve in the 1980s into the figure of the starving victim in the discourse of human rights.

Still, the superiority, for their purposes, of the aesthetics of fiction over the factual treatise, does not explain why the group of disaffected intellectuals that came to be known as the New Philosophers needed Solzhenitsyn at the moment that they did, why totalitarianism had to be denounced at that moment by people who had hardly given it a thought up until then. After all, the translation of the *Gulag Archipelago* into other languages and national situations—the United States, Germany, Italy—in no way unleashed the kind of repercussions and media outpouring that occurred in France. The answer, as I've already suggested, lies in the need to put an end to the memory of May '68, the need to make of all those political discussions and actions the expression of an immense, collective illusion, relegated definitively to a long-ago past.

54. Bernard-Henri Lévy, cited in Paugham, *Génération perdue*, 176.

The fortuitous "fit" between the New Philosophers' rhetoric of sound bite urgency, their casting of themselves as persecuted or romantic "beau tenebreux" dissident personalities, and the media demands of condensation and spectacularization did not go unnoticed at the time. (A joke circulating in Paris in the mid-1970s maintained that the only criterion for being a New Philosopher was looking good on television.) The ecstatic media showcasing of early pronouncements by the New Philosophers—themselves increasingly well-ensconced as individuals at the head of various radio and publishing organs—tended to frame the form taken by any critiques of their discourse and recuperate these into the serialized spectacle of the 1970s, the one entitled "the French intellectuals' trial of Marxism." Thus the authors of an early critique, *Contre la nouvelle philosophie*, which attempted, mistakenly, to refute the New Philosophers at the level of ideas, found themselves swept up into the spectacle immediately, appearing before they knew it as guests on *Apostrophes*, debating on the air and inadvertently helping the "New Philosophy" attain a kind of substance or legitimacy as a school of thought.[55] (*Apostrophes*, where the careers of so many future "media intellectuals" were launched, had its first broadcast in January 1975). Gilles Deleuze reluctantly but vigorously entered the fray, pronouncing the thought content of the New Philosophers to be, in a word, "nulle"—an empty content or "travail de cochon" structured on gross and meaningless binaries (law/rebellion, power/dissidence, good/evil) with whose vacuity it was impossible to engage. The content, in any case, he argued, was unimportant; it was not that which was being staged. The only object of their discourse was the assertion of a megalomaniacally self-important subject of enunciation, the disabused "we," a collective subject founded first and foremost on a repudiation of May '68:

> the theme that was already present in their first books: the hatred of '68. It was about who could best spit on '68. It is in function of that hatred that they constructed their subject of enunciation: "We, as those who made May'68 (??), we can tell you that it was stupid, and we won't do it again." A rancor against '68, that's all they are selling.[56]

Hatred perhaps, but couldn't the past be put to some use, the hay somehow be spun into gold? Couldn't the heritage of May be assumed and denied at once? The political climate of the mid-1970s offered an array of

55. See Francois Aubral and Xavier Delcourt, *Contre la nouvelle philosophie* (Paris: Gallimard, 1977).

56. Gilles Deleuze, "A propos des nouveaux philosophes et d'un problème plus général," supplement to *Minuit*, 24, May 1977.

possible reasons to shed an *ancien militant* past that had become increasingly cumbersome: the upcoming electoral campaigns of 1977 and 1978, the emergence, in Germany and Italy, of the figure of the "terrorist" with whom one would not want to be confused. Critics like Robert Linhart and Dominique Lecourt were quick to point out the way in which the official ideology of dissidence mounted by the New Philosophers amounted to a "moral rearmament of capitalism" by shifting attention away from the masses of Algerian workers on the outskirts of French cities to the plight of a few well known scientists and intellectuals, the dissidents of Eastern Europe.[57] But in the special issue of *Révoltes Logiques* published to coincide with the tenth anniversary of May, *Les Lauriers de Mai*, Danielle and Jacques Rancière, who had shared with several of the New Philosophers the same political trajectory from Althusser through the Maoism of post-May, offered the most nuanced analysis of the New Philosopher phenomenon. By neither allowing their argument to be determined by the high polemical style of the New Philosophers, nor falling into a denunciatory rhetoric of "betrayal" and "opportunism" like the one wielded with such gusto a few years later by Guy Hocquenghem, these authors turned away from the level of opinionated debate toward an historicizing, dialectical focus on the shifts and turns taken by the Maoist movement and its relation with intellectuals in the crucial years of May's aftermath. They concentrated, in other words, on the conditions of possibility in the immediate French past that allowed something like the New Philosophers and their brand of ethical conservatism to emerge. Their article (as well as the rest of the *Révoltes Logiques* issue on May, and an earlier critique of André Glucksmann by Jacques Rancière) is virtually unique in the writing in France of the period in attempting an intricate and informed history of the recent past, a critical history that while not participating in the posturing and repudiations of the "lost generation," goes a long way toward situating those repudiations.

The Rancières argue that the New Philosophers' invocation of the stage set of world history and their own disillusionment (linked to the "discovery" of the Gulag) is not the motivation for their pronouncements but rather its alibi—an alibi in part for their inability to come to terms with the recent past in France. This past includes not only May but the years that brought the immediate struggles of '68 in France to a conclusion around 1973; after, that is, the 1972 killing by a security guard of Maoist Renault worker Pierre Overney failed to elicit any mass-scale protest on the part of

57. See Robert Linhart, "Western 'dissidence' ideology and the protection of bourgeois order," in *Power and Opposition in Post-revolutionary Societies* (London: Ink Links, 1979), 249–60; Lecourt, *Dissidence ou révolution?*

workers, after the large waves of workers' struggles had faded, and the two organizations of the extreme left had broken up, either by self-dissolution (the *Gauche prolétarienne*) or by changing lines (the Ligue Communiste Révolutionnaire). For the Rancières, the emergence of the New Philosophers amounted to a perverse and distorted *reprise* of the *gauchiste* dream of uniting the voice of the intellectual to the speech of the people; as such, it could only be understood by examining the complex vicissitudes of the relation between intellectuals and the people—the rise and fall of the thematics of equality—that had been at the forefront in May. At the most basic level, the New Philosophers represented intellectuals who, in the old Maoist phrase, had once gotten down off their horses in May to gather the flowers, but who were once more firmly back in the saddle, reclaiming the specificity and prestige of a social category that May had disrupted and put into question. And by restoring to the category of intellectual the prestige and specificity that had been shaken by May, they were resuscitating the particular conception of the social that had authorized it. Claude, one of the Comité d'Action members interviewed by Nicolas Daum in his 1988 book, gives a vivid description of the role of intellectuals during the May-June events. Simply put, they had no role:

> In any case, intellectuals, during May '68, were like everyone else, they got on the moving train, they went down into the streets at the same time as everyone else. After the mass movement they could write all the analyses they wanted, but they had foreseen absolutely nothing, no more than did the CGT or de Gaulle.[58]

Intellectuals, in other words, had no specific place in May, no particular role; they were like everyone else, part of the crowd, the *pègre*—not representing any larger corporate or professional body, not self-designating *as* intellectuals. Like everyone else, they did not represent a concrete social category, but merely an agent at work with other agents, on the street, inscribed in the same project. In fact, it was their very refusal to self-identify as intellectuals that motivated their actions, a point reiterated many years later by Maurice Blanchot:

> When some of us took part in the May '68 movement, we hoped to preserve ourselves from any pretension to singularity, and in a certain way we succeeded in not being considered exceptional, but like everyone else. So much did the force of the anti–authoritarian movement render it easy to forget particularities, and to not allow the young, the old, the unknown, the too well known, to be distinguished the one from the

---

58. Claude, cited in Daum, *Des révolutionnaires dans un village parisien*, 172.

other, as if despite the differences and the incessant controversies, each person recognized himself or herself in the anonymous words written on the walls—words which even if they happened to be elaborated in common, were never, in the end, proclaimed to be the words of an author, being everyone's and for everyone, in all of their contradictory formulations. But this, of course, was an exception. . . .[59]

And, indeed, it was an exception; during the three or four years that followed May, *gauchiste* militants operated in a very different context, one defined equally by the waning of hopes for mass-level combativity in the factories and a severe state crackdown on political activity under Pompidou and Marcellin. (In the fall of 1970, more than sixty militants from the ex-GP alone were in prison). These were years, in other words, of political failures and the emergence of new internal contradictions and a new hardening of attitude within militant action. The need to go underground, for example, after political groups had been outlawed, helped cause the return of something like the political professional; authoritarian, or at least hierarchical structures were reintroduced into militant organizations that had resisted these up until this point. The rise of the professional militant tended to define politics once again as a separate, specialized sphere—a definition shared by both bourgeois democracies and Leninist parties. Thus, one symptom of the recomposition of power in militant organizations was a growing separation between one set of truths or body of knowledge, those that people who have responsibilities within the organization have access to and that are kept a secret between them, and another set of truths, for "the others." It was in this embattled context that an opportunity began to emerge for intellectuals to reassume a specific and autonomous role by lending their prestige or notoriety *as* intellectuals to protect and further various militant causes—causes that included organizing against police repression, for example (the *Secours rouge*), or for popular justice tribunals, publicizing the cause of militants on trial, supporting immigrants or investigating prison conditions—a range of militant activities whose scale and persistence necessitated the introduction of a feature entitled "Agitations" in the daily *Le Monde*. (It ran until 1973.) The best known instance of this, of course, was the assumption by Sartre of the editorship of *La Cause du Peuple*, after its editors, Jean-Pierre Le Dantec and Michel Le Bris, were arrested; charged with crimes against the state and incitement to theft, arson and murder; and sentenced to prison. Similarly, Simone de Beauvoir became titular editor of *L'Idiot International* as well, in order to protect its diffusion. The goal here for the intellectual

---

59. Maurice Blanchot, *Les intellectuels en question* (Paris: fourbis, 1996), 60.

was not the older model of "speaking for" the people, but rather simply that of assuring, by protecting revolutionary journalism targeted for censorship and seizure by Marcellin, the access to expression of multiple and varied voices of exploited communities, the "popular voice." This was the voice that, for Sartre, writing about his relationship to the Maoists and *La Cause du Peuple* in 1972, "the bourgeois class could not hear. It tolerated that revisionaries speak *to it* about the masses, but not that the masses *speak about themselves* without caring whether or not they are heard."[60] Sometimes the mobilization of what Jean Chesnaux called "intellectuels de service" amounted to a purely iconic brokering of their prestige by professional militants who did not bother to involve those whose names were being used in the preparation of a given activity, nor inform them of what was at stake.[61] But ascertaining the political value of various fronts or struggles is not, for the Rancières five years later, of primary interest. Their focus is rather on the *role* of the "intellectuel de service," a role that by giving back autonomy and specificity to the intellectual in militant struggle ironically opened the door to the intellectual's resuming his traditional pre-May status. It was through this open doorway that the New Philosophers would come crowding after 1975: the intellectual or philosopher reborn as unified subject (a false collective actually, the generational "we" as comprised of individual "I"s), endowed with authority—in fact, endowed with even more authority than they once could have claimed: the authority of being the makers of history and seismologists of the future.

If the New Philosophers embodied the restoration of the intellectual to his pre-May position as champion of freedom against domination, it was

60. Jean-Paul Sartre, introduction to Manceaux, *Les Maos en France*, 10.

61. Jean Chesnaux, "Gadgets éphémères, slogans oubliés, 'militants' effrontés," mimeographed text from 1973, "exclusively destined for interior circulation within the left movement." Thus in May 1971, for example, an African militant from the *Gauche prolétarienne* was threatened with deportation; intellectuals were mobilized to defend him by occupying an immigration office, only to learn later that the militant had been "punished" for betraying the GP and purged; no explanation was offered to those who had opposed his deportation and whose presence had gained the GP three lines in *Le Monde* under the rubric, "Agitations." In late 1971 and early 1972, a group of Parisian intellectuals including Chesnaux and Jean-Pierre Faye mobilized to support Maoist struggles against work-related accidents in the ship-building yards of Dunkerque. (See Jean-Pierre Faye et le groupe d'information sur la répression, *Luttes de classes à Dunkerque* (Paris: Galilée, 1973). They made three trips to the site without being able to determine whether or not a mass level of local workers' struggle existed behind the Maoists "out in front." For Chesnaux, at least, for whom the Maoists had once proved a real sensitivity in their relations with the masses, a revolutionary creativity and a talent for locating new arenas for struggle, a certain bitterness began to set in regarding these new forms of "populist elitism," the gadgets and secrecies resorted to by increasingly "professionalized" militants. Like many militants at this moment, Chesnaux would gravitate toward what the Maoists too easily called "secondary" struggles—women, regional movements, the Larzac—movements, which in fact had a much greater popular base.

with several important modifications. Whereas an older humanist "Sartrian" intellectual assumed a universal voice to "speak for the people," he or she did so acknowledging (and agonizing over) the contradictions between the aspirations of intellectuals and those of different popular movements. Domination, in the pre-May analysis, was conceived of in class terms. The pre-May Sartrian intellectual was "inassimilable everywhere," torn by perpetual contradictions and dissensions, constrained to live on the margins of the disfavored classes without ever being able to join them. "It isn't by saying that I'm no longer petit-bourgeois," wrote Sartre in 1965,

> that the intellectual can join with workers. But rather, on the contrary, by thinking: I am petit-bourgeois; if in order to try and resolve *my* contradiction, I have gone over to the side of the working class and the peasants, I have not for all that ceased being petit-bourgeois. Simply, by criticizing myself and by becoming more and more radicalized, I can refuse, inch by inch—without it interesting anyone else but myself— my petit-bourgeois conditioning.[62]

The New Philosopher, on the other hand, by virtue of having once "gotten off the horse" and united with the people in revolt, claimed to have overcome all those contradictions in a harmonious and vaguely spiritual unity or oneness with the popular masses, sharing with them the place of "nonpower" in a world where domination is no longer that of class against class, but rather that of a world now riven into stark ethical polarities: power and resistance, the state and civil society, good and evil. His past militancy also conferred upon him the function of "incarnating the real" in a way that the old humanist Sartrian-style intellectual never aspired to. Peter Dews has best showed the way in which the New Philosophers, in their battle with a certain kind of Marxism, used a conveniently vague Foucauldian vocabulary of power "with its abandonment of class analysis in favor of the vision of a complex of forces that continually disaggregate and coalesce."[63] If power is a kind of homogenous current, circulating indiscriminately through the social body, then it is never a question of whose power or for what purpose, as Dews points out, since the "purpose" of power can now only be its own expansion. The extension of the concept of power to all social relations makes it void of any political content. "The apparently radical shift entailed by the discovery that, since relations of power are everywhere, 'everything is political,' was swiftly followed by the discovery that the revolution may no longer be desirable, and that we

62. Jean-Paul Sartre, *Plaidoyer pour les intellectuels*, in *Situations VIII*, 421.
63. Dews, "Nouvelle Philosophie and Foucault," 165.

are consequently 'living the end of politics.' "[64] Strategists of ideological revolution like André Glucksmann, author of the 1968 text, *Stratégie de la révolution*, are transformed into theorists of spiritual revolution, and May becomes proleptically the founding moment of that genealogy. It becomes, in other words, a moment of individual, spiritual transformation, at the origin, now, of the turn to the ethical in French thought that is still with us today.

While none of the New Philosophers' texts has endured as a philosophical work, it was probably Glucksmann's 1975 *La cuisinière et le mangeur des hommes* that laid the groundwork for such a spiritual transformation by introducing a new "legend of the people" with whom the intellectual could effectively and mystically unite.[65] The all-suffering "pleb" in the writings of Glucksmann, was powerful by virtue of his political powerlessness, his dramatic weakness, his resistance that, in its hopelessness, acquires an aura of spiritualism if not divine grace. In fact, it was his inability to produce his own political structures or organizations—something that would have inevitably compromised him in the entanglements of "power"—that guaranteed the unsullied, natural purity of his innocent will to resist. Like "the proletariat" for the Marxist intellectual, the "pleb" offered a legend of the people who would "guarantee the rigor of our discourse and our action";[66] the intellectual, that is, could still be authorized in his discourse by "those below." But by authorizing his discourse with the suffering of the far-away inmate of the Russian Gulag, Glucksmann had become the voice of those who will never contradict him, the voice of those destined (and praised) for remaining, precisely, forever without a voice. For the pleb as the pure essence of rebellion is neutralized as soon as he sets himself a positive goal, as soon as he enters into the ambiguities of political action. In Rancière's analysis, Glucksmann had accomplished a discourse constructed on the silence of the masses, on their plaintive and pathetic cry. Pathos, as Kenneth Burke reminds us, increases in direct proportion to the perceived inarticulateness or muteness of the victim. As such, Glucksmann's authority is founded on nothing more than the lone voice of the masses' interpreter.

The "trial of Marxism" and the discourse on the Gulag thus served many purposes, the first and foremost of which was to effect the conversion of certain *gauchistes* and allow them to acquire a prominent role in the new post–May scene of intellectual power. The references to dissidents in

64. Dews, "Nouvelle Philosophie and Foucault," 166.

65. See André Glucksmann, *La cuisinière et le mangeur des hommes. Essai sur les rapports entre l'Etat, le marxisme, et les camps de concentration* (Paris: Seuil, 1975). Twenty thousand copies of this book were sold the year it came out.

66. Jacques Rancière, "La bergère au goulag," *Révoltes Logiques* 1 (winter 1975): 108.

the Eastern bloc serve primarily to settle accounts with their own past. What is more, their claim to occupy the powerless place of "dissidence," unaligned with political parties and situated transcendentally outside of the state, allowed them to deny the very real power and privilege they had already begun to wield in their positions within the communications industry. But it also saved them from having to confront the frustrations, disappointments, and growing contradictions they had encountered in their own militant experience in the aftermath of May: contradictions between the people as imagined and the people as encountered, contradictions between militant hierarchy and the dynamics of democratic contestation. It was these disillusions, the Rancières suggest, far more than a tardy awakening to the horrors of Marxism, that are at the heart of Glucksmann's reading of Solzhenitsyn. Speaking for the silent pleb in a far-away Russian camp was certainly easier than all of the difficulties surrounding representation that militants had encountered negotiating a conjuncture between student struggles and popular struggles; the figure of the "pleb," as Rancière points out, by signifying the negativity or refusal that each of us carries within him or herself, enables "a liquidation by simple denial of the object and aspirations of struggles as well as all the problems encountered: in the place of a reflection on the will to suppress the rigidity of social places, appears a critique of the Marxist critique of the division of labor."[67] By way of the blank page that is the "pleb," the New Philosopher simply suppresses the divisions that present an obstacle to his own mastery, arriving ultimately at the conclusion that the division of labor—with all of its hierarchies and its built-in limitations of peoples' capacities—is a good thing.

The price paid for acquiring their new role as the incarnation of a (newly spiritualized) May was of course the history of the May movement itself. For one clear effect of the New Philosopher phenomenon was to delay any pursuit or realization of concrete investigations into the movement:

> To show socialist revolution as an idea put into the heads of workers by master-thinkers intent on universal domination is perhaps the best way to no longer question oneself about the content of popular movements, their roots and their ideals, nor the history of the grass-roots of revolutionary movements, nor the illusions and disillusions formed in the meeting between revolutionary intellectuals and popular struggles. Perhaps what is at stake in the *gauchiste* critique of Marxism is much less the question of oppression in the east or the menace of Marxist power

67. Danielle and Jacques Rancière, "La légende des philosophes," 24.

here than it is the liquidation—in the juridical sense—of the history of
May and post May.[68]

By liquidating that history, the ten years separating May from its re-
writing evaporate, leaving little behind but the revisionist refashioning
of May as a spiritual/cultural transformation—one whose good-natured-
ness and elastic plurality can still be affirmed when necessary and molded
to whatever purpose it might serve in the years to come.

From antitotalitarian to neolibertarian to neoliberal: the politics remain consistent from the first emergence of the New Philosophers
in the 1970s to their *reprise* in the 1980s: verbal support for voiceless
"marginals" accompanied by a deep commitment to bourgeois liberalism. And while none of their individual works has endured, the rhetorical tone they perfected—ranging from indignation bordering on hysteria
to a muted mystical inflection—continues to dominate the proclamations
and assertions of media intellectuals in France today. Where the New
Philosophers in their first guise labored to counteract and ultimately re-
place the figure of the worker with the all-suffering and silent pleb, the
anti-third-worldists of the 1980s—many of the same people—take on the
figure of the colonial other, modifying its features into that of the adopt-
able child, the people-object, in need of emergency rescue. A whole new
imaginary of the third world comes into play as the painstaking work
of re-establishing their moral credentials after '68 reaches fruition for
many reformed *gauchistes*. But the new third world imaginary is not, as
I have suggested, completely new, but rather a *reprise:* the discovery of
humanitarian adventure and ambulance-politics remobilizes neoromantic
colonialist tropes, the old themes of departure and leaving gray Europe
behind. Rescue operations in extreme situations—floods and famines—
offer the only "pure" choice, one untainted by politics, as well as the only
"pure" victim. Yet even at the time some critics noticed that denunciations
of third -world totalitarianism on the part of the media intelligentsia were
almost invariably directed against left-wing regimes; Pinochet's Chili and
Reagan's attack on Grenada, for example, elicited no calls for emergency
interventions.

When Hocquenghem wrote his pamphlet against the ex-Maoists who
had rallied to power in 1985, he was one of just a few virulent voices of
critique in an ambiance of overwhelming, media-sponsored intellectual

68. Ibid., 22.

consensus. In the interview he contributed to Elisabeth Salvaresi's collection only two years later, the possibility for the kind of critique he had mounted in his book, he maintained, had largely disappeared :

> It all changed. When I wrote that book, there was a debate at the level of ideas. The people who had decided to renounce the sentimental *gauchisme* and utopias of their youth thought themselves obliged to legitimate their change. That's why I could write the book: because editorials, articles, writings existed by those people, the Bizots, the Julys, the Kouchners . . . claiming, for example, to be against the revolts in the third world. There was still a quarrel, and their repudiation took an ideological form, that of a veritable crusade that had lasted since 1977, the era of the New Philosophers, until 1984. Since then there is no longer any debate at all. . . . They feel stronger—and they are— and then, they no longer have any enemies. In the end this makes for a kind of ideological calm. . . . Not that they have revised their militaristic, pro-business ideas. But simply that they no longer feel the need to militate with the same energy for those ideas. . . .[69]

Hocquenghem is describing a situation where ideas and the power to express them have become coterminous, where the doxa—the relatively systematic set of expressions, words, frameworks, and images that set the limits for what is in fact thinkable and sayable—on May are now firmly in place. The attitude of critique or its very possibility—the soul of '68— has at this moment been lost. The enthusiastic conversion by some ex-*gauchistes* to the values of the market has been successfully disguised as a "cultural" or "spiritual" revolution, and May, it seems, can be renarrated now as the founding moment of this trajectory. By 1988, in "Le Procès de Mai," Kouchner no longer needs to acknowledge—let alone combat or take a distance from—the third-worldism of his past and that of many others. He can simply construct the history as if it never happened.

69. Hocquenghem, cited in Salvaresi, *Mai en héritage*, 23–24.

CONSENSUS AND ITS UNDOING

As the twentieth anniversary of May '68 neared, the dwindling list of witnesses to just a few authorized spokesmen, the corrosion of forgetting, and the disinformation at work in representations like "Le procès de Mai" had made May into something of a cipher. Disembodied, increasingly vague in it contours and plural, even inchoate in its aims, it was thus more available to treatment as a purely discursive phenomenon: a set of ideas rather than a political event, a disembodied spirit or ethos rather than an alternative social form. But if it was a cipher, it was still a *necessary* cipher. As the major reference point in recent French collective memory, May's fluctuating role in any narrative of postwar French history called for it to be anchored once and for all in a relationship of genetic continuity to the present and to the political exigencies of the hour. In the late 1970s, ex-*gauchistes,* many of them former Maoists, had advanced an image of May as the point of origin of a purely spiritual or "cultural" revolution—a "cultural revolution" ideologically very distant from the Cultural Revolution in China that had once filled their thoughts. Building on that interpretation, May now had to be proleptically refashioned into the harbinger of the 1980s—a present characterized by the return to the "individual," the triumph of market democracies, and an attendant logic linking democracy necessarily *to* the market, and the defense of human rights.

Thus, Gilles Lipovetsky, one of the group of new "new philosophers" who emerged in time for the twentieth anniversary, to propose a somewhat refined version of the moral reading advanced by the ex-*gauchistes,* argued that "under the sign of revolution, 'the 68 spirit' only pursued the weighty tendency of the privatization of existences." He continues: "Not only is the spirit of May individualist, but it contributed in its manner . . . to accelerating the arrival of contemporary narcissistic individualism, largely indifferent to grand social ends and mass combats."[1] May, in other words, contributed to creating a time-less and eternal era where even the *idea* of discontinuity and historical change has been evacuated, with the sole exception of the discontinuity that distinguishes this now indefinite present of the individual from the now definitively archaic past that once allowed the possibility of discontinuity and historical change and even knew instances of such changes. Completely deterritorialized, May becomes one with a stage of capitalism that denies any succeeding historical stages. By giving birth to a smooth and fractureless postmodernity, the '68 generation had, in effect, made themselves into the last generation.

Actors or agents pursue; can a "spirit" pursue? In fact, no—spirit manifests itself, shows itself, and because spirit shows itself, the course it follows is predetermined. May is no longer the affair of actors making choices or of people speaking in particular ways in particular settings, but rather the affair of an ethereal "spirit" given the expansive power to extend like some uncircumscribed but necessary magma from the 1960s to the 1980s, uniting the two eras into one continuous narrative of progress in the long march of democratic individualism. To make something called the "spirit of May" the protagonist of the narrative is to first attribute to May, without any clear justification, certain social "effects" of the present, and then to make those effects into May's essence, effectively recuperating that essence. Far from constituting a rupture, May, in this view, becomes "a moment of adaptation in the modernity of a slumbering capitalism, a moment of self-regulation."[2] May becomes capitalism's spring cleaning.

Only a few commentators remarked on the fantastic genealogy and peculiar theory of history that was proposed in a view of May as promoter of contemporary individualism, as actively contributing to the privatization of existences. At its most basic level, this was a genealogy in which, as Jean-Franklin Narot suggested, mere temporal succession has taken the place of causal historical relations. What comes before is the cause; what comes after is the effect or the product: the characteristics of the 1980s are *in* '68, because '68 came chronologically before so it must have engendered them.[3] At work is a philosophy of history according to which the past exists only to better justify and magnify the present.

Despite, or perhaps because of, this distorted causality, the Lipovetskian view of May achieved a virtual consensus in the 1980s—its traces are still with us today in contemporary suggestions that Internet tech-

1. Gilles Lipovetsky, "'Changer la vie' ou l'irruption de l'individualisme transpolitique," *Pouvoirs* 39 (1986): 99, 98.
2. The phrase is François Dosse's. See his "Mai 68, mai 88: les ruses de la raison," *Espaces Temps* 39/39, special issue, *Concevoir la Révolution. 89, 68, Confrontations* (1988): 45–49.
3. See Narot, "Mai 68 raconté aux enfants."

nology or the contemporary "communication revolution" are somehow in direct continuity with or "prefigured" by the 1960s. Consensus, in the literal meaning of the term, means an agreement on the evidence, the sensory givens of the situation, but it is precisely the "sensory givens" that are absent from the interpretation advanced in one version or another by Lipovetsky, Alain Minc, Luc Ferry and Alain Renaut in the 1980s.[4] The consensus, in fact, depends on that absence, on the agreement to ignore the sensory givens. During the twentieth anniversary commemorations on television, for example, very little could in fact be *seen* of May; documentary footage of street violence screened in 1978 was not shown on television in 1988. Without visual or auditory evidence, the frontal political strivings of May, the ferocious anti-Gaullism, the general strike of 9 million people, could very well have never occurred. And despite the consensus interpretation's emphasis on May's importance in engendering contemporary individualism, its authors showed not the slightest curiosity about the groups or individuals who had acted in the May uprisings. No attempt was made in their works to ascertain what the actors in May thought, what they wanted to do, what words they used, what meanings they assigned to their own actions. How much easier, indeed, is the philosopher's task of producing the "meaning" of an event when the voices of its actors are absent? Abstract speculation produced at such a vast distance from the speech and practices of May's actors can result only in abstraction in the service of abstraction. The dismal and often dizzying result is a full "hegemony of the word, a circularity of commentary"[5] in the words of historian Jean-Pierre Rioux as he sized up the state of affairs regarding the discourse on May at the end of the 1980s. With the matter or materiality of May erased, arguments circle back on themselves, and the proof of the conciliatory nature of May becomes, as Isabelle Sommier so astutely points out, the consensus that has been reached about *that* interpretation.[6]

If actors succeed, however loosely, in edging back into their own narrative, "the ruse of History" is there to sweep the ground out from under them. The results of your actions were the very opposite of what you intended! Poor imbeciles. You thought you were acting in conflict against capitalism, but through the victory of an anarchist "ruse of History," your efforts were a (if not *the*) key step in accomplishing the peaceful synthesis

4. See Alain Minc's theory of "capitalisme soixantehuitard" in *L'avenir en face* (Paris: Seuil, 1984); Lipovetsky, "Changer la vie," and *L'ère du vide* (Paris: Gallimard, 1983); Ferry and Renaut, *La pensée 68.*

5. Rioux, "A propos des célébrations décennales du mai français," 49–58.

6. See Isabelle Sommier, "Mai 68: Sous les pavés d'une page officielle," *Sociétés Contemporaines* 20 (1994): 63–82.

of all social relations (economic, political, and cultural) under the aegis of the market. If you had not acted at all (like, say, the Norwegians or the Spanish, who had no '68), capitalist modernization would have still assured the results (lifestyle or cultural in nature) we see around us today. Women would still have come to wear slacks instead of skirts, just as they have done in Norway or Spain; French people would still have begun to systematically "tutoyer" each other. But by being so misguided as to have acted to try to undermine or suppress capitalism, you actually hurried it along!

Régis Debray, from an allegedly different ideological position, had already, ten years earlier, at the time of May's tenth anniversary, used the same narrative emplotment whereby everything gets played out behind the actors' backs, off-stage, as it were, where the "ruse of Capital" lumbers along, engineering continuities and repercussions that can only escape the actors' knowledge. In fact, capitalist modernization, as the subject or protagonist of Debray's somewhat derisive narrative, is given all the lines and wields all the plot's power. The ruse of capital uses the aspirations and logic of militants against themselves, producing the exact result unwanted by the actors: opening up France to the American way and to American-style consumption habits. Debray's characterization of May's goals is, interestingly, identical to that of Lipovetsky: "the emancipation of the individual." Successful in that goal, May actually ends up undoing those constraints that were slowing down the extension of commodity logic throughout the social field in France. May, in Debray's words, was the "cradle of a new bourgeois society."[7]

Lipovetsky's version is quite similar:

> A revolution without an historical project. May is a cool uprising without deaths, a revolution without a revolution, a movement of communication as much as a social confrontation. The days of May, on the other side of the violence of the hot evenings, reproduce less the schema of modern revolutions strongly articulated around ideological stakes than they prefigure the postmodern revolution of communication. The originality of May is in its astonishing civility: everywhere discussions take place, graffiti blooms on the walls . . . communication is established in the streets, the amphitheaters, in the neighborhoods and factories, everywhere where it is usually lacking. It was about liberating the individual from the thousands of alienations that weigh daily upon him. . . . A liberation of speech . . . May '68 is already a personalized revolt, a

7. See Régis Debray, *Modeste contribution aux cérémonies officielles du dixième anniversaire* (Paris: Maspero, 1978). Excerpts translated as "A Modest Contribution to the Rites and Ceremonies of the Tenth Anniversary," *New Left Review*, 1st ser., no. 115 (May–June 1979): 46.

revolt against the repressive authority of the State, against the bureaucratic separation and constraints incompatible with the free development and growth of the individual.[8]

It is interesting to note in passing how much the trope of "civility" (here
astonishing civility) or "conciliation"—Kouchner's peaceful conversation
across the barricades—is predicated on the often explicit denial of the
literal deaths that occurred in May–June, not to mention the many suicides
in the years that followed. Though the number of deaths is small by some
standards—seven, by the recent count of one historian—it is striking how
consistently commentators, beginning with Raymond Aron, echoed here
by Lipovetsky, and more recently by Pierre Nora, reiterate the falsehood
that "no one died in '68."[9]

No one died, it appears, and the "individual," that fully formed entity
with knowledges, desires, and beliefs, is "liberated" and engendered by
May to henceforth become the basic unity of evidence. The "individual"
guarantees the absence of ideology: the "I" as supposed bearer of a greater
level of authenticity in its opposition ("the individual against the system"
is Renaut and Ferry's encapsulation of May, identical to that of Lipovetsky
and Debray) to any "we," the latter now rendered inevitably bureaucratic,
ideological, and repressive, a figuration of the State or the Party (and *not*,
incidentally, of the corporation).

Free or lateral "communication"—the word occurs three times in this
brief passage—between individuals merges, for Lipovetsky, with the free
circulation of the market; it is through the dominant trope of "communication" and its cognates (civility, liberation of speech, free exchange)
that the energies of May find themselves harnessed to the market logic
of the 1980s. But what is meant by the liberation of speech for Lipovetsky? Building on a common cliché of May's "verbal delirium"—derived,
primarily, from the graffiti Lipovetsky evokes in this passage—May as a

8. Lipovetsky, *L'ère du vide*, 244–45. Pierre Nora essentially adopts the Lipovetsky interpretation, with a slight spin, in the concluding sections of his *Lieux de mémoire:* "[This was] the true
birth of the 'society of the spectacle,' which it was the express purpose of the 'events' of May to
overthrow." "The Era of Commemoration," 611.

9. Michelle Zancarini-Fournel gives the figure of seven deaths in " 'L'autonomie comme
absolu,' " 139. Lipovetsky again: "Without deaths or traitors . . . May '68 presents itself as a
soft 'revolution.' " Cited in " 'Changer la vie' . . . ," 94; Raymond Aron, writing in 1983: "Alone
among historic days, those of '68 did not spill blood; the French did not kill each other." Cited
in Bernard Pivot and Pierre Boucenne, "15 ans après Mai 68: Qui tient le haut du pavé?" in
Lire 93 (May 1983): 20. Pierre Nora: "After it was over, everyone wondered what had actually
happened in terms of revolutionary action, of history in the Hegelian sense, written in letters of
blood. Not only was there no revolution, but nothing tangible or palpable occurred at all." "The
Era of Commemoration," 611.

festival of ludic self-expression becomes the *frère semblable* to 1980s consumerism. 1980s interpretations of May like Lipovetsky's relied heavily on the graffiti at the expense of any other "texts" or documentary evidence. Reducing the language of May to a few poetic phrases—"It is forbidden to forbid" or "beneath the paving stones, the beach"—considerably facilitates May's assimilation to a 1980s social vision of a society free from archaic conflict and social confrontation.

And yet if new forms of contact and solidarity existed in May between people previously separated, it was not, of course, thanks to the media but rather the result of active destruction of forms of mediation that had kept people up until then in enforced segregation. In other words, if the brief use by militants during May of *reconverted* media at a moment when the usual organs of "vertical" or bourgeois communication—the mainstream press, the state-run television, the official government spokesmen, the whole particular class order incarnated by the state—had been put out of service, if this creative subversion can be rewritten in the 1980s as prefiguring the superior harmony of the interaction of particular egoisms forming a marketplace, then perhaps it is best to return to Sartre's observation that the power of the students lay not in their seizure of speech but rather in their refusal of it. The refusal of speech was just as much a part of May culture as its seizure. After all, it was the refusal to negotiate with the state on the part of insurgents ("no dialogue between *matraqueurs* and *matraqués*"), the refusal of what one tract called "the stinking *seduction* of dialogue,"[10] that accelerated the disarray and terror of the state; negotiation would, after all, have kept conflict within limits tolerated by the system. Repentant former militants, chatting on the commemoration shows twenty years after, in this sense literally volunteered the dialogue with the state that was refused at the time. In a text written just after the events, Sartre developed the theme of the "refusal of speech" by discussing the students' critique of what we used to call in the United States—there is no apt French equivalent—the "relevance" issue. He refers to their impatience with the meta-discursive level of cultural analysis, the piling on of cultural mediations and interpretations—that is, the belief in the ability of culture to provide resolutions: "words that comment upon other words and so on and so forth into infinity."[11] As a functionary in the word trade,

10. Tract dated circa May 20, 1968, signed "Les enragés de Montgeron" and entitled "Le Crachat sur l'Offrande!" The passage reads: "In the stinking *seduction* of the 'dialogue' we recognize the ultimate mask worn by repression-recuperation. Fetid breath beneath a dripping smile—recycled police trickery: the extended hand prolongs the *matraque* while the congealed spectacular culture of yesterday and today asphyxiates how much more surely than tear gas. *SPIT ON THE OFFERING!*" Cited in Schnapp and Vidal-Naquet, *Journal de la commune étudiant*, 580.

11. See Jean-Paul Sartre, "La jeunesse piégée," in *Situations VIII*, 239–61.

a student's refusal to produce "discourse about discourse," amounts to the refusal to speak *as* a student. It is tantamount to going on strike: the blissful silence of the factory when the workers shut down their machines or the hissing and booing of the workers at Billancourt responding to the terms of the Grenelle negotiations. To refuse to speak as students or to express the interests of students ("We had no interest in student affairs")[12] is a necessary part in demanding instead to speak the language of *common* affairs, the language that is the carefully guarded prerogative of professionals. It is a necessary step in tearing politics away from those who have a monopoly on it and who make it their *métier*. It was precisely the refusal to act *as* students, the refusal to demand *"des gommes et des crayons"* ["erasers and pencils"], that incensed Minister of the Interior Raymond Marcellin. Writing in 1969, he recounts undercover information he has obtained on "one of the last meetings of the *lycéen* 'action committees,' [a meeting] organized around four themes. What was the first theme? The reform of the *lycées* or the university? No, the struggle against imperialism."[13] The reaction of professionals like Marcellin—de Gaulle, Pompidou and crew, and their police—to the questioning of the sphere of specialized politics on the part of students and workers did not in any stretch of the term resemble either "astonishing civility," or a quasi-Habermasian moment of transparent communication, or, for that matter, the false universality of liberal humanism. The sphere of communication doesn't open by itself. Opening it to the more or less large number of people who have no access to speech is symbolically, if not physically, violent, and beset with all the violence of the specificity of political action. Students sought far less to "express themselves" than to invent a name that might encompass themselves, along with workers and farmers, as having been excluded from the affairs of government.

As even the most cursory examination of the tracts assembled by Schnapp and Vidal-Naquet makes clear, students and workers in May went about this struggle, using the language of the then-dominant Marxist vulgate: a language that spoke of a social world divided between, on one side, the bourgeoisie, and on the other, the proletariat. The language of May is the language of these tracts, of small publications in often ephemeral journals, of mimeographed texts from all kinds of groups and organizations whose faded print shows the wear of the stencil and whose pathos increases in relation to the number of spelling mistakes, the texts

12. Jean-Marc Bougereau reiterates this statement on the television show "Paris, 24 mai 1968," "Histoire d'un jour" series, prod. Maurice Dugowson (1985) and again on the BBC radio show "Field of Dreams."

13. Raymond Marcellin, *L'ordre public et les groupes révolutionnaires* (Paris: Plon, 1969), 49.

of neighborhood and factory "action committees" that often survived well beyond May—the language of their meetings, of their endless and often confused discussions.

> And so I kept everything, as though it were impossible for me to get rid of that heavy, cumbersome litter that I had accumulated over the years. As if it were vital that I conserve the tracts, posters, journals, brochures, bulletins. . . . And it is. For if I didn't have these scraps of paper, how would I have proof that those years really existed, that they had been really lived by me and by others, by thousands of others and not just by the few more or less repentant, more or less amnesiac "revolutionaries" who, having become media stars during the 1980s, arrogated to themselves the monopoly on representation and on what was said about those years.[14]

In documentary footage shown on television in 1978 but unscreened in 1988, one can hear discussions in the courtyard of the Sorbonne, under enormous portraits of Mao and Guevara, between young and old debating the value of workers' councils; one can hear lycéens demanding not the right to express themselves as "individuals," but to be able to freely organize in the schools in support of fellow students expelled for circulating a text of *Le déserteur* in the high schools.[15] Even commentators sympathetic to the "liberation of speech" interpretation of May, like Michel de Certeau, are forced to admit that such "liberation" took place within the strict confines of a very tight vocabulary: "The 'contesters' were often reproached for expressing themselves with very limited intellectual means. 'Two dozen words': consumer society, repression, contestation, the qualitative, capitalism, and so on. The fact is exact."[16] In fact, it is so true that an embarrassed Daniel Cohn-Bendit appearing on television in the 1980s and forced to comment on footage of his younger self speaking at a meeting the language of '68 is, in his will to distance himself from his earlier incarnation, obliged to invent on the spot a new slogan: "Sous la langue de bois, le désir" (Beneath the stereotyped political discourse, desire).[17] Speaking now in the new *langue de bois* of the "lost generation," he continues: "Our ideas were right, but our discourse was false, it was

---

14. Storti, *Un chagrin politique*, 53.

15. See "Les lycéens ont la parole," a documentary episode of *Dim Dam Dom*, prod. Pierre Zaidline (1968). Is the text in question Boris Vian's anti–Algerian War song, or is it Jean-Louis Hurst [Maurienne]'s "novel" by that title, first published by Minuit in 1960? In either case, both texts had been seized and censored by the government.

16. Michel de Certeau, *The Capture of Speech* (Minneapolis: University of Minnesota Press, 1997), 29–30.

17. Daniel Cohn-Bendit, cited in "Paris, 30 mai 1968," part 2 of the Dugowson documentary.

the *langue de bois.*" In other words, the stereotypical Marxist phrases we spoke were just the manifest content; the latent meaning was desire and individual self-expression, the hidden truth, the hidden meaning of May, waiting to break out. The leftist language of class, what was in fact the speech and vehicle of the movement, must be ignored as something that *blocked* the more authentic May from emerging—the May of soul, individual desire and spirituality. The actual language of the 1960s must be forgotten or denied, because what we really meant to say we could in fact only express later, in the new language of the 1980s.

One advantage of eliminating or failing to consider the dominant language of May is that the door is then open to overt ventriloquism: one can substitute or lend whatever language one pleases to May's actors. The most bizarre exercise in this kind of ventriloquism to emerge during the hypocrisy of the Mitterrand years was Luc Ferry and Alain Renaut's pamphlet, *La pensée 68,* about which one is tempted to paraphrase Mary McCarthy and say that everything about the title is a lie, including the "La." Especially the "La." The "La" implies wrongly that the event had a coherence and a unity and even more wrongly a "thought" corresponding to it. (The name of that thought, incidentally, is "anti-humanism": the book's subtitle, "Essai sur l'anti-humanisme," a more accurate description of the book's contents, would undoubtedly have sold fewer books). Even today, a young person curious about the intellectual foundations of the movement might be tempted by the title or by the lovely bright red Fromanger print on the cover, to select this book. But the authors nowhere elucidate the relation between the book's title and subtitle, or between the political events of 1968 and the intellectual trend called "anti-humanism" (a composite "ideal type" of thought represented by the work of four of what the authors call "philosophistes," Derrida, Lacan, Foucault, and Bourdieu) they are concerned with denouncing. Renaut and Ferry had to ignore a biographical relation of those thinkers to May, for good reason, since, as Dominique Lecourt and others have pointed out, the thinkers chosen by Renaut and Ferry to treat were each left speechless by '68.[18] Derrida, for example, showed the utmost reservation during the events, and Foucault, in Tunisia, was not even present at all for the insurrection.[19]

18. See Lecourt, *Les piètres penseurs,* especially 38–51. Lecourt provides a thorough critique of *La pensée 68,* arguing that "there was never a unity of thought among the groups that unleashed May. . . . Only after the fact, almost twenty years later, thinkers seeking notoriety forged the *fiction* of a unity to better channel and orient toward their philosophical positions the backlash of political thought that began after 1976 . . . there never existed anywhere a '68 thought,' neither before, during or after May."

19. See Michel Foucault, *Dits et Ecrits, 1964–1988,* vol. 4 (Paris: Gallimard, 1994), 78: "During the month of May 1968, as during the period of the War in Algeria, I was not in France: always a little out of step, on the margins."

Pierre Bourdieu, who would go on to be extremely active and central to the organization of intellectuals in support of workers during the November–December 1995 strikes in France, did not, according to Christine Delphy, one of the members of his *équipe de travail* in 1968, show the same level of initiative or political solidarity during May. He did not, in other words, "get on the moving train."[20] Louis Althusser, an anti-humanist thinker inexplicably *not* treated by Renaut and Ferry, was hospitalized during May, and, as Cornelius Castoriadis commented on the question of Lacan, "No one in Paris in the 1960s in his right mind who knew something of the person and his writings, would have dreamed that Lacan could have had anything to do with a social and political movement."[21] Thus, while any number of "thinkers" were active in '68—Mascolo, Sartre, Lefebvre, Chesnaux, Blanchot, Duras, and Faye among them—the "anti-humanist" thinkers were, if anything, left in a kind of disarray by the political events. Lacan, for one, went so far as to comment about the demonstrators that they were lost souls in search of a father or "aspiring toward a master."[22]

Nor is any link established between the writings or thought of these intellectuals and the events of May, beyond the most vague chronological "simultaneity'" (i.e., that these writers wrote during the 1960s). On the basis of this chronological relationship, Ferry and Renaut argue, the writings, like the event, must be considered "symptoms" of a unique phenomenon: the rise of contemporary individualism. Again, the absence of analysis of '68 culture, language, or history is complete. The only militant cited in *La pensée 68*—not surprisingly, Daniel Cohn-Bendit—is quoted in a footnote effectively contradicting the book's argument: "People wanted to blame Marcuse as our mentor: that's a joke. Not one of us had read Marcuse. Some of us read Marx, maybe Bakunin, and among contemporary writers, Althusser, Mao, Guevara and [Henri] Lefebvre. The political militants of the March 22nd group have almost all read Sartre."[23] A reader's confusion could only be heightened by Renaut and Ferry's reluctant refusal to deny a "humanist" aspect to May, though what they mean by "humanist," in this context, seems to be limited to the no-

---

20. See Christine Delphy, "La Révolution sexuelle, c'était un piège pour les femmes," *Libération*, May 21, 1998, 35. Delphy recounts that the Bourdieu *laboratoire* at the center for European sociology at the CNRS was the only one that continued working during May; Bourdieu asked his researchers to remain at their desks photocopying his works to be distributed to the demonstrators.

21. Cornelius Castoriadis, "Les mouvements des années soixante," *Pouvoirs* 39 (1986): 110.

22. See Jacques Lacan, *Séminaire XVII* (Paris: Seuil, 1991), 239: "As revolutionaries, what you are aspiring to is a master."

23. Daniel Cohn-Bendit, *La révolte étudiante*, 70, cited in Luc Ferry and Alain Renaut, *French Philosophy of the Sixties* (Amherst: University of Massachusetts Press, 1990), xviii.

tion of "the individual against 'the system.' "[24] Were the manifestly humanist slogans of May inspired then by their exact philosophical opposite? Among the commentators driven to exasperation by the book, few were as outspoken as Cornelius Castoriadis, for whom '68 was nothing if not an event that put into question precisely the reifying structures underlying the ideas now being labeled, twenty years later, as " '68 thought":

> It is strange to see the work of a group of authors who became fashionable after the *failure* of '68 and the other movements of the period and who played no role in even the most vague "sociological" preparation of the movement, being called " '68 thought" today. Both because their ideas were totally unknown to the participants and because they were diametrically opposed to their implicit and explicit aspirations. . . . Renaut and Ferry are totally nonsensical: for them '68 thought is anti-'68 thought, the thought that built its mass success on the ruins of the '68 movement and in function of its failure.[25]

Given the book's failure to argue any relationship between May and their chosen thinkers, most of the book's reviewers simply made no reference at all to 1968 in their reviews.[26] Thus, a favorable review by François Furet begins by admitting that "the reference to May '68 is not indispensable to its [the book's] intelligence."[27] Reviewers who, continuing to take the title at face value, expected to learn something about May '68, complained angrily about the way in which the events themselves had been dissolved into the authors' fulminations about anti-humanism, and attributed a purely ideological, rather than theoretical, aim to the pamphlet.[28] That is to say, they read it above all as a political polemic. By suggesting an ultimately fallacious amalgam between what Althusser would call two "semi-autonomous" orders of reality, the authors sought to kill two birds with one stone, that is, to bury May and denounce anti-humanism. After a series of exhausting intellectual contortions they arrive back at the old Aronist position: both "phenomena," the event and anti-humanist thought, must be liquidated to clear a place for the liberal

24. Ferry and Renaut, *La pensée 68*, xxi.

25. Castoriadis, "Les mouvements des années soixante," 110, 113–14. Elsewhere, Castoriadis commented, "L. Ferry and A. Renaud got their numbers reversed: their *'68 thought* is in fact *'86 thought*." "L'auto-constituante," *Espaces Temps* 38/39 (1988): 55.

26. See, for example, Raymond Boudon, "Sciences sociales: Des gourous aux journalistes," *Commentaire* 35 (autumn 1986) or Olivier Mongin, "Le statut de l'intellectuel: Fou ou conseiller du prince?" *Cosmopolitiques* 2 (Feb. 1987).

27. See François Furet, "La grande lessive: L'homme retrouvé," *Nouvel Observateur*, June 13–19, 1986, 114–15.

28. See, for example, Gérard Guegan, "Touche pas à Mai 68," *Le Matin*, Dec. 20, 1985, 27; or Marcel Bolle de Balle's review in the *Revue de l'Institut de Sociologie* 3/4 (1985).

philosophy of human rights that, in the eyes of the book's authors, France in the 1960s was wrong, even criminal, to have ignored.

The question of whether May '68 affirmed or put into crisis the structuralist thought of the 1960s was perhaps best put back into perspective by a phrase written on the blackboard of a Sorbonne classroom during May '68, a phrase that Lucien Goldmann was fond of citing: "Structures don't go down into the streets."[29] People—not structures—make history, and beyond that, being for or against structuralism is not what causes hundreds of thousands of people to descend into the streets. Sartre had already dismantled a kind of "political illiteracy," as he called it, similar to the one exemplified by Renaut and Ferry in *La pensée 68*, when he responded to a journalist's analysis of the "thought" of Daniel Cohn-Bendit being a melange of Thomas Carlyle and Friedrich Nietzsche. The "thought" of Cohn-Bendit, taken as a synecdoche for the movement in general, must for Sartre be thought that is the product of an action. The problems thought confronts are those practical, pragmatic, and theoretical questions raised in the immediacy of a specific situation—for example, the problem of what can or should be the role of an activist minority. Despite theories proposed by Lenin, Blanqui, or Rosa Luxemburg, there is no metahistorical solution to the role of an activist minority in an insurrectionary movement, and the movement must think through the problem in its lived situation. What role, asks Sartre, could Carlyle or Nietzsche possibly play in all this?[30]

The notion that a mass movement like May could be subsumed into any one organization, "leader," or, especially, into any one thinker or school of thinkers, continues to produce distorted interpretations and claims within the literature on May. The invisible hand of Marcuse, whose works were unread in France until after May, when they began to sell at a rapid rate, continues to be evoked as managing or directing from afar the events in Paris.[31] Occasionally, such "political illiteracy" is advanced by the thinker himself. Before his death, the Situationist Guy Debord was given to making increasingly megalomaniacal pronouncements about his own role in "causing" the insurrection, speaking, for example of "the grave responsibility that has often been attributed to me for the origins, or even the command, of the May 1968 revolt," and, finally, "admitting to being the one

29. Lucien Goldmann, cited in Elisabeth Roudinesco, *Jacques Lacan* (Paris: Fayard, 1993), 444.

30. See Jean-Paul Sartre, "Les Bastilles de Raymond Aron," in *Situations VIII*, 175–92.

31. The French edition of Marcuse's *One Dimensional Man* was published during May 1968 and sold 350,000 copies in two months; by the end of June, the Drugstore Saint-Germain was selling 500 copies a day. See Patrick Combes, *La littérature et le mouvement de Mai 68. Ecriture, mythes, critique, écrivains, 1968–1981* (Paris: Seghers, 1984).

who chose the time and direction of the attack."[32] Debord's 1967 *Société du spectacle* and the journal he collaborated on, *Internationale Situationniste* (published between 1958 and 1969) undoubtedly helped perform an intellectual task of demolishing and desacralizing of bourgeois consumer society for the elite readership who had access to these texts in the early 1960s. But it was the disturbances of 1968 that made *La société du spectacle* known and read. While a Situationist pamphlet like "De la misère en milieu étudiant" (written not by Debord but by Mustapha Khayati), widely distributed in Strasbourg and beyond in 1966, reached a large readership, other Situationist texts were only read by large numbers of people *after* '68 in an effort to come to terms with or understand what had occurred.

Perhaps the most accurate assessment of the aims of *La pensée 68*'s authors is announced in a blurb on the current edition's back cover: "This book, which was at the center of a big polemic, bears witness to a change in intellectual generations." The "packaging" of the polemic, as Pierre Macherey recently observed, is at one with the book's "thought"; that is, both rely entirely on the transposition of the marketing concept of "generation" and other journalistic techniques into the field of philosophy, such that the new generation emerges fully formed to render the previous one obsolete. Get out so that we can take your place.

Who are the new generation? They "are" nothing but those who are no longer . . . what? Here, the ex-*gauchistes* would have filled in the word "blind," while the moral philosophers might substitute, as Ferry and Renaut and friends did in a subsequent pamphlet, the label "Nietzschean"[33] or, more elaborately, they might come up with a phrase like "We are those who are no longer under the influence of poisonous 'master thinkers.' . . ." By this negative or reactionary self-definition, and by that alone, we are authorized to say "we": a new alliance, a public pact—"our philosophical generation"—is sealed by those who recognize themselves as members of a generation. But to be nothing more than "the new generation," Macherey points out, isn't to express anything much more than the absolute exigency to *not* be something—a resentment disguised as a position. The motivations of such a pronouncement are clearly more ideological than theoretical, in that supposedly fundamental theoretical stakes are being measured according to momentary, passing criteria. These motivations include an accession to philosophical power through forming alliances—"we," the union of "moral" or "ethical" philosophers—alli-

---

32. Guy Debord, cited in Anselm Jappe, *Guy Debord* (Berkeley: University of California Press, 1999), 46, 100.

33. See A. Boyer, A. Comte-Sponville, V. Descombes, L. Ferry, R. Legros, P. Raynaud, A. Renaut, and P. A. Taguieff, *Pourquoi nous ne sommes pas nietzschéens* (Paris: Grasset, 1991).

ances that can be broken as soon as it comes to the moment of actually sharing power. In addition, the "new generation" seeks a relegitimation of philosophy as a discipline against the abusive theoretical procedures of "suspicion" or "deconstruction"—in other words, a contribution to the maintenance of philosophical order that is, as Bernard Lacroix observed, a specific contribution to the maintenance of order itself.[34] Their intention, clearly stated around the concept of "generational conflict" or "rupture," is to restore or relegitimate, in the name of the new 1980s generation, universalist ideals indispensable to the functioning of a democratic republic, ideals characterized as having been abandoned by the older generation, now definitively rendered, in the journalistic or marketplace vocabulary favored by Renaut and Ferry, *"passéiste"* (lost in the past) or *"en désuetude"* (obsolete). And it is here, Macherey notes, that the contradiction in their enterprise becomes the clearest. For the implicitly historicist presuppositions inherent in the notion of "to each generation its own ideas" can hardly be called universalist. If this were so, then thought would then become something that happens without ever being transmitted or communicated, since the necessary rupture between generations would erect an impassible divide. "The history of thought does not, as our journalist professors would have us believe, amount to the succession of philosophical generations."[35]

In Jean-François Vilar's 1993 novel, *Nous cheminons entourés de fantômes aux fronts troués*, the narrator, a press photographer, comes across a photograph of May 1968 that he himself had taken twenty years earlier. It was his first published photo:

A photo of May 68. The courtyard of the Sorbonne, just liberated— or given back, according to some—May 13th. I'm coming back from Denfert. Night is falling. A piano has already been set up. After the demo, friends are wandering around the citadel, dead tired, with that incredulous expression of the victor on their faces. Some of them have gotten together and are sitting on the chapel steps. Helmets and bottles. Fake street urchins and genuine political commissars. We all knew each other, formed, hammered out together at UNEF. We like each other, we detest each other with that inexpiable hatred that links those who

34. See Bernard Lacroix, "À contre-courant: Le parti pris du réalisme," *Pouvoirs* 39 (1986): 117–27.

35. See Macherey, *Histoires de dinosaure*, especially 183–206. A longer version of Macherey's critique, which includes an astute and detailed reading of the philosophical content of their argumentation, entitled "Réflexions d'un dinosaure sur l'anti-anti-humanisme," can be found in a supplement to *Futur antérieur, Le gai renoncement* (Paris: L'Harmattan, 1991), 157–72.

are not building the same identical embryo of the future and necessary revolutionary party. The 'Italians,' the Trots, the Maoists, the anarchists, the spontaneists, the Bordighists, the archeo-situationists, the
Posadists, the ones who are against all tendencies and a few others besides. It's dusk, the moment of grace, the pause between one historic
demo and the next soviet General Assembly. . . .

Marc is in the photo, in the middle of almost all the big mugs of the
era. There he is, almost thin, Lissac glasses, Bodygraph suit. Behind
him, not far away but off to the side, is Jeanne.

She is hard to make out, one would have had to have been there
the moment the photo was taken to identify her with any certainty.
Black bangs, a smoky gaze, her hand covering her mouth (cigarette between her fingers) hiding the bottom of her face (she didn't like the
shape of her mouth). Marc and she had been married for a few months
when May exploded. Her name is not mentioned in the photo caption.
Two years later, as a result of the crises, the suicide attempts, the running away, the encroaching gesticulations, the fastidious depressions, a
habituée of all the psychiatric couches and all the cures, she was committed. . . . To Ville-Evrard. . . .

After May, [Marc] had become, in the Leninist terminology then
prevalent, what was called a "professional revolutionary." Barely
twenty-five years old, he was a Maoist. More precisely: a Maoist-
Stalinist. The people's war faction, new partisans, CGT-Kollabo (the K
was important, it gave that *boche* effect), etc. Frequently Marc had to go
into hiding. When this happened he was sheltered by fellow travelers,
well-known intellectuals, untouchable themselves. . . .

Jeanne was doing badly, like everyone. She used to say, laughing,
"I suffer from communism's delay." Since I saw her infrequently I
could measure how quickly her features were coming undone. I never
thought, as others did, other comrades, that Marc behaved badly with
her. No one behaved well in the days after May.[36]

The itineraries of two lives, roughly sketched out, from the moment of
the May events forward through the difficult aftermath when, it seems,
no one acted well, each person sent back brutally, with the dissolution of
the movement and its forms of collectivity, to his or her own private life,
each attempting to survive isolation and marginalization on the one hand,
illegality on the other. Marc, a recurrent character in Vilar's detective novels, is now the highly successful editor of *Le Soir*, a newspaper originally

---

36. Jean-François Vilar, *Nous cheminons entourés de fantômes aux fronts troués* (Paris: Seuil,
1993), 100–102.

christened *Le Grand Soir* when it began publication shortly after May. At that time, Marc had been a *gauchiste* leader, who, during his brief imprisonment in August 1968, wrote a book with a title the narrator recalls as "something like *Today: The Incendiary Hour.*"[37] In those days, whenever the narrator and Marc exchanged correspondence of any kind—vacation postcards or polemical treatises—they would sign off with "fraternal communist greetings." Marc's political trajectory from the days of communist fraternity to the novel's present in 1989 is nicely summed up elsewhere in the novel when Marc (he was "no longer the street-smart reporter he knew how to be. He had become a power, avid for respectability"[38]) telephones the narrator from the editorial desks high atop the Springer conglomerate building in Berlin. It was this very institution that had been the target of the first violent demonstration in which Marc and the narrator had participated together in February 1968. (The demonstrations against Springer alluded to in the novel actually occurred. The Springer conglomerate, which Karl Dietrich Wolfe, head of the German SDS, once famously called a "money-making instrument of hate," controlled 85 percent of the West German press output in 1968).

The character of Marc is, of course, instantly recognizable to most readers as a thinly veiled pastiche of Serge July, a name, a personality whose contemporary professional success as the editor of *Libération* has facilitated the production of many of the contemporary images or phrases —"a generous but naive idealism," "from revolution to reform," "individualism," "communication" and above all, "generation"—through which '68 has been subsequently re-encoded:

> He had renounced one by one those follies [of May] and several others. Without a complex. Without cynicism. They were to be counted up as the profits and losses of—Marc was very fond of this notion—a "generation." Out of that largely collective foolishness an intelligence of the time could be distilled and delivered. *Le Soir* was the expression of that intelligence or at least its tribunal.[39]

The character of Jeanne, however, has no known "personality" behind her as model and appears throughout the passage as someone struggling to attain representability and failing—becoming representable, "a figure of May," that is, only by chance and only through her progressive defiguration. Already in the shadows and off to the side in the photo, her features half hidden, she is part of a circle of intimacy and camaraderie that existed

37. Ibid., 177.
38. Ibid., 65.
39. Ibid., 178.

then—marriage, friends, a common political formation, a whole alternative form of political sociability whose traces, now, are nearly impossible to find. No one outside that circle knew her or would be able to identify her in the photo whose caption does not record her name. But the circle, the collective organizations or a life lived collectively, has come undone, and where Marc becomes a "figure" in post-May society, Jeanne does not merely continue to live anonymously, she in fact loses ground, her features over time disintegrating through madness, disregard and forgetfulness, her itinerary lost as the group disbands. Prompted by the photo, the narrator phones Marc to inquire after Jeanne and learns that she has indeed, a year earlier, succeeded in taking her own life. Her illness, in her own half-ironic words, is a political one: "I suffer from communism's delay." She suffers from being out of sync with her times, off track, like so many others in the Giscard years of "change without risk"; her death is the death of nobody in particular.

Like the woman factory worker at the center of the images captured in *La reprise du travail aux usines Wonder,* Jeanne may be taken as at once the figure of the undoing of collectivity and of the corrosion that accompanies the forgetting of that collectivity. She represents the anonymous militants of May and those lost in May's aftermath: the suicides, depressions, and despairs of those who became derailed, horrorstricken or dumbfounded by the reversals and recuperations that transpired after May—those who didn't embrace the forward march of modernity, those who were inexorably caught between trying to make something continue that had lost its momentum and trying to reintegrate back into a society they had so forcibly rejected and tried to bring down.[40] And though the narrator, unlike some of his comrades, refuses to assign personal moral guilt for Jeanne's illness to Marc, the author, Vilar, on the other hand, yokes the two opposing trajectories together in a marriage, thereby seeming to suggest that the problem of "representability" in narratives of May must be understood dialectically. At the level of representation, that is, Marc becomes an historical figure *at the price* of Jeanne; a newspaper like *Libération,* by helping "fix" the movement and locate it in a small group of pseudo-leaders, has engaged in an exercise of control and neutralization.

40. See, for example, René's response to the question of how he lived the end of the movement: "Despair is a big word. I no longer had hope there would be a revolution, another May '68, or that the movement would continue. All that breath of liberty that I had felt so strongly had passed. I had ideas that I couldn't apply, nor could I apply ideas that weren't mine. It was impossible for me to integrate and go to work in a society I had criticized so much, that I had wanted destroyed. . . . I continued to drag about in anarchist milieux, in the end these dried up. Like the CA, things worked well in the beginning, then little by little disintegrated, we were fewer and fewer, our activities became more scattered, the meetings became more and more just friends getting together." Cited in Daum, *Des révolutionnaires dans un village parisien,* 213.

Marc, at the center of the photo, has succeeded, attained privilege, developed his enunciatory position, "become a big professional,"[41] because he *already was* those things, was already in intimate relations with and geographic proximity to power, could already force his way to the loudspeaker at any number of *assemblés générales*, and he conserves these powers now by exercising control over the function of representability. Similarly, Jeanne's annihilation transpired not just because of her psychological fragility; it was prolonged and extended by an enormous amount of narrative labor on the part of those who had come to dominate the representation of the movement, labor that continued to render her insignificant or invisible, to reduce her to nothing. Jeanne's case is severe because she literally does not survive May's upheaval and its aftermath. But how many others, who, remaining alive, and negotiating in a host of different ways the constraints of the real, the crushing of political hope and its slow displacement over time onto other initiatives—how many of these have watched their own history being expropriated from them? Are celebrities like Marc the truth of the movement or the tree that hides the forest? Does media recognition in the present alone give one the right to speak about a collective past?

Patrick Rotman and Hervé Hamon's aptly titled *Génération* was one of the books most responsible for fixing the May movement into a patented "Who's Who." When the first volume was published in 1987, *Libération* gave it a glowing review and a four-page spread complete with interviews and life stories of the authors, two progressive journalists. The reviewer, Laurent Joffrin, praised the book's portrait of "a generation of baby-boomers," "irrepressible individualists," and "zealots of anticommunism," who "mad for politics, find themselves, twenty years later, almost all engaged in culture or communication."[42] The review's title, "Generation: An Inside Look" (*Un regard intérieur*) already created a somewhat voyeuristic expectation in the reader of having access to the secret, inner life of stars or celebrities, or at least of overhearing high *gauchiste* gossip.

Written in a racy "factional" or "true novel" style, the book made it plain that *Génération*'s authors had not given too much thought to the complexities of representing a mass movement. The political significance of their choice to limit their cast of characters entirely to Parisian student leaders is not simply a matter of the enormous initial exclusions such a choice perpetuates—exclusions of workers, farmers, and other provincials, people in their forties or older, among many others. To reduce a social movement to a few supposed leaders or trademarked repre-

41. Vilar, *Nous cheminons*, 65.
42. Laurent Joffrin, "Génération: un regard intérieur," *Libération*, March 23, 1987.

sentatives—what Isabelle Sommier calls "the family photo-album tendency"[43]—is an old tactic of confiscation: thus reduced, any collective
politics loses its power by being localized and therefore controllable. An
editorial published in 1969 in the anarchist journal *Noir et Rouge* showed
the mechanisms of such a tactic to be already in full sway only months
after the events of May and June drew to a close:

> [The bourgeoisie] has "personalized" outrageously, knowing how prof-
> itable this method is in the long run. For some, May was uniquely a stu-
> dent revolt, the students were just Nanterre students, Nanterre was the
> "March 22nd" group, and this last was just Daniel Cohn-Bendit. For
> others, the workers' strike was just about salary demands, the workers
> were just the CGT, and the CGT was just Seguy. . . . Thus, no possible
> discussion: some people were fanatically following a German-Jewish
> adventurist, others were calmly obeying their "union bosses." No mix
> between workers and students: let's firmly hold on to the division be-
> tween intellectual and manual labor.
>
>   Wasn't it all better than that?[44]

But in the late 1980s there was a new political significance to be gained
from Rotman and Hamon's decision to grant the characters they choose
(and only them) a full biography, a complete life story extending from
before, during, through post-May, and up to the present in the form of an
epilogue. Only they, in other words, are given the chance to grant meaning or coherence to their existence, to have a sequential life, to look back,
frequently with condescension, from the perspective of a forty-year old,
on their distant juvenile convulsions and naivetés. In this way *Génération*
helped put into place the picture that all that remained of '68 was the
trajectory of certain student leaders, particularly those who had learned
their lesson, those who were happily communing now in a strict adherence to the order of things and had abandoned all or part of the political
energy of May, notably any solidarity with workers or the third world.
And by a kind of circular logic, it was the present ("almost all engaged in
culture or communication") that seemed to have determined the choice
of those people the book elevated to "leadership" positions in its narrative of the events of May. Only those individuals, in other words, who
had risen from the Latin Quarter directly into starring roles in the media or culture industry, were "exemplary" of May. And May, in turn,
becomes depoliticized: a "cultural revolution," a revolt in communication. The teleology of a particular version of the 1980s *"soixante-huitard"*

43. Sommier, "Sous les pavés," 64.
44. Cited in "L'extraordinaire," *Noir et Rouge* 44 (April–May 1969): 1.

thus determined the authors' rendition of what transpired in '68, making May, to a certain extent, "a school or apprenticeship in manipulation"[45] — the phrase is Patrick Demerin's—from which one successfully graduates. And, as Isabelle Sommier remarks, such a representational choice takes on enormous political efficacy to the extent that the witnesses designated (or self-designated, in the case of the commemorations) as representative or exemplary appear because of their own social position in the present *as* incarnations of the ruse of history, living demonstrations of the vanity of '68. Martine Storti's anger is typical of the suspicion, if not rage, that greeted the authors' choice of rendering May in the form of "the exemplary itinerary":

> I remember how angry I became reading Hervé Hamon and Patrick Rotman's book, *Génération*, that came out at the end of the 80s. At the beginning of the second volume, we are told about an episode that took place in 1969, in Paris, at the lycée Louis-le-Grand. At lunchtime, a "far-right commando group" attacked the establishment, and a high school student had his hand ripped open by a grenade. Taken to the hospital, the hand was amputated. We will never know the name of that high school student who, undoubtedly, was not judged worthy of escaping from anonymity. But we find out in return absolutely everything about one of his *lycée* comrades, Antoine de Gaudemar, who at the moment of the book's publication in 1988, was a journalist at *Libération*.[46]

From the perspective of Storti, *Génération* and the series of television documentaries based on the book, produced by Rotman and Hamon and screened in 1988, together with the other television commemorations of May, were engaged in fabricating a "generation" out of a tiny clique of individuals, leaving the experience of thousands by the wayside. Political representativity and media representativity had become synonymous. "Rare were those, among the hundreds of thousands, even millions of French who had lived the hopes and expectations of the '68 years, who recognized themselves in the destiny of the *'médiatiques.'*"[47]

What *Génération*'s generation accomplished was a purely cultural revolution. That Joffrin's review in *Libération* certified and reiterated Rotman and Hamon's master tropes of "generation" and "cultural revolution" with a few well-chosen biological metaphors was not surprising. After all, *Libération* itself was widely recognized as—in the words of Paul

45. Patrick Démerin, "Mai 68–Mai 88. Choses tues," *Le Débat* 51 (Sept.–Nov. 1988): 173–78.

46. Storti, *Un chagrin politique*, 15–16.

47. Demerin, "Mai 68–Mai 88," 175.

Thibaud—"the daily where 'the generation of '68' has found a place to express itself and a manner in which to express itself."[48] Already in his celebrated editorial on the occasion of May's tenth anniversary, *Libé*'s director, Serge July, had opened with a well-placed biological metaphor "branding" the generation: "From this point on, like the bulls in any cattle-breeding ranch, we wear an indelible mark: we are part of a generation."[49] Joffrin himself in 1993, having become editor in chief at *Libération*, would confide in an interview, not without a certain amount of pride, that *Libération* had attained an objective that its founder, Jean-Paul Sartre, may not have wanted: "We were the instrument of capitalism's victory over the left."[50] In the interest of that victory, nothing could be more essential than attempting to control and depoliticize the interpretation of 1968. Joffrin's review of *Génération* denies any political dimension to the revolt, likening the political language of May to an unnatural and unnecessary appendage obscuring the cultural and modernizing aims of the movement: "the slogans of a revolutionary symbolic that they *grafted onto* their movement often expressed it badly" (my italics). The cultural aims are given an authentic, well-nigh organic status, to which the political becomes just an arbitrary, laboratory addition. The generation itself is granted by Joffrin all the natural force of a world historical tidal wave: "Born in penury, grown up with the society of abundance, they were destined to bring down, like a huge groundswell, each of the dikes—familial, scholarly, cultural—that a still rural nation elevated in front of them." Already the generational trope encompasses the whole forward movement of capitalist modernization—a modernization that is natural and "destined." When the second volume of *Génération* appeared a year later, its authors had swept the individual itineraries of the first volume up into a single collective destiny, and the generation's role in incarnating burgeoning progress was made even clearer. Far from revolting against capitalism, the generation acted to force a blocked and backward France into the future. Reviewing the second volume in *Libération*, Jean-Michel Helvig praised its tracing of "a generational route, both vivid and confused, where one reads perhaps better than anywhere else the chaotic process of the modernization of contemporary France."[51]

Génération, the book of heroes, quickly became the best-selling popular account of the '68 years in France. Along with the television commemora-

48. Paul Thibaud, "De la politique au journalisme: *Libération* et la génération de 68. Entretien avec Serge July," *Esprit*, May 1978, 2.

49. Serge July, *Libération*, May 18, 1978.

50. Laurent Joffrin, France 2, June 2, 1993. Cited in Serge Halimi, *Les nouveaux chiens de garde* (Paris: Editions Liber-Raisons d'Agir, 1997), 50.

51. Jean-Michel Helvig, "Le roman du gauchisme," *Libération*, Jan. 8, 1988.

tions of the 1980s, it succeeded in reducing the number of representations, or rather in reducing what was sayable about '68, to one tiny, ideological trope: the family or generational saga. As Sartre reminds us, ideology means simply the thorough way in which our reflexes have been conditioned by the dominant narrative forms and models. Ideology, he writes,

> doesn't mean a philosophical system . . . it has to do with an apparatus constructed and interiorized in such a manner that it is impossible, or at least very difficult, to form a thought that is not a specification of the model, and even more difficult to pass from an idea structured by those schemas to ideas that don't belong to the system.[52]

Guy Hocquenghem was, as we saw, among the first to read the usage of the term "generation" on the part of his former comrades in the late 1970s at the level of a symptom, to see the word as the first sign of their renunciation of the movement. Early on, he announced his abhorrence for the term and his refusal to be swept up into the paradoxically elite membership it connoted. Such generational auto-affirmation was all the more difficult to stomach since it arose precisely at the moment when those proclaiming it were visibly acceding to the back corridors of mainstream institutional power. Martine Storti, in her memoir of the '68 years, is also careful to distinguish her own representational strategy from the generational doxa: "I wrote this narrative in order to recount a singular path, which I don't claim to be exemplary. I do not incarnate my generation, or rather, I incarnate it neither more nor less than others do."[53] In his introduction to the French translation of Karl Mannheim's classic essay, "The Problem of Generations," Gérard Mauger asks whether the usage of the term, in effect, "tends to substitute a 'new' vision of the social world riven by age for the 'traditional' Marxist representation divided by class."[54] If so, this would certainly help account for some of the appeal of the term in '68 literature. Mannheim begins his essay by dividing the existing literature on the subject into two camps: a positivist, mostly French one, and a "romantic-historical," primarily German. Positivists, he states, are attracted to the concept of generation because it provides a general law to express the rhythm of historical development, based on the biological law of life span. The concept sets up a comprehensible, measurable form for understanding directly the framework of human destiny, as well as the changing patterns of intellectual and social currents, in biological terms

---

52. Jean-Paul Sartre, *L'idiot de la famille*, vol. 3 (Paris: Gallimard, 1972), 222.

53. Storti, *Un chagrin politique*, 14.

54. Gérard Mauger, "Préface à la traduction de Karl Mannheim, *Le problème des générations*" (Paris: Nathan, 1990).

operating within a unilinear conception of progress. The Germanic view, on the other hand, adopted a qualitative rather than quantitative treatment of the concept, seeking the "inner aim" of a generation, the "interior" rather than the mechanistic temporality of the coexisting generations that make up an epoch. That "inner aim" or "interior temporality" was something phenomenological, something that could not be measured but only experienced—something that, in its most extreme Heideggerian version, is indistinguishable from "the very stuff and substance of Fate":

> Fate is not the sum of individual destinies, any more than togetherness can be understood as a mere appearing together of several subjects. Togetherness in the same world, and the consequent preparedness for a distinct set of possibilities, determines the direction of individual destinies in advance. The power of Fate is then unleashed in the peaceful intercourse and the conflict of social life. The inescapable fate of living in and with one's generation completes the full drama of individual human existence.[55]

Peculiarly, perhaps, the trope of "generation" that solidified in the 1980s as the dominant model of '68—extending even, as we have seen in our discussion of the intervention of Ferry and Renaud, into the realm of philosophy—draws from both the positivist and the romantic-historical tendencies described by Mannheim. The positivist, biologistic view underlies all of the various schematic psychological reductions of the social movement to "family saga": the old, familiar functionalist explanation of the "generation conflict," sons versus fathers, as the motor of history—an explanation of '68 that emerged almost instantaneously as the events transpired. Developmental psychology, of the kind popularized by Erik Erikson in the United States, saw social upheaval as the necessary part—the functional safety valve, as it were—in guaranteeing a process of continuity in what Mannheim calls a unilinear conception of progress. Children, by means of "acting out," end up confirming all the more strongly their parents' endowment; thus, contestation is useful, functional, a rite of passage to the status of adulthood. History is reduced to the mechanical, rhythmic, evolutionary unfolding of sociobiological destiny.

From the romantic, Heideggerian side, the weight of collective destiny or "Fate" could be attributed later to any number of the "results" or "effects" of which May now would have been the cause: from the rise of Lipovetskian individualism, to the modernization of France, or the

---

55. Martin Heidegger, *Sein und Zeit*, cited in Karl Mannheim, "The Problem of Generations," in *Essays on the Sociology of Knowledge* (London: Routledge and Kegan Paul, 1952), 282.

end of communism—all results, it bears mentioning, that would seem to preclude something "like May" from ever happening again. Rotman and Hamon usefully provide an epilogue to their second volume that rehearses an inventory of many of the "lessons of May": "Our generation was generous, the bearers of very strong moral values that were perverted by politics";[56] or "Our generation overthrew the cultural foundations of French society";[57] or "I belong to a generation that lived a formidable mutation amidst follies that were revealed to be fruitful."[58]

Generation (the book and the trope) offered something for everyone: a highly romanticized, even heroic life story, and a deterministic socio-logical framework that happily affirmed the old tribal or anthropological notion of the liminality of adolescence giving way to inevitable reaggrega-tion into the adult world of the division of labor. Happy, that is, because youth, no matter how turbulent, passes; it is circumscribed and transitory by definition. And if the revolt attributed to youth does *not* pass, then this is because one has not outgrown adolescence. Youth's transitoriness is what lies concealed in plain sight in the past tense used in the title of Daniel Cohn-Bendit's 1986 book (and television series based on the book), *Nous l'avons tant aimée, la révolution* (The Revolution—We loved it so much). All young people revolt, it's part of being young. Works like Cohn-Bendit's took up the task of extending the trope of generation to the planetary level: "In 1968 the planet embraced itself. As though a universal slogan had been followed. In Paris as in Berlin, in Rome or in Turin, the paving stone became a symbol of a generation in revolt."[59] On the thirtieth anniversary of May the image of '68 as a planetary generational conflict could be found again in this May 1998 editorial in *Le Monde:*

> Around the year 1968, in all the Western world, there appears on the public scene a new collective character: the adolescent class of age . . . it affirms itself in opposition to the adult world. It is the first example in history of an international movement whose basis is belonging to the same generation.[60]

56. Jean-Paul Ribes, cited in Hervé Hamon and Patrick Rotman, *Génération*, vol. 2, *Les années de poudre* (Paris: Seuil, 1988), 636. See also vol. 1, *Les années de rêve* (Paris: Seuil, 1987).

57. Tiennot Grumbach, cited in Hamon and Rotman, *Génération*, vol. 2, p. 639.

58. Serge July, cited in Hamon and Rotman, *Génération*, vol. 2, p. 636.

59. Daniel Cohn-Bendit, *Nous l'avons tant aimée, la révolution* (Paris: Barrault, 1986), 10. Despite the expansiveness of his image, Cohn-Bendit presents a decidedly urban-centric view of global '68. As Claude Rives remarks, the paving stone is an urban phenomenon; in the coun-tryside, the cart-load of manure in front of the prefecture was more common, even if the con-frontations with the police were just as violent. See his "Le viticulteur du pays d'oc," *Le Monde,* May 27, 1998, 13.

60. Dominique Dhombres, "La révolte de la jeunesse occidentale," *Le Monde,* May 12, 1998.

Edgar Morin, largely credited with originating the interpretation of '68
as a "youth revolt," and, as such, with postulating the determinism and
dynamism of a "class of age," tried to do so by giving a new spin to the
idea of age cohort as determinative by arguing the formation of a new class
of age that does not correspond to the old traditional manifestations.[61]
But in this he is not so far from the depoliticizing remarks of his fellow sociologist, Raymond Aron, who saw '68 as the pure expression of
socio-hormonal frustration, a biological convulsion: "youth in general . . .
we are in the presence of a phenomenon which is as much biological as
social."[62] The new "class" of adolescence that appeared in France in the
1960s, according to Morin, occupies a modern vacuum between childhood
and adulthood. Morin marshaled a number of sociological facts to support
the idea of the new modern vacuum, including the extension of the period
of time of schooling before the entry into the adult world, accompanied by
a demographic increase in the number of youth taking advantage of newly
democratized opportunities in higher education. But has this "modern
vacuum" in the West since disappeared or been superceded by another
kind of adolescence? If not, then why has the extreme politicization of
youth in France in the 1960s not occurred again to anywhere near the same
degree? Why have "youth" not continued to perform as political subjects?
Nothing in the hypostatic sociological category of "youth,"—even a new,
modern "youth"—can explain why French youth (and many others, both
non-French and non-youthful) tried to take politics into their own hands
in 1968. And if the sociological category can't explain that, what good is
the category? In this sense, Morin's notion of a "youth movement" is but
a barely improved version of the equally ideological category, "student
movement," an entity-notion that suggests at least three things: that the
entire social level of students constituted itself as a political actor, that
its intervention into society constituted an irreversible given, and that it
expressed interests recognizable as "student interests." On the latter, it is
worth recalling the vehemence with which militants at the time refused
to see themselves in this light, resisting attempts to be identified with any
one function—be it "student" or "consumer," or least of all, perhaps, the
"cher téléspectateur" of Gaullist television. "There is no student problem
any longer," reads a tract from mid-May, "The student is not a valid notion. . . . Let us not be enclosed within a pseudo-class of students. . . ."[63]
Of the hundreds of posters produced in the popular studio of the Beaux-
Arts school, almost none, as Pierre Vidal-Naquet noted at the time of the

61. See Edgar Morin, in "Mai 68: complexité et ambiguïté," *Pouvoirs* 39 (1986): 71–80.
62. Aron, *Elusive Revolution*, 40.
63. "Thèses de la commission 'Nous sommes en marche,'" Censier, salle 453 (May 13–20 1968).

events, makes an allusion to the existence of a student movement; almost every one is inscribed within the political struggle against the Gaullist regime and in a rhetoric of solidarity with workers' struggles and the general strike.[64]

The concept of "generation," Mannheim thought, provided a useful alternative to class for locating people socially. Perhaps this is why categories like "youth" or "generation" became so useful as marketing categories, locatable "niches" (the Pepsi generation, the youth market) to be targeted by advertising and media *matraquages*. The Situationists recognized this fact early on when they denounced "youth" as an overrated socioeconomic category, a purely merchandising notion; Pierre Macherey, as we've seen, reiterated this idea when he characterized the invention of the "new generation of philosophical thought" on the part of Renaud, Ferry, and others as a pure marketing device. "Students," "youth," and "generation" dissolve politics into sociology by positing distinct, circumscribable social locations, a definitive residence for the movement. And yet '68 was about nothing so much as the *flight from* social location. May brought together socially heterogeneous groups and individuals whose convergence eroded particularities, including those of class and age. It realized unpredictable alliances across social sectors. The uncontrollable transversal extension of the movement, its highly protean and unforeseen development, the way it spread across the majority of the social space in France—it is the fear of this "mass" quality of May, I believe, that lies behind the will to reduce it subsequently to a strict "age effect," to the agency of an ersatz sociological category like "youth" (or its substitutes, "generation" or "students") on the part of sociologists, on the one hand, or to the agency of "pseudoleaders" on the part of journalists and the media, on the other. In fact, the personalizing of the student leaders is but the flip side of the generalizing of concepts like "youth" or "generation." The anxiety generated by the reconquest of the street by anonymous people fuels both personalization and sociological abstraction. As Jean-Franklin Narot remarked, the subversive potential of the movement lay in the way it created something like a "chain reaction of refusal" across the entire social field, the way it was, finally, irreducible to any framework or organizational location. Its potential lay in its escaping "not only institutions but the mastery of the protagonists themselves."[65] A movement that began by disarticulating "sociology" and its functionalist version of the social was succeeded by sociology's triumphant reaffirmation. The reduction of '68 to a sociobiological agent, "youth," once again reasserts a naturalist def-

64. See Schnapp and Vidal Naquet, *Journal de la commune étudiant*, 549.
65. Narot, "Mai 68 raconté aux enfants," 182.

inition of politics and conflict wholly at odds with the May movement, a determinism that produces a politics that abolishes politics.

A reprisal, unlike a commemoration, always arrives unscheduled. When, in the winter of 1995, anonymous people again took to the streets in France in huge numbers, there was no possibility of confusing the movement that had erupted with anything resembling a "youth" insurrection. At the center of the tenacious and combative winter strikes that brought hundreds of thousands of supportive demonstrators to the streets once again was the figure of the state railway worker, the *cheminot*— and a worker on the brink of retirement at that, battling the government about the terms of his pension. Yet what began as a set of partial or local demands on the part of public sector workers soon mushroomed into a mass popular uprising with enormous political ramifications. "For the first time in a rich country," wrote one editorialist in *Le Monde*, "we are witnessing today in reality a strike against globalization, a massive and collective reaction against financial globalization and its consequences."[66]

The uprising was provoked by the announcement of a government plan, designed by Prime Minister Alain Juppé, to introduce a kind of additional tax to pay off the social security debt; the plan also called for raising the number of years before state workers could have access to their pensions and for transferring control over social expenditure, particularly in health care, from employer/employee organizations to the government— reforms designed to bring France in line with the international financial establishment. The mainstream media on the whole, as well as the usual array of court and screen intellectuals whose names and faces had by this time achieved a kind of ubiquity—André Glucksmann, Alain Finkielkraut, Pascal Bruckner, Bernard-Henri Lévy, Françoise Giroud, *Libération*, Jacques Julliard, *L'Esprit*, the Fondation Saint-Simon people—leapt to congratulate, in a text published in *Le Monde*, "a fundamental reform going in the direction of social justice."[67] *Libération* went so far as to greet the announcement of the plan with an admiring front page headline: "Juppé l'Audace!" (Juppé the Bold!).[68] But railway workers, joined by significant numbers of workers in the postal service, public utilities, education and health services, and financial administration, saw it differently and 2 million public sector workers went out on strike. For

66. Erik Izraelewicz, "La première révolte contre la mondialisation," *Le Monde*, Dec. 9, 1995.
67. "Pour une réforme de la Sécurité Sociale," *Le Monde*, Dec. 3–4, 1995. The pro-Juppé petition was launched in part by the journal *Esprit*. Among the first hundred to sign were Rony Brauman, Pierre Rosanvallon of the Fondation Saint-Simon, Alain Touraine, and Jacques Julliard.
68. *Libération*, Nov. 16, 1995.

them the plan represented a crucial step along the greased path toward an Americanized system of social benefits: minimal health services and shaky pensions. The Juppé plan was in their view a frontal attack on the national health system and "public services"—those sectors entirely privatized in the American system but in France not totally subservient to market forces. The strike rendered Juppé's position analogous to that of Margaret Thatcher or Ronald Reagan in their first years in office: just as Thatcher in England had initiated her program of "reforms" by crushing the miners' strike, and just as Reagan had inaugurated his conservative revolution by breaking the air-traffic controllers' strike and firing 16,000 workers, so Juppé and Chirac had to adopt a position of non-negotiation and smash the strike in France. Public sector workers were not alone in viewing the conjuncture in this way. Throughout November and December, hundreds of thousands of people, oblivious to the inconveniences a transportation strike ushers into everyday life, took to the streets in support of striking workers and against the plan. Such demonstrations had not been seen in France since May 1968. In some ways they were even larger and more massive.

May '68—the comparisons were inevitable. Mavis Gallant reports in her chronicle of May and June 1968 that in Paris the bookstore shelves were empty of books about the Paris Commune in those two months— suddenly all of her friends, it seems, were busy reading Lissigaray and other historical accounts of the Commune and its demise.[69] In the winter of 1995, the figure of May 1968 haunted the prose of journalists and the slogans of demonstrators. "Instructors and Teachers, in Solidarity and Indignant, Remember a Certain Month of May," read one December headline in Le Monde.[70] Another article noted: "As in May '68, the red flag flew out over the campanile of the Benedictine station overlooking Limoges. As in several other cities, references to the "student spring" were obligatory, especially among the most experienced demonstrators."[71] But it was the government, above all, that seemed to see the specter of May hovering over the movement. Casting about for a way to counteract the increasing volume of demonstrators, the neo-Gaullist government of Jacques Chirac (who himself, as head negotiator of the Grenelle Accords, is rumored to have brought a revolver stuffed into his belt to one of the negotiation meetings) recalled de Gaulle's successful conjuring up of pro-government supporters and "Committees of Defense of the Republic" to

69. A re-edited version of Prosper-Olivier Lissigaray's classic work, Histoire de la Commune de 1871, had appeared in the Petite Collection Maspero in 1967.
70. Michel Braudeau, "Les enseignants, solidaires et indignés, se souviennent d'un certain mois de mai," Le Monde, Dec. 9, 1995.
71. "Le mouvement est plus suivi dans l'ouest du pays," Le Monde, Dec. 7, 1995, 7.

rally around him on May 30, 1968.[72] But the attempt to repeat history failed miserably. Chirac's organization set up analogous committees of antistrike "Angry Consumers," made up of people fed up with the lack of public transportation. But these committees never took off. When only 2,000 people showed up at the first pro-government rally, the plan was immediately scrapped.

Very little about the '95 strikes actually recalled May directly. In 1968, the country came to a complete halt. In 1995, a paralysis of sorts was created by the lack of transportation, but private industry workers, while supportive of the public sector workers, did not join in the strike as they had in 1968. Students were far less directly involved in the winter movement. As in 1968, established political parties were reduced by events to the status of worried onlookers; unlike May, however, the unions, for the most part, went along with the tide. The geography of the revolt differed as well. While significant provincial street battles and work stoppages—more significant, many would say, than the theatrics going on in Paris—occurred during '68, the '95 strikes were characterized by provincial revolts of an amplitude not seen in May, a political dynamic born independently of the center, the Paris region, where the strikes and demonstrations were in scope and quantity much less impressive. The '95 movement was largest in cities like Toulouse, Nantes, Montpellier, and Bordeaux—a movement of national amplitude and general interest developed in a decentered fashion, generating mostly from the south and the west. As Pascal Nicolas-Le-Strat points out, the provincial dimension of '95 could not be reduced to a dialectic of regionalists versus Paris ; this was not the eternal fight against centralism fueled by the resentment of the periphery. Rather, the local revolts—in Rouen, in Nice—were worth something in and of themselves and were, in fact, something new: a political dynamic born independently of the center and yet managing to attain a unifying, national character.[73] The '95 movement also introduced tactics and practices in conducting the strike distinct from May practices. In 1968, striking workers tended to stay tied to their workplaces, secluded from other workers and students within their own occupied factories. One of the novelties of the '95

72. See Jean-Louis Soux, "Sous les mots, les fantasmes de mai 1968," *Le Monde,* Dec. 3–4, 1995, 9. For Chirac as an armed negotiater of the Grenelle Accords, see Jean-Marie Colombani, *Le résident de la république* (Paris: Stock, 1998), 48; Philippe Alexandre, *L'Elysée en péril* (Paris: Fayard, 1969), 156–67.

73. See Pascal Nicolas-Le-Strat, "Sujets et territoires du mouvement social (Marseille, Nantes, Toulouse et les autres)," *Futur-Antérieur,* nos. 33–34 (1996/1): 113–26; see also Alain Bertho's article in the same issue. The best accounts of the '95 movement are in Daniel Singer, *Whose Millennium? Theirs or Ours?* (New York: Monthly Review Press, 1999), and Christophe Aguiton and Daniel Bensaïd, *Le retour de la question sociale: Le renouveau des mouvements sociaux en France* (Lausanne: Editions page deux, 1997). I have relied primarily on these accounts for my own.

movement was the new level of interbranch communication and coordination. In any number of provincial cities, different combative sectors would meet together every morning—in the train locomotive depot in Rouen, for example—to discuss the next steps of the movement.

But it was probably appropriate that it should be Daniel Cohn-Bendit who would try to put into place the "official" terms of the comparison between May '68 and the '95 revolts, manipulating both events in such a way that a distorted version of May could be used to discredit what had now turned into the largest political uprising in France for a quarter century. Writing in the newspaper where Raymond Aron had published his own denunciations of May, Le Figaro, Cohn-Bendit contrasted "the movement of modernization in 1968" to "the conservative movement of 1995," the latter summed up, in his view, by the slogan, "Don't touch our gains."[74] (Recently Cohn-Bendit has been quoted as pleading, "Let's all be more human and less political.")[75] In his comparison of the two events, all of the sociobiological trappings of the '68 movement as "generation"—its speed, youthfulness, and forward-thinking audacity—were mobilized to create in the '95 movement their opposite: the aging pensioner's anachronistic attempt to cling to the past, his trepidation about the future. Cohn-Bendit's comparison does double duty: by attempting to reinforce the consensus image of May as a modernizing movement, marching in step with the rhythms of the world market, the strikes of '95 can then be seen as anachronistic anomalies, archaic in their wishes and concerns, mentally out of sync, out of touch with global realities in their retreat back into a national framework—in a word, retrograde and conservative.

The problem was that May, in the consensus version fabricated in the 1980s, was supposed to have rendered any revitalized workers' movement or outbreak of mass democratic participation definitively obsolete. May, after all, at least in Aron's view, was supposed to be the last of the misguided nineteenth-century insurrections, a tired sham replay and posturing by students in need of historical drama but condemned instead to psychodrama. And yet now something was happening again—something that the organs of Anglo-Saxon modernity looked upon with contempt and horror: "Strikers in the millions, battles in the streets: the events of the last two weeks in France make the country resemble a banana republic in which a besieged government tries to impose the politics of austerity on a hostile population."[76] Something that should by all means be quickly taken in hand—if it could not be brought to an end, it could at least be

74. Daniel Cohn-Bendit, Le Figaro, Dec. 11, 1995.
75. Daniel Cohn-Bendit, Libération, April 6, 1999.
76. The Economist, Dec. 9, 1995, cited in Halimi, Les nouveaux chiens de garde, 71.

interpreted as the last of the last gasps, the very last archaic strike of a century now reaching its end. Cohn-Bendit's statement summed up the viewpoint of the service intelligentsia to which he now belonged. Many of the original signers of the text supporting the Juppé plan (including, in addition to the names already mentioned, several others like Alain Touraine and Claude Lefort known for their writings about '68), dismayed and unhinged by the unending series of demonstrations throughout the country, sought to validate their early position by following Cohn-Bendit's line and labeling the strikes "corporatist" and above all, archaic or backward-looking. Bravely, it seems, these intellectuals would be the realists, clear-eyed, unsentimental, and cognizant of economic necessity. They would stand up against aging workers who, after all, were exhibiting nothing more than their own pathetic retreat from the modern world, their fear of moving forward into a liberal society expanding, as anyone with eyes could see, everywhere in the world. They would courageously combat the retrograde egalitarian fantasies and irrationalities of workers and those who supported them. They would make of the 1995 strikes an eruption of nostalgia in the ongoing narrative of the disappearance of class and conflict in a modern consensus democracy like France. Night after night on the evening news viewers were treated to journalists, experts, and intellectuals echoing the government position and each other; Serge Halimi, in his book on the contemporary French media, evokes typical television scenarios from those months: "debates" staged between four media intellectuals, each of whom is a supporter of the Juppé plan; or television anchors, each making over 120,000 francs a month, interrogating railway workers in their fifties, whose monthly salary hovered around 8500 francs, accusing them of being "privileged."

But the government, the experts, and the court intellectuals were caught short by the extent, enthusiasm, and endurance of the popular support for the movement—proof that particular or local demands by strikers were being interpreted as pertaining to the general interest, proof that those in the private sector felt the public employees were fighting for them as well. "We are no longer fighting for ourselves," said one railway worker after the first week of the strike, "We are on strike for all wage-earners. To start with, I was on strike as a train driver, then as a railway worker, then as a public sector worker, and now it's as a wage earner that I am on strike."[77] An alternative group of intellectuals—Bensaïd, Vidal-Naquet, and Bourdieu among the 560 who eventually signed—wrote a counter-manifesto to the one issued by the pro-government forces to this

---

77. CFDT activist cited in P. Barets, "Journal de grève. Notes de terrain," *Actes de la Recherche en Sciences Sociales* 115 (1996): 12.

effect, stating that the strikers "in fighting for their own social rights . . . are fighting for equal rights for all: women and men, old and young, the jobless and the wage-earners, workers with special statute, employees of the state or of the private sector."[78] The strike forced the government to negotiate, and to back down on a number of its programs, notably the extension of years of service before pensions, and the reorganization of the railways. The government did not yield, however, on the central issue of social spending.

The winter strikes of 1995 were not the fulfillment of some unrealized potential unleashed in May '68. Nothing in May/June 1968 announced a political program that could be fulfilled at a later date, nor a developmental path along which the strikes of 1995 or other subsequent events would occur as foreseeable episodes in a necessary chain. Nor did '68 provide a "model" that could be repeated, successfully or unsuccessfully, later on. But each event in its status as interruption of the established order was a political event claiming a new way of formulating equality—outside of the State, outside of the parties—and each enacted politics as a polemic around social equality. The division separating the politico/mediatic/intellectual elite from "the workers" or "the people" in the winter of 1995 made the polemical division at the heart of '68 newly visible. The 1995 strikes sought to overcome the chasm separating "those who know"—the experts, the technocrats of which Juppé was an almost caricatural example—from those who are considered incapable of knowing or of understanding the steady droning language of the strong franc, the single currency, the corporate balance sheets—of understanding, in other words, the whole air of economic necessity given to liberal politics as well as their own predestined inability to achieve such understanding. And in so doing, the strikes reopened the chasm of May, and tore open the consensus that had congealed across the surface of the '68 events.

And there were other signs that a new conjuncture had been reached in France, a new impatience with the liberal order, a questioning of the reigning ideology—or what had come to be called in the 1980s, when the word "ideology" had itself become too ideological to mention—"la pensée unique." At a popular level, one tangible manifestation of disquiet was the readiness with which people in France bought and read books critiquing the naturalized laws of the economy; a number of these works became the best-sellers of the late 1990s. In the countryside, the radical activities of

78. Le Monde, Dec. 6, 1995, 30. Other signers of the statement supporting the strike included historians and scholars noted for their work on 1968 like Danièle Linhart, Jacques Kergoat, and René Mouriaux.

the agricultural union, the Confédération Paysanne, and its leader, José Bové, were and continue to be greeted with strong popular support, both in France and abroad. Among older intellectuals, there were signs of a growing awareness that the history of the past thirty years—their own political and intellectual history beginning with 1968—had to be recovered and in some sense wrested from the confiscation that history had undergone. Thus, a number of polemical alternative histories were published in the late 1990s by left intellectuals—Gilles Châtelet, Pierre Macherey, Emmanuel Terray, Dominique Lecourt, Françoise Proust among them—who had been largely silent, or writing within their academic specializations, or keeping themselves in reserve in other ways up until this point. At the same time, a number of scholars like Isabelle Sommier and Michelle Zancarini-Fournel began to turn their attention to serious historical study of the 1960s.

Each of these developments followed and will follow its own temporality, but for now they have created a space of simultaneity, a still fragile but increasingly substantial undermining of the liberal closure of history and thought announced with such fanfare in 1989. And each represents in its own way a demand for an accounting with the past, and specifically, with '68. Young historians now are perhaps following the chronological demands of their métier, the professional trajectory that has given us, after Vichy, a wealth of new investigations of the Algeria years and the beginnings of a reconsideration of the French 1960s. Their project is defined perhaps in part by the historian's notion that the events of the 1960s have at last "entered history," that sufficient temporal distance now separates our time from then so that a kind of professional objectivity can prevail. The historian's project overlaps with but clearly differs from that of older intellectuals who lived those events and who are now making a claim on analysis, a claim to recover their own past and that of others—thirty years later, after suffering what they view as the hijacking and distortion, during the 1970s and 1980s, of their own experience. And in the case of Bové and the Confédération Paysanne, something closer to an unbroken link of continuity, of "unfinished business" unites that group's activism to the '68 years. For their forms of agricultural politics originate not so much in the urban *gauchisme* of '68, but in the radical *travailleurs/paysans* organizations of Bernard Lambert in Brittany during the early 1960s.

The 1995 strikes—and after them Seattle and the other recent manifestations of political eventfulness whose nebulous affinities are now being traced in the emerging refusal, at a mass level, of the new liberal world order structured by the marketplace—these events created and continue to create a new optic on 1968. Along with the intellectual and political developments in other registers, they enlarge the frame through which May can now be viewed at the same time that they sharpen the focus in such a way that the lost figures of May, the colonial subject and the worker, regain a clearer definition. And with the return of these figures, the frontal anti-capitalism of the movement, the class struggle of the years surrounding May '68, from the end of the Algerian War through to the Lipp strikes of the mid-1970s, comes into view. In France in 1995, when workers and others massively refused the future being naturalized before them by "those who know," that refusal of a certain future had repercussions on the past as well. It transformed the event of '68 from a fact into a force, a force free now to be displaced and return again in quite dissimilar but related events. It threw a wrench into the story of May as a great cultural reform, as a rendezvous with modernity, as a birth of the new individualism. It brought an end, that is, to the end of May, by giving it a new afterlife, the contours and rhythms of which are still before us.

ABBREVIATIONS

CA   comité d'action. Grass-roots militant organization created in the course of the events. Based in neighborhoods, campuses, factories, or in particular sectors.

CAL   comité d'action lycéen. Born at the end of 1967 out of the anti–Vietnam War organizations CVB and CVN. Early membership most often drawn from militants of far left youth movements who had broken with young Communists because of the soft attitude of the PCF toward the Vietnam War. Among their journals were *Barricades* and *La Commune*. The CALs frequently renamed their schools: for example, the *lycée Thiers* became the *ex–lycée Thiers* and then the *lycée de la Commune de Paris*.

CDR   Comité pour la défense de la république. Gaullist citizen support groups, created by Charles Pasqua.

CFDT   Confédération française démocratique du travail. The second largest French trade-union grouping. More *gauchiste* than the CGT.

CGT   Confédération générale du travail. Largest French trade union grouping, closely allied with the PCF.

CRS   Compagnies républicaines de sécurité. Riot police.

CVB   Comité Viêt-nam de base. Organization supporting the Vietnamese people, instigated by the Maoist groups, the PCMLF, and the UJC (ml) in May 1967. Disappears after May '68.

CVN   Comité Viêt-nam national. Founded in November 1966 to bring together the movements and organizations opposed to the war in Vietnam, except for the Maoists. Organizes important anti–American demonstrations in 1967–68; disappears after May '68.

FER   Fédération des étudiants révolutionnaires. Trotskyist group.

FHAR   Front homosexuel d'action révolutionnaire. Informal movement created in 1971 under the auspices of the MLF; disappears around 1976.

FLN   Front de libération nationale algérien

FNL   Front nationale de libération vietnamien

FO   Force Ouvrière

FUA   Front Universitaire Antifasciste

GP   Gauche prolétarienne. Maoist organization issuing from the UJC (m-l). Edits *J'Accuse,* and then *La Cause du Peuple.* Originates in the autumn of 1968 and self-dissolves in 1973.

IDHEC   Institut des Hautes Etudes Cinématographiques

IS	Internationale Situationniste. Group founded in 1958, publishes journal by the same name. Produces critique of contemporary society focused on the commodity form and image culture (theorized as "the society of the spectacle"). Publishes a widely read pamphlet immediately before May '68, *De la misère en milieu étudiant*.
JCR	Jeunesse Communiste révolutionnaire, born in April 1966 from a split within the UEC. Published a monthly journal, *L'Avant-Garde Jeunesse*. Trotskyist, well disposed to Castro, active in the CVN. Well represented in the provinces: Caen, Rouen, Rennes, Marseille. Dissolved by the government in June 1968. Regroups in September around a new journal, *Rouge*.
LC	Ligue communiste. Founded in 1969 by militants from the former JCR. Dissolved by Raymond Marcellin on June 21, 1973.
LCR	Ligue communiste révolutionnaire. Founded in 1974, takes over where the LC left off. Continues publication of *Rouge*.
MLF	Mouvement de la libération de la femme. Created in August 1970, bringing together three large tendencies (Féministes révolutionnaires, Psychanalyse et politique, Femmes en lutte) and numerous small journals and groups. Disappears in 1981.
PCMLF	Parti communiste marxiste leniniste de France. Maoist organization operating along democratic centralist lines, advocating pro-Chinese positions, created in 1967.
OAS	Organisation de l'armée secrète. Colonialist paramilitaries in Algeria.
ORTF	Office de radiodiffusion télévision française
PCF	Parti communiste français
SNESUP	Syndicat national de l'enseignement supérieur
UEC	Union des étudiants communistes. Student union allied with the PCF. The oldest of the "groupuscules" of UNEF. Its journal was *Le Nouveau Clarté*.
UJC (m-l)	Union des Jeunesses Communistes (Marxiste-Leniniste). Also born of a split within the UEC in November 1966 at the Ecole Normale Supérieure on the rue d'Ulm. Pro-Chinese, active in creating contacts with workers' milieux. Self-dissolves in autumn 1968, giving birth to the GP and the VLR.
UNEF	Union national des étudiants de France. Student union that underwent a move to the left in the context of mobilizations against the Algerian War and university reforms.
VLR	Maoist group born out of the dissolution of the UJC (m-l) in opposition to the moral puritanism of the GP. Edits the journal *Tout*. Self-dissolves in 1973.

BIBLIOGRAPHY

Printed Sources

Action, nos. 1–47 (1968–69).

Aguiton, Christophe, and Daniel Bensaïd. *Le retour de la question sociale: Le renouveau des mouvements sociaux en France*. Lausanne: Editions page deux, 1997.

Aisenberg, Andrew. *Contagion: Disease, Government, and the "Social Question" in Nineteenth-Century France*. Stanford: Stanford University Press, 1999.

Alexandre, Philippe. *L'Elysée en péril*. Paris: Fayard, 1969.

Alland, Alexander. *Le Larzac et après: L'étude d'un mouvement social innovateur*. Paris: L'Harmattan, 1995.

Alleg, Henri. *La question*. Paris: Minuit, 1958. Reprint with new afterword by Jean-Paul Sartre, Paris: Minuit, 1961.

————. *The Question*. Trans. John Calder. New York: Braziller, 1958.

Analyses et documents, no. 154 (May 18, 1968) "De la lutte étudiant à la lutte ouvrière"; no. 155 (June 7, 1968) "De l'occupation des usines à la campagne électorale"; no. 156 (June 27, 1968) "Le mouvement de mai: De l'étranglement à la répression."

Andro, P., A. Dauvergne, and L.-M. Lagoutte. *Le Mai de la révolution*. Paris: Julliard, 1968.

Arguments, nos. 1–27/28 (1956–62).

Aron, Raymond. *Mémoires: 50 ans de réflexion politique*. Paris: Julliard, 1983.

————. *La révolution introuvable*. Paris: Fayard, 1968.

————. *The Elusive Revolution: Anatomy of a Student Revolt*. Trans. Gordon Clough. New York: Praeger, 1969.

Artous, Antoine. *Retours sur Mai*. Paris: La Brèche–PEC, 1988.

Aubral, François, and Xavier Delcourt. *Contre la nouvelle philosophie*. Paris: Gallimard, 1977.

Autogestion, nos. 1–42 (1967–78).

"Avec Dionys Mascolo. Du Manifeste des 121 à Mai 68." *Lignes*, no. 33 (March 1998).

Backmann, René, and Claude Angeli. *Les polices de la nouvelle société*. Paris: Maspero, 1971.

Badiou, Alain. Interview. "Penser le surgissement de l'événement." *Cahiers du Cinéma*. Special issue, "Cinéma 68," May 1998, 10–19.

Bardèche, Maurice. *Défense de l'Occident*. Paris: Editions Nouvelles Latines, 1968.

Baynac, Jacques. *Mai retrouvé*. Paris: Robert Laffont, 1978.

Beauvoir, Simone de. *La cérémonie des adieux. Entretiens avec Jean-Paul Sartre, août–septembre, 1974*. Paris: Gallimard, 1981.

————. *Adieu: A Farewell to Sartre*. Trans. Patrick O'Brian. New York: Random House, 1984.

219

Bedarida, Francois, and Michael Pollak, eds. "Mai 68 et les sciences sociales." *Cahiers de l'IHTP,* no. 11 (April 1989).

Bénéton, Philippe, and Jean Touchard. "Les interprétations de la crise de Mai-Juin 1968." *Revue Française De Science Politique* 20, no. 3 (June 1970): 503–44.

Bensaïd, Daniel. *Moi la révolution: Remembrances d'une bicentenaire indigne.* Paris: Gallimard, 1989.

—————. *Le sourire du spectre: Nouvel esprit du communisme.* Paris: Editions Michalon, 2000.

Bensaïd, Daniel, and Alain Krivine. *Mai si!* Paris: PEC-La Brèche, 1988.

Bensaïd, Daniel, and Henri Weber. *Mai 1968: Une répétition générale.* Paris: Maspero, 1968.

Bertho, Alain. "La grève dans tous ses états." *Futur-Antérieur,* nos. 33–34 (Jan. 1996): 63–78.

Biard, Roland. *Dictionnaire de l'extrême gauche de 1945 à nos jours.* Paris: Belfond, 1978.

Blanchot, Maurice. *L'Entretien infini.* Paris: Gallimard, 1969.

—————. *Les intellectuels en question. Ebauche d'une réflexion.* Paris: fourbis, 1996.

—————. "La rue." Anonymous tract, June 17, 1968. Reprinted with attribution, *Lignes,* no. 33 (March 1988): 144.

—————. "Sur le mouvement." *Les Lettres nouvelles,* June–July 1969. Reprinted in *Lignes,* no. 33 (March 1998): 163–83.

Boudon, Raymond. "Sciences sociales: Des gourous aux journalistes." *Commentaire,* no. 35 (autumn 1986).

Boyer, A., A. Comte-Sponville, V. Descombes, L. Ferry, R. Legros, P. Raynaud, A. Renaut, and P. A. Taguieff. *Pourquoi nous ne sommes pas nietzschéens.* Paris: Grasset, 1991.

Braudeau, Michel. "Les enseignants, solidaires et indignés, se souviennent d'un certain mois de mai." *Le Monde,* Dec. 9, 1995.

Britton, Celia. "The Representation of Vietnam in French Films Before and After 1968." In *May '68: Coming of Age,* ed. D. L. Hanley and A. P. Kerr, 163–81. London: Macmillan, 1989.

Broyelle, Claudie. *La moitié du ciel. Le mouvement de libération des femmes aujourd'hui en Chine.* Paris: Denoël, 1973.

Broyelle, Claudie, and Jacques Broyelle. *Le bonheur des pierres, carnets rétrospectifs.* Paris: Seuil, 1978.

Broyelle, Claudie, Jacques Broyelle, and Evelyne Tschirart. *Deuxième retour en Chine.* Paris: Seuil, 1977.

Bruckner, Pascal. *Le sanglot de l'homme blanc.* Paris: Seuil, 1983.

—————. *The Tears of the White Man: Compassion as Contempt.* Trans. William R. Beer. New York: Free Press, 1986.

Bulletin de Liason Inter-Comités d'Action (B.L.I.C.A.), July 22, 1968.

Cahiers de la Gauche Prolétarienne (1970–71).

Cahiers du Cinéma. Special issue, "Cinéma 68," May 1998.

Cahiers du Forum-Histoire, nos. 1–10 (1976–78).

Cahiers de Mai, nos. 1–40 (1968–73).

Cahiers Marxistes-Leninistes (Feb. 1966, April 1966, Jan.–Feb. 1967).

Cassou, Jean. *Art et contestation.* Brussels: La Connaissance, 1968.

Castoriadis, Cornelius. "L'auto-constituante." *Espaces Temps,* nos. 38/39 (1988).

————. *Mai 1968: La Brèche: Premières réflexions sur les évenéments*. Paris: Fayard, 1968.

————. "Les mouvements des années soixante." *Pouvoirs* 39 (1986).

Castoriadis, Cornelius, and Claude Chabrol. "La jeunesse étudiant." *Socialisme ou Barbarie*, no. 34 (March 1963): 46–58.

La Cause du Peuple, no. 1 (1968); no. 32 (1970); nos. 34, 36, 38 (1971).

Certeau, Michel de. *La prise de parole et autres écrits politiques*. Paris: Le Seuil, 1994.

————. *The Capture of Speech and Other Political Writings*. Trans. Tom Conley. Minneapolis: University of Minnesota Press, 1997.

Châtelet, Gilles. *Vivre et penser comme des porcs. De l'incitation à l'envie et à l'ennui dans les démocraties-marchés*. Paris: Exils Editeur, 1998.

Chesnaux, Jean. "Gadgets éphémères, slogans oubliés, 'militants' effrontées." Mimeograph.

————. "Réflexions sur un itinéraire 'engagé.'" *Politiques*, no. 2 (spring 1992): 1–10.

————. "Vivre en mai. . . ." *Les lettres nouvelles* (1969).

Cohen-Solal, Annie. *Sartre, 1905–1980*. Paris: Gallimard, 1985.

————. *Sartre: A Life*. Trans. Anna Canagni. New York: Pantheon, 1987.

Cohn-Bendit, Daniel. *Nous l'avons tant aimée la révolution*. Paris: Barrault, 1986.

Cohn-Bendit, Daniel, and Gabriel Cohn-Bendit. *Le gauchisme—remède à la maladie sénile du communisme*. Hamburg: Rowohlt Taschenbuch Verlag, 1968.

Collectif Vietnam de Jussieu. "Loin du Vietnam!" *Les Temps Modernes*, no. 344 (March 1975): 1196–16.

"Colloque sur Mai 68: Paris, May 17, 18, 1978." *Le Peuple*, no. 1041 (July 1–15, 1978).

Colombani, Jean-Marie. *Le résident de la république*. Paris: Stock, 1998.

Combes, Patrick. *La littérature et le mouvement de Mai 68. Ecriture, mythes, critique, écrivains, 1968–1981*. Paris: Seghers, 1984.

Comité d'action bidonvilles. Tract dated June 4, 1968.

Comité d'Action Écrivains/Étudiants/Travailleurs, tract, May 26, 1968.

Comité d'Action Étudiants-Écrivains au Service du Mouvement. *Comité* 1 (Oct. 1968). Excerpts rpt. in Dionys Mascolo, *A la recherche d'un communisme de pensée*. Paris: fourbis, 1993. 299–322.

————. "Un an après, le comité d'action écrivains-étudiants." *Les Lettres nouvelles*, June–July 1968, 143–88. Reprinted in Dionys Mascolo, *A la recherche d'un communisme de pensée*, 323–63. Paris: fourbis, 1993.

Comité d'Action Travailleurs-Étudiants. "Les élections: que faire?" Tract dated June 15, 1968.

Comité d'Action Travailleurs-Étudiants/Censier. Undated tract, but after May 26, 1968.

Comité de vigilance sur les pratiques policières. *POLICE: Receuil de coupures de presse*. Paris: Charles Corlet, 1972.

"Concevoir la révolution. 89, 68, confrontations." *Espaces Temps*, nos. 38/39 (1988).

CFTC. "Face à la repression." Mimeographed pamphlet (Oct. 30, 1961).

Critique communiste. Special issue. "Mai 68–Mai 78" (1978).

Daeninckx, Didier. *Le bourreau et son double*. Paris: Gallimard, 1986.

————. *Meurtres pour mémoire*. Paris: Gallimard, 1984.

Daniel, Jean and André Burgière, ed. *Le tiers monde et la gauche*. Paris: Le Seuil, 1979.

Daum, Nicolas. *Des révolutionnaires dans un village parisien*. Paris: Londreys, 1988.

Le Débat, no. 39 (March–May 1986). "Y-a-t'il une pensée 68?" Nos. 50, 51 (May–Aug. 1988, Sept.–Oct. 1988). "Le mystère 68."

Debray, Régis. *Modeste contribution aux discours et cérémonies officiels du dixième anniversaire.* Paris: Maspero, 1978.

———. "A Modest Contribution to the Rites and Ceremonies of the Tenth Anniversary." Trans. John Howe. *New Left Review*, 1st ser., no. 115 (May–June 1979): 45–65 (excerpts from the Maspero publication).

Deleuze, Gilles. "A propos des nouveaux philosophes et d'un problème plus général." *Minuit*, no. 24 (supplement to main volume) (May 1977).

Delphy, Christine. "La révolution sexuelle, c'était un piège pour les femmes." *Libération*, May 21, 1998.

Démerin, Patrick. "Mai 68–Mai 88. Choses tues." *Le Débat*, no. 51 (Sept.–Oct. 1988): 173–78.

Des soviets à Saclay. Paris: Maspero, 1968.

Descamp, Christian. "Jean Chesnaux, historien du présent et de l'avenir." *Le Monde dimanche* (Sept. 4, 1983).

"Le devenir de Mai." *Lignes*, no. 34 (May 1998).

Dews, Peter. "The 'New Philosophers' and the End of Leftism." In *Radical Philosophy Reader*, ed. Roy Edgley and Richard Osborne, 361–84. London: Verso, 1985.

———. "The *Nouvelle Philosophie* and Foucault. *Economy and Society* 8, no. 2 (May 1979): 127–71.

Document L'Idiot International. *Minutes du procès Geismar.* Paris: Hallier, 1970.

Dollé, Jean-Paul. *L'insoumis: Vies et légendes de Pierre Goldman.* Paris: Grasset, 1997.

Dreyfus-Armand, Geneviève. "L'arrivée des immigrés sur la scène politique." Lettre d'information, no. 30. *Les années 68: Événements, cultures politiques et modes de vie.* CNRS, Institut d'Histoire du Temps Présent (June 1998).

———. and Laurent Gervereau, eds. *Mai 68: Les mouvements étudiants en France et dans le monde.* Paris: BDIC, 1988.

Droz, Bernard, and Evelyne Lever. *Histoire de la guerre d'Algérie, 1954–1962.* Paris: Seuil, 1984.

Dugrand, Alain, ed. *Black Exit to 68: 22 nouvelles sur mai.* Paris: La Brèche-PEC, 1988.

Duprat, François. *Les journées de mai 68: Les dessous d'une révolution.* Intro. and afterword by Maurice Bardèche. Paris: Nouvelles Editions Latines, 1968.

Durandeaux, Jacques. *Les journées de mai 68.* Paris: Desclée de Brouwer, 1968.

Duras, Marguerite. "20 mai 1968: Texte politique sur la naissance du Comité d'Action Etudiants-Ecrivains." In *Les yeux verts*, 59–70. Paris: Cahiers du cinéma, 1996.

———. "20 May 1968: Description of the Birth of the Student-Writer Action Committee." In *Green Eyes*, trans. Carol Barko, 53–62. New York: Columbia University Press, 1990.

Einaudie, Jean-Luc. *La bataille de Paris: 17 octobre 1961.* Paris: Seuil, 1991.

L'Enragé, nos. 1–12 (1968).

Epistemon. *Les idées qui ont ébranlé la France. Nanterre: Novembre 1967–juin 1968.* Paris: Fayard, 1968.

Erhel, Catherine, Mathieu Aucher, and Renaud de La Baume, eds. *Le procès de Maurice Papon.* 2 vols. Paris: Albin Michel, 1998.

Eribon, Didier. *Michel Foucault.* Paris: Flammarion, 1989.

Esprit, July–Aug. 1976, Sept. 1976, May 1998.

Faye, Jean-Pierre, et la groupe d'information sur la répression. *Lutte de classes à Dunkerque*. Paris: Editions Galilée, 1973.

Ferry, Luc, and Alain Renaut. *La pensée 68. Essai sur l'anti-humanisme contemporain.* Paris: Gallimard, 1985.

———. *French Philosophy of the Sixties: An Essay on Antihumanism*. Trans. Mary H. S. Cattani. Amherst: University of Massachusetts Press, 1990.

Fields, A. Belden. "French Maoism." In *The 60s without Apology*, ed. Sohnya Sayers et al., 148–77. Minneapolis: University of Minnesota Press, 1984.

———. *Trotskyism and Maoism: Theory and Practice in France and the United States.* Brooklyn: Autonomedia, 1988.

Finkelstein, Norman. *The Holocaust Industry*. London: Verso, 2000.

Finkielkraut, Alain. *La défaite de la pensée*. Paris: Gallimard, 1985.

Foccart, Jacques. *Le général en Mai. Journal de Elysée.* Vol. 2, 1968–69. Paris: Fayard, 1998.

Foucault, Michel. *Dits et écrits, 1964–1988.* Vol. 4. Paris: Gallimard, 1994.

Forestier, Patrick. "Les impostures du tiers-mondisme." *Paris-Match*, Feb. 22, 1985, 3–21.

Fraser, Ronald. *1968. A Student Generation in Revolt*. London: Chatto and Windus, 1988.

Fromanger, Gérard. "L'art, c'est ce qui rend la vie plus intéressante que l'art." *Libération*, May 14, 1988, 43.

Furet, François. "La grande lessive: L'homme retrouvé." *Nouvel Observateur*, June 13–19, 1986, 114–15.

———, ed. *Terrorisme et démocracie*. Paris: Fayard, 1985.

Gallant, Mavis. "The Events in May: A Paris Notebook—I." *New Yorker*, Sept. 14, 1968, 58–124.

———. "The Events in May: A Paris Notebook—II." *New Yorker*, Sept. 21, 1968, 54–134.

Garde rouge, nos. 1–8 (1966–67).

Garnier, Jean-Pierre, and Roland Lew. "From the Wretched of the Earth to the Defence of the West: An Essay on Left Disenchantment in France." Trans. David Macey. *The Socialist Register* (1984): 299–323.

Gastaut, Yvan. *L'immigration et l'opinion en France sous la Ve république.* Paris: Seuil, 2000.

Gavi, Philippe, Jean-Paul Sartre, and Pierre Victor. *On a raison de se révolter*. Paris: Gallimard, 1974.

"Les Gauchistes." *La NEF*, no. 48 (June–Sept. 1972).

Geismar, Alain, Serge July, and Erlyn Morane. *Vers la guerre civile*. Paris: Editions et Publications Prémières, 1969.

Giorgini, Bruno. *Que sont mes amis devenus? (Mai 68–été 78, dix ans après)*. Preface by Félix Guattari. Paris: Savelli, 1978.

Glucksmann, André. *La bêtise*. Paris: Grasset, 1985.

———. *La cuisinière et le mangeur d'hommes. Essai sur les rapports entre l'Etat, le marxisme, et les camps de concentration.* Paris: Seuil, 1975.

———. *1968: Stratégie et révolution en France*. Paris: Christian Bourgois, 1968.

Goldman, Pierre. *Souvenirs obscure d'un juif polonais né en France*. Paris: Seuil, 1975.

Gombin, Richard. *Les origines du gauchisme.* Paris: Seuil, 1971.

Goslin, Richard. "Bombes à retardement: Papon and 17 October." *Journal of European Studies* 28 (1998): 153–72.

Goulinet, Isabelle. "Le gauchisme enterre ses morts." Mémoire de maitrise en histoire. Université Paris I, Panthéon-Sorbonne, 1993.

Gretton, John. *Students and Workers: An Analytical Account of Dissent in France, May–June 1968.* London: MacDonald, 1969.

Guegan, Gérard. "Touche pas à mai 68." *Le Matin,* Dec. 20, 1985, 27.

Guin, Yannick. *La Commune de Nantes.* Paris: Maspero, 1969.

"Haine de la nostalgie." *Lignes,* no. 35 (October 1998).

Halimi, Serge. *Les nouveaux chiens de garde.* Paris: Editions Raisons d'Agir, 1997.

Hallier, Jean-Edern. *La cause des peuples. Une autobiographie politique.* Paris: Seuil, 1972.

Hamon, Hervé, and Patrick Rotman. *Génération.* Vol. 1, *Les années de rêve.* Paris: Seuil, 1987.

———. *Génération.* Vol. 2, *Les années de poudre.* Paris: Seuil, 1988.

———. *Les porteurs de valises. La résistance française à la guerre d'Algérie.* Paris: Albin Michel, 1979.

Hanley, D. L., and A. P. Kerr, eds. *May '68: Coming of Age.* London: Macmillan, 1989.

Harvey, Sylvia, ed. *May '68 and Film Culture.* London: BFI Publications, 1978.

Helvig, Jean-Michel. "Le roman du gauchisme." *Libération,* Jan. 8, 1988.

Hempel, Pierre. *Mai 68 et la question de la révolution: Pamphlet.* Paris: Librairie "La Boulangerie," 1988.

Hocquenghem, Guy. *L'après-Mai des faunes.* Preface by Gilles Deleuze. Paris: Grasset, 1974.

———. *Lettre ouverte à ceux qui sont passés du col Mao au Rotary.* Paris: Albin Michel, 1986.

Hollier, Denis. "1968, May. Actions, No! Words, Yes!" In *A New History of French Literature,* ed. Denis Hollier, 1034–40. Cambridge: Harvard University Press, 1989.

Internationale Situationniste, nos. 1–12 (June 1958–Sept. 1969).

Internationale Situationniste. *De la misère en milieu étudiant considéré sous ses aspects économique, politique, psychologique, sexuel et notamment intellectuel et de quelques moyens pour y remédier.* 1966. Paris: Champ Libre, 1976.

Izraelewicz, Erik. "La première révolte contre la mondialisation." *Le Monde,* Dec. 9, 1995.

Jameson, Fredric. *Brecht and Method.* London: Verso, 1998.

———. "On Cultural Studies." In *The Identity in Question,* ed. John Rajchman. New York: Routledge, 1995.

———. "Periodizing the 60s." In *The 60s without Apology,* ed. Sohnya Sayres et al., 178–209. Minneapolis: University of Minnesota Press, 1984.

Jappe, Anselme. *Guy Debord.* Berkeley: University of California Press, 1994.

Jarrel, Marc. *Eléments pour une histoire de l'ex-Gauche Prolétarienne. Cinq ans d'intervention en milieu ouvrier.* Paris: NBE, 1974.

Joffrin, Laurent. "Génération: Un regard intérieur." *Libération,* March 23, 1987.

Julliard, Jacques. "Le tiers monde et la gauche." *Nouvel Observateur,* June 5, 1978.

Kaplan, Leslie. *Depuis maintenant: Miss Nobody Knows.* Paris: P.O.L., 1996.

Kessel, Patrick. *Le mouvement "maoiste" en France: Textes et documents 1968–1969.* 2 vols. Paris: Union générale d'édition, 1972, 1978.

Khilnani, Sunil. *Arguing Revolution: The Intellectual Left in Postwar France.* New Haven: Yale University Press, 1993.

Krivine, Alain, and Daniel Bensaïd. *Mai Si! 1968–1988: Rebelles et repentis.* Paris: PEC-La Brèche, 1988.

Labro, Philippe, ed. *"Ce n'est qu'un début."* Paris: Editions et publications premières, 1968.

———. *"This Is Only a Beginning."* Trans. Charles Lam Markmann. New York: Funk and Wagnalls, 1969.

Lacan, Jacques. *Séminaire XVII.* Paris: Seuil, 1991.

Lacoste, Yves. *Contre les anti-tiers-mondistes et contre certains tiers-mondistes.* Paris: La Découverte, 1985.

Lacroix, Bernard. "A contre-courant: Le parti pris du réalisme." *Pouvoirs* 39 (1986): 117–27.

Lambert, Bernard. *Les paysans et la lutte de classe.* Paris: Seuil, 1970.

Langlois, Denis. *Les dossiers noirs de la police française.* Paris: Seuil, 1971.

Lecourt, Dominique. *Dissidence ou révolution?* Paris: Maspero, 1978.

———. *Les piètres penseurs.* Paris: Flammarion, 1999.

Le Dantec, Jean-Pierre. *Les dangers du soleil.* Paris: Les Presses d'Aujourd'hui, 1978.

Lefebvre, Henri. *L'irruption de Nanterre au sommet.* Paris: Anthropos, 1968.

———. *The Explosion: Marxism and the French Revolution.* Trans. Alfred Ehrenfeld. New York: Monthly Review Press, 1969.

———. *Le temps des méprises.* Paris: Stock, 1975.

Le Roux, Hervé. *Reprise: Récit.* Paris: Calmann-Lévy, 1998.

———. Interview with Serge Toubiana. *Cahiers du Cinéma,* March 1997, 50–55.

Levine, Michel. *Les ratonnades d'octobre.* Paris: Ramsay, 1985.

Leys, Simon. *Les habits neufs du président Mao: Chronique de la révolution culturelle.* Paris: Champ Libre, 1971.

Liauzu, Claude. *L'enjeu tiersmondiste: Débats et combats.* Paris: L'Harmattan, 1987.

———. "Mémoire, histoire et politique: À propos du 17 octobre 1961." *Tumultes,* no. 14 (April 2000): 63–76.

———. "Le tiersmondisme des intellectuels en accusation." *Vingtième Siècle,* no. 12 (Oct.–Dec. 1986): 73–80.

Libération May 1978; May 1988; May 1998.

Lidsky, Paul. *Les écrivains contre la commune.* Paris: Maspero, 1970.

Linhart, Robert. *L'établi.* Paris: Minuit, 1978.

———. "Evolution du procès de travail et luttes de classe," *Critique Communiste.* Special issue, *Mai 68–Mai 78,* 1978.

———. "Western 'Dissidence' Ideology and the Protection of Bourgeois Order." In *Power and Opposition in Post-revolutionary Societies,* trans. Patrick Camiller, 249–60. London: Ink Links, 1979.

Linhart, Virginie. *Volontaires pour l'usine. Vies d'établis, 1967–1977.* Paris: Seuil, 1994.

Lipovetsky, Gilles. "'Changer la vie' ou l'irruption de l'individualisme transpolitique." *Pouvoirs* 39 (1986).

———. *L'ère du vide: Essais sur l'individualisme contemporaine.* Paris: Gallimard, 1983.

"Loin du Vietnam." *Cinéma,* January 1968, 37–55.

Luxemburg, Rosa. *The Mass Strike, the Political Party and the Trade Unions.* Trans. Patrick Lavin. New York: Harper Torchbook, 1971.

Macherey, Pierre. *Histoires de dinosaure. Faire de la philosophie, 1965–1997.* Paris: PUF, 1999.

————. "Réflexions d'un dinosaure sur l'anti-anti-humanisme." Supplement to *Futur-Antérieur,* "Le Gai renoncement," 157–72. Paris: L'Harmattan, 1991.

Magri, Lucio. "Réflexions sur les événements de Mai—I." *Les Temps Modernes,* nos. 277/278 (Aug.–Sept. 1969): 1–45.

————. "Réflexions sur les événements de Mai—II." *Les Temps Modernes,* no. 279 (Oct. 1969): 455–492.

Manceaux, Michèle. *Les Maos en France.* Preface by Jean-Paul Sartre. Paris: Gallimard, 1972.

Mandarès, Hector, ed. *Révo cul dans la Chine pop: Anthologie de la presse des Gardes rouges (mai 1966–janvier 1968).* Paris: Union générale d'éditions, 1974.

Mannheim, Karl. *Essays on the Sociology of Knowledge.* London: Routledge and Kegan Paul, 1952.

Mao Tse-tung. *Selected Works of Mao Tse-tung.* Vol. 3. Peking: Foreign Languages Press, 1965.

Marcellin, Raymond, *L'importune vérité.* Paris: Plon, 1978.

————. "Objectifs et méthodes des mouvements révolutionnaires d'après leurs tracts et leurs journaux." (August 1968).

————. *L'ordre public et les groupes révolutionnaires.* Paris: Plon, 1969.

Marshall, Bill. *Guy Hocquenghem: Beyond Gay Identity.* Durham: Duke University Press, 1997.

Maspero, François. "Comment je suis devenu éditeur." *Le Monde,* March 26, 1982.

————. "In Reference to the Police in Front of Our Bookstore." Tract distributed by the bookstore of Editions Maspero, Sept. 1968.

————. Interview by Guy Dumur. "Maspero entre tous les feux." *Nouvel Observateur,* Sept. 17–23, 1973, 58–60.

————. Interview by Jean-Francis Held. *Nouvel Observateur,* Aug. 24–30, 1966, 26–30.

————. Interview. "Le long combat de François Maspero." *Nouvel Observateur,* Sept. 27, 1976, 56–60.

Mauger, Gérard. " 'Etudiants, ouvriers, tous unis!' (Eléments pour l'histoire des avatars d'un mot d'ordre)." *Les Temps Modernes,* no. 370 (May 1977): 1879–97.

————. Introduction. Karl Mannheim. In *Le problème des générations,* trans. Gérard Mauger and Nia Perivolaropoulou, 7–18. Paris: Nathan, 1990.

Maupeou-Abboud, Nicole de. *Ouverture du ghetto étudiant: La gauche étudiante à la recherche d'un nouveau mode d'intervention politique.* Paris: Anthropos, 1974.

Mauss-Copeaux, Claire. *Appelés en Algérie. La parole confisquée.* Paris: Hachette, 1998.

Medec, François le. *L'aubépine de mai: Chronique d'une usine occupée.* Nantes: 1988.

"Mémoires et histoires de 1968." *Mouvement social,* no. 143 (April–June 1988).

Minc, Alain. *L'avenir en face.* Paris: Seuil, 1984.

Monchablon, Alain. "Le mouvement étudiant," Lettre d'information, no. 6. Institut d'Histoire du Temps Présent (Sept. 1995).

Le Monde. May 1968; May 1978; May 1988; Nov.–Dec. 1995; May 1998.

Mongin, Olivier. "Le statut de l'intellectuel: fou ou conseiller du prince?" *Cosmopolitiques* 2 (Feb. 1987).

Moreau, Jean. "Les 'Maos' de la gauche prolétarienne." *La Nef,* no. 48 (June–Sept. 1972): 77–103.

Morin, Edgar, Claude Lefort, and Jean-Marc Coudray [Cornelius Castoriadis]. *Mai 1968: La Brèche: Premières réflexions sur les événements.* Paris: Fayard, 1968.

Mouriaux, René, Annick Percheron, Antoine Prost, and Danielle Tartakowsky, eds. *1968: Exploration du Mai français.* 2 vols. Paris: L'Harmattan, 1992.

Mouvement du 22 mars. *Ce n'est qu'un début, continuons le combat.* Paris: Maspero, 1968.

Narot, Jean-Franklin. "Mai 68 raconté aux enfants. Contribution à la critique de l'inintelligence organisée." *Le Débat,* no. 51 (Sept.–Oct. 1988): 179–92.

Nicolas-Le-Strat, Pascal. "Sujets et territoires du mouvement social (Marseille, Nantes, Toulouse et les autres)." *Futur-Antérieur,* nos. 33–34 (1996/1): 113–26.

Nizan, Paul. *Les chiens de garde.* Paris: Maspero, 1974.

Noir et Rouge: Cahier d'Études Anarchistes-Communistes, nos. 1–46 (1956–70).

Nora, Pierre. "L'ère de la commémoration." In *Les lieux de mémoire.* Vol. 3, pp. 4687–719. Paris, Gallimard, 1997.

————. "The Era of Commemoration." In *Realms of Memory.* Vol. 3, pp. 609–37. Trans. Arthur Goldhammer. New York: Columbia University Press, 1998.

————, ed. *Essais d'égo-histoire.* Paris: Gallimard, 1987.

Notre arme c'est la grève. Travail réalisé par un collectif de militants du comité d'action qui ont participé à la grève de Renault-Cléon du 15 mai au 17 juin 1968. Paris: Maspero, 1968.

"Nouveau fascisme, nouvelle démocratie." *Les Temps Modernes,* no. 310 bis (1972).

Novick, Peter. *The Holocaust in American Life.* Boston: Houghton Mifflin, 1999.

"Où en sommes-nous avec Mai 68?" *Nouvelle Revue Socialiste,* no. 76 (Aug.–Sept. 1985).

Papon, Maurice. *Les chevaux du pouvoir, 1958–1967.* Paris: Plon, 1988.

Passerini, Luisa. *Autobiography of a Generation: Italy, 1968.* Trans. Lisa Erdberg. Middletown, Conn.: Wesleyan University Press, 1996.

Partisans, nos. 1–68 (1961–72).

Paugham, J., ed. *Génération perdue.* Paris: Robert Laffont, 1977.

Péju, Paulette, ed. *Les ratonnades à Paris.* Paris: Maspero, 1961.

Perrault, Gilles. *Un homme à part.* Paris: Bernard Barrault, 1984.

————. *Les parachutistes.* Paris: Seuil, 1961.

Perrier, Jean-Claude. *Le roman vrai de Libération.* Paris: Julliard, 1994.

Perrot, Michelle. *Les ouvriers en grève.* 2 vols. Paris: Mouton, 1974.

Pesquet, Alain, *Des Soviets à Saclay?* Paris: Maspero, 1968.

Peuchmaurd, Pierre. *Plus vivants que jamais.* Paris: Robert Laffont, 1968.

Le Peuple Français, nos. 1–10 (1971–80).

Pivot, Bernard, and Pierre Boucenne. "15 ans après Mai 68: Qui tient le haut du pavé?" *Lire,* no. 93 (May 1983).

Pompidou, Georges. *Pour rétablir une vérité.* Paris: Flammarion, 1982.

Poulantzas, Nicos. *State, Power, Socialism.* Trans. Patrick Camiller. London: Verso, 2000.

Pouvoirs 39 (1986).

Queysanne, Bruno. "Les étudiants français et la crise de l'université bourgeoise." *Révolution*, no. 4 (Dec. 1963): 6–12.

Rajsfus, Maurice. *Mai 68: Sous les pavés, la répression (mai 1968–mars 1974)*. Paris: le cherche midi, 1998.

———. *Le travail à perpétuité*. Paris: Manya, 1993.

Rancière, Danielle, and Jacques Rancière. "La légende des philosophes (les intellectuels et la traversée du gauchisme)." *Révoltes Logiques*. Special issue, *Les Lauriers de Mai ou les Chemins du Pouvoir, 1968–1978* (Feb. 1978): 7–25.

Rancière, Jacques. *Aux bords du politique*. Paris: La fabrique, 1998.

———. *On the Shores of Politics*. Trans. Liz Heron. London: Verso, 1995.

———. "La bergère au goulag," *Révoltes Logiques* 1 (winter 1975): 96–111.

———. "The Cause of the Other." Trans. David Macey. *Parallax*, no. 7 (April–June 1998): 25–34.

———. "Democracy Means Equality." Interview. Trans. David Macey. *Radical Philosophy*, no. 82 (March/April 1997): 29–36.

———. "Les hommes comme animaux littéraires." Interview. *Mouvements*, no. 3 (March–April 1999): 133–144.

———. *The Ignorant Schoolmaster: Five Lessons in Intellectual Emancipation*. Trans. Kristin Ross. Stanford: Stanford University Press, 1991.

———. *The Nights of Labor*. Trans. Donald Reid. Philadephia: Temple University Press, 1989.

Reader, Keith. "The Anniversary Industry." *Screen* 26, no. 3 (summer 1988): 122–26.

Reader, Keith, and Khursheed Wadja. *The May 1968 Events in France: Reproductions and Interpretations*. London: St. Martin's Press, 1993.

Reid, Donald. Introduction. to *The Nights of Labor*, by Jacques Rancière. Philadelphia: Temple University Press, 1989.

———. "The Night of the Proletarians: Deconstruction and Social History." *Radical History Review* 28–30 (1984): 445–63.

Révoltes Logiques, nos. 1–15 (1975–81).

Révolution (1963–64).

Ricoeur, Paul. *La mémoire, l'histoire, l'oubli*. Paris: Seuil, 2000.

Rieffel, Rémy. *La tribu des clercs: Les intellectuels sous la Ve République, 1958–1990*. Paris: Calmann-Lévy, 1993.

Rifkin, Adrian. Introduction to *Photogenic Painting/La Peinture photogénique*, ed. Sarah Wilson. London: Black Dog Press, 1999. 21–59.

Rifkin, Adrian, and Roger Thomas, eds. *Voices of the People: The Social Life of "La Sociale" at the End of the Second Empire*. Trans. John Moore. London: Routledge and Kegan Paul, 1988.

Rioux, Jean-Pierre. "A propos des célébrations décennales du mai français." *Vingtième Siècle*, no. 23 (July–Sept. 1989): 49–58.

———. *La guerre d'Algérie et les français*. Paris: Fayard, 1990.

Rioux, Jean-Pierre, and Jean-François Sirinelli, eds. *La guerre d'Algérie et les intellectuels français*. Paris: Editions Complexe, 1991.

Ross, Kristin. *The Emergence of Social Space: Rimbaud and the Paris Commune*. Minneapolis: University of Minnesota Press, 1987.

———. *Fast Cars, Clean Bodies: Decolonization and the Reordering of French Culture*. Cambridge: MIT Press, 1995.

————. "Lefebvre on the Situationists: An Interview." *October* 79 (winter 1997): 69–84.

————. "Watching the Detectives." In *Postmodernism and the Re-reading of Modernity*, ed. Francis Barker et al. Manchester: University of Manchester Press, 1992. Reprinted in *Postmodern Literary Theory*, ed. Niall Lucy. London: Blackwell Press, 1999.

Roudinesco, Elisabeth. *Jacques Lacan. Esquisse d'une vie, histoire d'un système de pensée.* Paris: Fayard, 1993.

Rousso, Henry. *Le syndrome de Vichy de 1944 à nos jours.* Paris: Seuil, 1987.

Salvaresi, Elisabeth, ed. *Mai en héritage.* Paris: Syros, 1988.

Samuelson, François-Marie. *Il était une fois "Libération."* Paris: Seuil, 1979.

Sarazin, James. *La police en miettes: Le système Marcellin.* Paris: Calmann-Lévy, 1974.

Sartre, Jean-Paul. *Les communistes ont peur de la révolution.* Paris: Editions John Didier, 1968.

————. *L'idiot de la famille.* 3 vols. Paris: Gallimard, 1972.

————. *Situations V.* Paris: Gallimard, 1964.

————. *Situations VIII: autour de 68.* Paris: Gallimard, 1972.

————. *Situations IX: mélanges.* Paris: Gallimard, 1972.

————. *Situations X: politique et autobiographie.* Paris: Gallimard, 1976.

————. *What Is Literature?* Trans. Bernard Frechtman. New York: Braziller, 1965.

Sauvageot, Jacques, Alain Geismar, Daniel Cohn-Bendit, and Jean-Pierre Duteuil. *La révolte étudiant.* Paris: Seuil, 1968.

Schnapp, Alain, and Pierre Vidal-Naquet. *Journal de la commune étudiant. Textes et documents. Novembre 1967–Juin 1968.* Paris: Seuil, 1969.

Seale, Patrick, and Maureen McConville. *Drapeaux rouges sur la France. Les causes, les thèmes, l'avenir de la révolution.* Trans. Jean-René Major. Paris: Mercure de France, 1968.

Singer, Daniel. *Prelude to Revolution.* New York: Hill and Wang, 1970.

————. *Whose Millennium? Theirs or Ours?* New York: Monthly Review Press, 1999.

Smith, William Gardner. *The Stone Face.* New York: Farrar, Straus, 1963.

Sommier, Isabelle. "Mai 68: Sous les pavés d'une page officielle." *Sociétés Contemporaines*, no. 20 (1994): 63–84.

————. *La violence politique et son deuil: L'après 68 en France et en Italie.* Rennes: Presses universitaires de Rennes, 1998.

Soux, Jean-Louis. "Sous les mots, les fantasmes de mai 1968," *Le Monde*, Dec. 3/4, 1995, 9.

Stora, Benjamin. *Appelés en guerre d'Algérie.* Paris: Gallimard, 1997.

Storti, Martine. *Un chagrin politique: De mai 1968 aux années 80.* Paris: L'Harmattan, 1996.

Stovall, Tyler. "The Fire Next Time: African-American Expatriates and the Algerian War." *Yale French Studies* 98 (2000): 182–200.

Talbo, Jean-Philippe, ed. *La grève à Flins.* Paris: Maspero, 1968.

Terray, Emmanuel. *Le troisième jour du communisme.* Paris: Actes Sud, 1992.

Thibaud, Paul. "De la politique au journalisme: *Libération* et la génération de 68. Entretien avec Serge July." *Esprit*, May 1978, 2–24.

Tout, nos. 1–16 (1970, 1971).

Trebitsch, Michel. "Voyages autour de la révolution: Les circulations de la pensée critique de 1956 à 1968." Proceedings from colloquium, "Les années 68." Institut d'histoire du temps présent. Nov. 18–20, 1998.

Tricontinental (1968–71).

U.N.E.F. and S.N.E. Sup. *Le livre noir des journées de mai (du 3 mai au 13 mai)*. Paris: Seuil, 1968.

"Une société sans mémoire?" *Vendredi*, Nov. 23–Dec. 6, 1979.

Viansson-Ponté, Pierre. *Histoire de la république gaulienne, Mai 1958–Avril 1969*. Paris: Fayard, 1971.

Vidal, Daniel. "Les conditions du politique dans le mouvement ouvrier en mai–juin 1968." In *Grèves revendicatrices ou grèves politiques?* ed. Pierre du Bois, 443–547. Paris: Anthropos, 1971.

Vidal-Naquet, Pierre. "Une fidélité têtue. La résistance française à la guerre d'Algérie." *Vingtième Siècle*, no. 10 (April–June 1986): 3–18.

———. *Mémoires*. Vol. 2, *Le trouble et la lumière, 1955–1998*. Paris: Seuil, 1998.

Vigier, Jean-Pierre. "The Action Committees." In *Reflections on the Revolution in France: 1968*, ed. Charles Posner, 199–211. Middlesex: Penguin Books, 1970.

Vive la Révolution, nos. 1–7 (1969–70).

Vilar, Jean-François. *Bastille tango*. Paris: Presses de la Renaissance, 1986.

———. *C'est toujours les autres qui meurent*. Paris: Actes Sud, 1997.

———. "Les murs ont la parole." *Rouge*, May 9, 1978, 8–9.

———. *Nous cheminons entourés de fantômes aux fronts troués*. Paris: Seuil, 1993.

———. "La prise de parole." *Rouge*, May 10, 1978, 8–9.

———. "Le temps des fossoyeurs." *Rouge*, May 11, 1978, 10.

Wolfreys, Jim. "Class Struggles in France. *International Socialism* 84 (1999): 31–68.

Zancarini-Fournel, Michelle. "'L'autonomie comme absolu': une caricature de Mai et des années 68." *Mouvements*, no. 1 (Nov.–Dec. 1998): 138–41.

———. "Histoire, mémoires, commémoration." Lettre d'information, 1. "Les années 68: évenements, cultures politiques et modes de vie." Institut d'histoire du temps présent. (Dec. 1994).

Zancarini-Fournel, Michelle, Geneviève Dreyfus-Armand, Robert Frank, and Marie-Françoise Lévy, eds. *Les années 68. Le temps de la contestation*. Brussels: Editions Complexe, 2000.

Zomponi, Francis. *In nomine patris*. Paris: Actes Sud, 2000.

———. *Mon colonel*. Paris: Actes Sud, 1999.

Films

Andrieu, Michel. *Le droit à la parole*. Documentary. Prod. La Lanterne, 1968.

Collectif Arc. *Citroen-Nanterre, Mai–Juin 1968*. Documentary, 1968.

———. *CA 13: Comité d'action du 13ème*. Documentary, June 1968.

Collectif de Cinéastes et travailleurs de Sochaux. *Sochaux 11 juin 1968*. Prod. Slon-Iskra, 1970.

Collective. *Cinétracts*. Prod. Slon-Iskra, 1968/70.

Goupil, René. *Mourir à trente ans*. 1982.

Groupe Medvedkine. *Classe de lutte*. Prod. Slon-Iskra, 1968–69.

———. *Nouvelle société, n. 5*. Prod. Slon-Iskra, 1969.

———. *Nouvelle société, n. 6*. Prod. Slon-Iskra, 1969.

————. *Nouvelle société, n. 7.* Prod. Slon-Iskra, 1969.

Groupe Medvedkine de Sochaux. *Les trois-quarts de la vie.* Prod. Slon-Iskra, 1971.

Jaeggi, Danielle, and Ody Roos. *Pano ne passera pas.* 1968.

Klein, William. *Grands soirs et petits matins. Mai 68 au quartier Latin.* Documentary, 1978.

Lawaetz, Gudie. *Mai 68.* Documentary, 1974.

Lebrun, Claude. *Mai 68 5 ans après.* Documentary, 1973.

Le Roux, Hervé. *Reprise.* Documentary, 1997.

Marker, Chris. *Le fond de l'air est rouge,* 1977.

————. *On vous parle de Paris: Maspero. Les mots ont un sens.* Prod. Slon-Iskra, 1970.

Marker, Chris, and Mario Marret. *A bientôt, j'espère.* Prod. Slon-Iskra, 1967.

Marker, Chris, Jean-Luc Godard, Joris Ivens, William Klein, Claude Lelouch, Alain Resnais, and Agnès Varda. *Loin du Vietnam.* Prod. Slon, 1967.

Rubbo, Michel. *Les enfants de Solzhenitsyne: Y a pas à dire, font du bruit à Paris,* documentary, 1979.

Thorn, Jean-Pierre. *Le dos au mur.* Prod. La Lanterne, 1980.

————. *Oser lutter, oser vaincre.* Documentary, 1969.

Willemont, Jacques, and Pierre Bonneau. *La reprise du travail aux usines Wonder.* June 1968.

Television and Radio

"La dernière année du Général." Patrick Berberis, prod. In series *Les brulures de l'histoire,* 1995.

"En terminale." Pierre Cardinale, prod. In series *Les chemins de la vie,* 1968.

"L'examen ou la porte!" Jean-Pierre Beaurenaut, dir. 1990.

"Field of Dreams." David Caute, ed. David Levy, prod. BBC Radio 4 program, broadcast January 20, 24, 1988.

Génération. Hervé Hamon, Patrick Rotman, and Daniel Edinger, prods. Series contains Françoise Prébois, *Paroles de mai;* Gilles Nadeau, *La révolution introuvable;* Jean Lassave, *Mai . . . Après;* Michel Fresnel, *La Commune étudiante.* 1988.

"Histoire de Mai." Pierre-André Boutang, André Frossard, prods. May 7, 14, 21, 28, 1978, Fr 3.

"Les lycéens ont la parole." Pierre Zaidline, prod. In series *Dim Dam Dom.* Moderated by Marguerite Duras, 1968.

"Mai: Connais Pas." André Campana, prod. In series *Vendredi.* Broadcast May 13, 1983, Fr3.

"Paris, 24 mai 1968," "Paris, 30 mai 1968," "Paris, 27 avril, 1969." Phillipe Alfonsi and Maurice Dogowson, prods. In series *Histoire d'un jour,* 1985.

"Le procès de Mai." Roland Portiche and Henri Weber, prods. May 22, 1988, TF 1.

"Radioscopie." Jean-Paul Sartre. Broadcast February 7, 1973.

"68 dans le monde." In series *Les dossiers de l'écran.* A2, May 2, 1978.

"Les Temps modernes." Herta Alvarez-Escudero, dir. In series *Qu'est-ce qu'elle dit Zazie?* 1997.

INDEX

1022222222222222222222222222222222222222